KARL BARTH

CHURCH DOGMATICS

A SELECTION

*the text of this book is printed
on 100% recycled paper*

KARL BARTH

CHURCH DOGMATICS

A SELECTION

With an Introduction by HELMUT GOLLWITZER

Translated and Edited by G. W. BROMILEY

HARPER TORCHBOOKS
THE CLOISTER LIBRARY
HARPER AND ROW, PUBLISHERS
NEW YORK

CONTENTS

v

EDITOR'S PREFACE

Although Karl Barth has an established name in the theological world, and even in wider spheres, the content and significance of his main work, the *Church Dogmatics*, are not so widely known or appreciated as they deserve. The vast nature of the work, and the extended process of composition, are partly responsible. In addition, the isolation of the war years, and the inevitable lag in translation, have proved contributory factors in English-speaking areas.

In the circumstances, it is natural that there should have been various attempts to introduce readers rather more gently to the *Dogmatics*. This is the purpose of Professor Gollwitzer in the present work, in which he has in view both a wider public, yet also students and pastors who feel the need of initial guidance. His method is not merely to select for purposes of information, but also to group under leading themes to serve the purposes of interpretation. He has also contributed a fine introductory essay which admirably helps to an understanding of the mature Barth of the *Dogmatics*.

It should be emphasised that, while the work may lead more general readers to a fruitful acquaintance with Barth, it cannot replace the *Dogmatics* for serious students. If the main themes and extracts are judiciously selected, they are necessarily inadequate to convey the full sweep or content of the work. Many important themes have to be excluded, and the extracts themselves are naturally torn from their more immediate setting. This does not mean that the total effect is misleading. No more competent or sympathetic guide could be desired than Professor Gollwitzer. It means that the work primarily serves its intended purpose of introduction and orientation, as also, it is to be hoped, of stimulation.

The Introduction has been independently translated,

together with the brief theses at the head of the various sections. The extracts from the *Dogmatics*, which have been numbered and indexed for the sake of easier reference, follow the authorised English translation of the relevant volumes (*C.D.*, I, 1—IV, 2), all of which are now available. In an Appendix three passages have been added from IV, 3, which was not yet available, even in German, when the original choice was made.

PASADENA, *Michaelmas*, 1960.

INTRODUCTION

" The theology of Karl Barth is beautiful. Not merely in the external sense that he writes well. He writes well because he unites two things, namely, passion and objectivity. And his passion is for the object of theology, and his objectivity that which is proper to so stimulating an object. Objectivity means immersion in the theme. And the theme of Barth is God as He has revealed Himself to the world in Jesus Christ according to the witness of Scripture. It is because Barth turns his glance wholly away from the state of faith and directs it to the content of faith . . . that he writes well, and ·we do not have to fear from him pastoral edification ; the matter builds up itself. But it is so captivating and challenging that true objectivity necessarily coincides with a penetrating but in no sense meretricious intensity. This union of passion and objectivity is the basis of the beauty of Barth's theology. Who in the last decades can be compared with him in the exposition of Scripture, not exegetically, nor in a biblicist sense, nor tendentiously, nor with pastoral rhetoric, but with such concentration on the Word that this alone shines out in its fulness and radiance ? And who has possessed such unwearying perseverance and vision, and possessed it because the matter itself unfolds and displays itself in all its greatness before him ? We have to go right back to Thomas to find a similar freedom from all tension or narrowness, or so complete a mastery of understanding and good temper, a good temper which in Barth often takes the form of humour, but more especially that of a pronounced taste for *tempo giusto*, of a lively rhythm. Barth can make it quite convincing that for him Christianity is something absolutely triumphant. He does not write thus because he has the gift of style but because he bears testimony, wholly objective testimony, to something which has to do with God and which therefore commands the very best style or writing. For Kierkegaard Christianity is otherworldly, ascetic and polemical. For Barth it is the awe-inspiring revelation of God, of the

I

eternal light shining over all nature and fulfilling every promise, God's eternal Yea and Amen to Himself and His creation." [1]

These words, which do honour not only to the one whom they extol but to a writer who did not allow confessional barriers to hinder him from such grateful acknowledgment, apply to a theological work of unusual force which for the last thirty years has deeply influenced the inner development of the Evangelical church in the German-speaking world, and which the many translations and reactions show to have aroused no less attention, agreement and disagreement in the Christian churches of other lands.

Since the time of the Reformation no Evangelical theologian has received so much notice from Roman Catholic theology as Barth; his work has created a new situation for the Evangelical-Roman Catholic debate. The development of the Ecumenical Movement would have been just as inconceivable' without his contribution as would the Christian resistance to German National Socialism, or the richly varied wrestling of Christians and churches with Communism in the Eastern European states. It takes effect in the decisions of the young missionary churches of Asia and Africa in face of nationalistic and syncretistic movements no less than in the countless weekly sermons at which both preachers and listeners are hardly conscious how different the preaching would be if it had not been preceded by this dogmatic work. Both as literature and scholarship it is a product of the desk, yet it has not been restricted to the literary or academic level, but has exerted an influence on the active life of the 20th-century Christian churches and the practical conduct of innumerable individual Christians. If it has not had such strong emotional accompaniments as the so-called awakenenings of the 18th and 19th centuries, its ultimate effectiveness will probably be no less powerful.

What are the prospects of Christianity to-day? What has it to say to-day and to-morrow in face and in the midst of the cataclysmic changes in which humanity is engulfed? How can there be renewal in our ossified or quickly ossifying Church organisations? How is Christianity to hold its own in competition with and under the assault of newly arisen political religions and reinvigorated older religions ? How is it to fulfil its mission in the technical world of the future ? What is this mission ? What is Christianity, the Gospel, Christian faith ? In Barth's writing there is no practicable prescription for answering these questions. He is not indeed the only one to face them and to say important things regarding them. But those who tackle them—and which of our contemporaries, Christian or non-Christian, can fail to do so ?—are well advised not to overlook Barth's contribution. Hence it is not surprising that from the very outset his way is surrounded and accompanied by the attention not only of theologians but of many who are not theologians or even Christians. Many of them as academic colleagues have immediately perceived the vital significance of this work for the situation of the physician at the sick-bed, the merchant in economic life, the judge and the politician. The particularity of the Christian message, its claim and promise, its difference from all that man can tell himself about life and death, this world and the next, along the ordinary paths of religion and philosophy, have seldom been expressed with such resoluteness, with such power of sustained thinking, or with such confidence in the centre of this message.

Theology is the exposition or expository presentation of the Christian message. This statement has many implications. Barth never wearies of working it out for himself and others. Its first implication is the humility of theology. Theology does not create or fashion its subject. Its subject is presented to it. It is there before it and apart from it. It must take it as it is, as it offers itself. It can only think after it, following its movements—for it is a living theme or subject and not a dead object. It can only obediently and pliantly adapt itself to its particularity, resolutely refusing to attempt to bring it into conformity with the categories, thought-forms, concepts and needs which all human thought always brings with it. This special, unique subject must rule, and everything else must serve and be glad to be able to do so. This is the basis of what seems at first sight to be the provocatively sharp rejection by Barth of what is called " natural theology," i.e., the acknowledgment of a general framework of thought, derived perhaps from a general concept of

3

science, an established anthropology, a presupposed philosophical system or some other given knowledge of God, reality and man, into the co-ordinated system of which the Christian revelation has to be fitted. Yet it was by this rejection at the end of the twenties, when he stood almost alone and broke with a two-thousand-year-tradition in Christian theology, that Barth established a bulwark against the specific adaptation of the Christian faith to the norms of a supposed Germanic race consciousness (cf. his own exposition of the so-called Barmen *Declaration* as given on pp. 54–65). Revelation is not one species in a genus. It is the *concretissimum* which cannot be fitted into anything else and must be the starting-point of thought. We are well on the way to understanding Barth when we learn with him to reverse the usual movement of thought from the general to the particular and to move instead from the particular—this particular—to the general.

To the humility of theology there also belongs the knowledge that it never controls its subject. The subject of theology for Barth is not just God but God in His revelation, and His revelation is present only in the message which the Church brings to men. This ongoing message is the real theme which theology presupposes as the basis of its own existence and on which it reflects. It is never able to do this fully. It never achieves more than provisional results. It never produces a system of pure doctrine in which the nature of Christianity is conclusively fixed for all time. Theology is a historical work. With the message itself, which always turns anew to new men and ages, it is always on the way, *theologia viatorum*, a pilgrim theology. In Barth's own thinking this is shown in his readiness continually to strike his tents before settling down too comfortably. From the first edition of his *Epistle to the Romans* in 1917 to the latest volume of the *Church Dogmatics* he has been engaged in ceaseless revision with constant surprises no less for himself than for contemporaries working with him, and we have not yet seen the last of these surprises—for he is still young in his seventies. His thinking is of great systematic force and sustained power of concentrated thought. His doctrine of reconciliation in particular is a marvel of architectonic beauty. Yet he is

4

not the creator of a system deducing from a single principle and therefore knowing everything in advance. It is because his thinking is a humble following that it is so alive, so vital.

If theology is exposition, this means concretely that it is bound to a text, to the text which the Church has recognised and acknowledged as the Canon, i.e., the standard, the normative, basic and exemplary form for the continuing delivery of its message, in other words to the Bible. Apart from Augustine, Luther and Calvin there has hardly been a great Christian thinker who has more clearly displayed the exegetical character of all theology, nor a dogmatic presentation of the Christian faith which has been worked out so clearly in terms of express exegesis of the whole content of the Bible. The small print exegetical passages in the *Church Dogmatics* are usually prepared by Barth before the composition of his own thematic expositions, though they are placed after them in the text. From this we infer that, if the temporal priority of exegesis shows the heteronomy, the dependence of theological thinking, its spatial priority in print shows its autonomy, freedom and individual responsibility, not as slavish repetition, but as the free expression, after humble listening, of its own understanding—the " freedom of those who are bound," according to the pregnant title selected by his friends, and forbidden by the German censor, for the volume prepared in 1936 in honour of his 50th birthday.[2]

Because theology is not free speculation but thinking which is referred to a specific place and set under concrete authority, the reader even of this selection must bear in mind that the theme rather than the author is responsible for many of the highly individual trains of thought which he finds. Barth's concern is not just with his own theology as a private view of things, or the programme of a theological school competing with other trends. His concern is always with the content of the Christian message. For Barth every sentence is as it were a proposal for the understanding of this message and it is accompanied by the question whether the message does not impose this understanding. Hence even when we come across very strange lines of thought it is as well not to reject them forthwith but first to ask whether they have any basis in the message itself.

Barth never strives after originality for its own sake. In many of his theses he has contradicted hoary Christian traditions, but he has never done so lightly, nor in proud and arbitrary opposition to the fathers. In no Evangelical dogmatics since the great works of the older Protestant orthodoxy is there such a mass of historico-theological material, not merely in the form of exposition but of discussion. In none is there more intensive wrestling not merely with the theology of the Reformation but with the fathers and the great thinkers of mediaeval Scholasticism. For this theology, listening to the Bible means also attentive listening to other men. Even in the case of the great opponent Schleiermacher there is a constant concern to know what positive lessons he may have to teach. The sharp blade which Barth uses in polemics is always in fact a very humane instrument, and leaves the final judgment to the One who alone is Judge. As he himself says (IV, 2, p. 570), the word conflict or " falling-out " " has to be used very cautiously and selectively in theology. We cannot wish to fall out with God, with Jesus Christ, with the Holy Spirit. We can only be glad and thankful that God is on our side. It is also better not to fall out with Holy Scripture or the Church as the communion of saints. And it is better that there should be no falling out in our relationship with our neighbours. But there is every cause . . . to fall out with oneself." This is practised by Barth even in relation to the period which he first opposed so vehemently, namely, the theology of the 19th century, to which he has devoted one of his finest books.[3] For him tradition is neither a burdensome yoke nor a divine dictate. It is the voice of the fathers and brethren to be heard both with gratitude and freedom. It does not prevent his venturing into the new and unknown. Yet he always finds satisfaction when he can say that for all the " critical freedom which I have had to exercise . . . I have always found myself content with the broad lines of Christian tradition " (IV, 2, p. xi).

This peace with tradition, so different from the hybris of the revolutionary, is the Catholic element in the *Church Dogmatics* as the critical freedom is the Protestant.

6

Ecumenical breadth is one of the most important characteristics of this work. In passages where the motifs of Roman
Catholic, Eastern Orthodox and Pietist theology are
explicitly or implicitly taken up and heard, the expert is
continually forced to ask himself whether what they try
to say is not better brought out here and better and more
biblically expressed. There can be no mistaking Barth's
Reformed origin. He never conceals his particular gratitude
to the much slandered and misunderstood Calvin. But
it would be foolish for this reason to describe him as a
Reformed or Calvinistic theologian in the narrower sense.
Confessional definiteness does not mean confessional con-
striction. The division of the Church into confessions is
abruptly described by him as a scandal for which there is
no justification (IV, 1, p. 675). Theology as a serious
matter must always be prepared firmly and uncompromisingly to say Yes and No. It must always be prepared to
take its place in the conflict of confessions. But it must
also recognise that confessional traditions " exist in order
that we may go through them (not once but continually),
but not in order that we may return to them and take up
our abode in them " (III, 4, Preface). Thus Barth as an
acknowledged heir of the Reformation has contributed
essentially to the rediscovery of the theology of Luther
and Calvin which is such a feature of the modern epoch
of Protestant theology, and yet, although often chidden for
his orthodoxy, he has powerfully opposed every orthodox
repristination. Hence it is not surprising that in debate
with Roman Catholics his theology is regarded on the one
side as the most consistent realisation of the intention of
the Reformation (E. Przywara) and on the other as the
opening up of " a new possibility of fruitful interconfessional
conversation " (R. Grosche), or indeed as both " the
strongest development of Protestantism and the closest
approximation to Catholicism " (H. U. von Balthasar,
J. Küng). Yet it is unmistakeably Protestant in its consciousness of the responsibility of the individual, whom
no tradition nor ecclesiastical court can relieve of the duty
of publicly stating what he has heard and perceived, and
who therefore, in the bold words of the Preface to the first
volume, must " in all modesty venture to be such a Church
in his own situation and to the best of his ability."

7

Theology is impossible without humility because the truth at issue is a person who says : " I am the Truth " (Jn. 14⁶). We cannot possess a person, or rather this person. If He gives Himself, He does not give Himself away. Because its subject is so intractable, theology is an enterprise which cannot guarantee its own success. Hence there are many passages in the *Church Dogmatics* in which the author reminds himself and his readers of the essential reserve laid upon this thinking. It cannot take place without prayer for the fulfilment of the promise by which it is initiated—a fulfilment which it cannot produce nor demand, but for which it can only pray as for free grace. If theology is not pointless chatter, if it is " different from Rabbinic learning or Greek speculation . . . then it is so at every point on the basis of election, and not otherwise " (I, 2, p. 349 ; cf. II, 1, p. 70 ff.). The appeal must be to no less than the supreme court, and confidence in the supreme help and assistance, if theology is to be a meaningful undertaking. This was the real meaning of the earlier designation " dialectical theology " by which Barth and his friends first came to be spoken of after the first world war. Barth himself has later said rather brusquely that the label was attached to them by spectators, and he himself has become increasingly reluctant to use the ambiguous term " dialectical." He certainly used it freely enough in his earlier period. But he never had in view a Hegelian dialectic, i.e., a method of successfully viewing things together, and therefore a triumph of thought over the contradictions of reality. What he meant was rather a confession of the brokenness of our thinking, to which only contradictory parts are given and which cannot hope to achieve the synthesis reserved for God alone. In his development reflection on this brokenness belongs to his earlier period, whereas later he has given greater emphasis to the promise given to human thinking as it may enter the service of the message. This has meant a yielding of the influence of the paradoxical thinking of Kierkegaard before the attempt to understand the unity of the divine action in the incomprehensibilities of the divine decisions.

For theology should seek in all humility to understand. If it is exposition, this implies that it has a subject. Hence there can be no question of a " blind and formless and inarticulate and irrational stirring " to which there corresponds on our side only a " blind and formless incitement or even pacification." Revelation is rather an event by which man becomes " one who sees and understands and knows," and can give " a logical answer corresponding to the logical attitude of God " (IV, 2, p. 313). Christian faith is as remote from irrationalistic mysticism as it is from a rationalism which posits the axioms of human reason as a measure of the possibility and actuality of God. It is essentially *fides quaerens intellectum*, faith seeking after understanding.[4] Revelation neither lulls the understanding nor eliminates it. It mobilises it, both humbling and yet also encouraging it. In the volumes of the doctrine of reconciliation especially Barth applies all the energy of his thinking to banish any suggestion of caprice or whimsicality from the understanding of divine grace. Rejecting modern irrationalism, against which we are warned by its dreadful fruits in the Third Reich, he honours man as a rational being (III, 2, pp. 419 ff.), and he particularly values revelation as that which is not in any sense a-logical but genuinely rational. In God there is no conflict between mystery and rationality. For this reason theology does not violate but recognises the mystery of God in its attempt to trace the wisdom of God in His acts.

Barth once wrote in 1922 that he had got over the childish ailment of being ashamed of theology,[5] and already in the Preface to the second edition of his *Epistle to the Romans* he points out that what awaits the reader is full-blooded theology. " If in spite of this warning non-theologians take up the book—and I know some who will understand its contents better than many theologians—I shall be very pleased ; for I firmly believe that its subject concerns everyone because its question is the question of everyone. Yet even with this audience in view I could not make it any easier. If I am not mistaken . . . we theologians best serve the interests of the laity if we do not expressly or purposefully address ourselves to them but keep to our calling like all honest workmen." His aim is not to be a prophet or renovator or reformer or revolutionary, but simply an honest workman, one who is charged by the Church to expound the Christian message in the service of this message and with a view to its better transmission. Convinced of the incomparable importance of this message for every man and age, and not least for our own age and its problems, he is sure that a life is not wasted if all its time and energy are devoted to the service of theology, and that this service is not incidental, and should not be rendered in a dilettante, rhetorical or sentimental manner, but must be undertaken only as sober work, with pitiless self-criticism, in the full strictness of the concept, without fearing the reproach of intellectualism, with the most highly intellectual eloquence and objective self-absorption. " Politics is the most manly of occupations next to theology," he could once write in relation to some political memoirs, thus showing how highly he esteemed his own task.

The theological work of Barth, therefore, is for a Christianity supremely threatened by arbitrariness and *allotria* an unmistakeable summons back to its true theme and task. Even the non-theological and especially the non-Christian reader, or the reader who does not regard himself as a Christian, finds himself invited to participate in objective thinking, though he must admit that no particular concession is made to him. If he reads impartially and with sufficient seriousness, he will hopefully note how often his own questions are treated. But they are not treated with express reference to him, nor with any anxious concern for particularly original or modern language. Barth has never dealt specifically with the demand so often put to the Church that it should more fully speak the language of the age, nor with the question so often discussed in Church circles how the Gospel should be preached to the modern man. But he has always thought that the question of content should take precedence of that of manner, that the correct recognition of what the Church has to say will also produce the right way of saying it, that if only it is correctly perceived the matter will speak for itself and create for itself an appropriate language. The fact that Barth rejects the attempt of " natural theology " frees him from any fear that there might be an age when it could be proclaimed either with triumph or sorrow that God is dead—an age, therefore, which might discard all earlier religious traditions and thus be unreceptive to the Gospel. Expecting receptivity to the Gospel only by the miracle of the Holy Spirit, he has implicit trust in this miracle, and does not therefore think in terms of ages which are more religious or more profane, closer to God or more distant from Him. The non-Christian can put no question which is not necessarily that of the Christian dogmatician as well. In solidarity with the non-Christian, he has no prior knowledge. He must begin from the very beginning with no presupposed consciousness of God. He must learn to spell out the message which comes to him as to every man. He must apply himself to understand its content, context and consequences. The fact that hearing is the only way to faith continually brings the Christian and the non-Christian into the same situation. Hence there is no reason for us to be concerned first with our own faith or lack of faith, but only with the unique theme which here breaks into the sphere of our lives as we are told of it. All the cards are on the table. Nothing more is required of any of us than in other branches of intellectual life, namely, seriousness of objective thought and living interest in the theme. The rest does not lie in the hands of men, whether they are the speakers or hearers, and therefore it cannot be forced by a particular method or mode of speech. If Barth's *Epistle to the Romans* was already sharply distinguished from the usual type of biblical commentary by its lively expressionistic style, this style was only the natural result of the overwhelming of the author by his great discoveries. In the event, and especially in the development of the successive volumes of the *Dogmatics*, Barth's style has more and more lost its prophetic quality, but also its academic flavour, which is most pronounced in the first. The language of the scholar has given way to that of direct presentation or even narration, the nature of the subject being such that it can " only be told " and not considered and described as a system (II, 2, p. 188). It is because the theme of this narration is as inexhaustible as it is enthralling that Barth is so eloquent, that his eloquence is never empty or merely rhetorical, that new expressions and comparisons continually occur to him, that the flow of his eloquence is so living and powerful and that he need not strive after modernity. If modernity of jargon is not found in his work, the passion of objectivity and " sober exuberance " (II, 1, p. 219) make his language genuinely modern.

His work did not begin at a professor's desk or with the aspirations of a young man of the new generation. The origins are to be found in the embarassment of an honest man in a Swiss parsonage who could have no more illusions as to the contrast between the claim of his work and its actuality. According to its claim as expressed in the tolling of the bell, preaching from the pulpit, the opening of the Bible and the administration of the sacraments, this work stands in the service of the intervention of another and eternal reality, being the place at which account has to be taken of this reality. But in actuality men were taking it up as a conventional task without the corresponding movement, so that it was valued like all other ecclesiastical activities and trends as the preaching of a culture which thought it meritorious to be Christian but saw to it in every possible way that there should be no genuine intervention to shake and question it. In actuality, therefore, the attack and claim which are so unmistakeable in the New Testament were muted and neutralised by the official recognition, the cultural integration and the social control of Christianity as a middle-class institution. In actuality the factory owners in the small industrial town of Safenwil in Aargau naturally expected the minister to be on their side in the bitter class war between them and their workers, and to use his preaching to summon the latter to good conduct, contentment and restraint from strike action. In actuality even the spiritual equipment which the young pastor had received from his theological teachers contradicted the task with which he found himself charged when he mounted the pulpit and opened the Bible.

In its resistance to the great attack on traditional dogma launched by the Enlightenment, the Protestant theology of the 19th century, on the basis of the Pietist movement and the Roman Catholic theology of the Counter-reformation, had very largely agreed in taking up a defensive position in which the truth of Christian faith was to be proved by demonstrating the indispensability of religious feeling to all higher humanity, it being also shown that all previous historical religions constitute an evolutionary ladder at the head of which stands Christianity, which embraces all their positive qualities and surpasses them in its spiritual and ethical development of the consciousness of God. In this way it seemed to be made clear that the most progressive civilisation and the highest religion, that Christianity, the West and progress all belong together, and that Christianity is an irreplaceable instrument for the humanisation of humanity which the century had adopted as its programme. The justification of Christianity had its roots, therefore, in that of religion generally, and this was accomplished by understanding it as an expression of the noblest need and the noblest assurance which man could discover in himself, as the revelation of his highest feature, his transcendentally related spirituality. If this defence did not find the hoped for response in the educated circles for which it was intended, it did at least give the representatives of Christianity the satisfaction of finding themselves in step with the march of civilisation and not of belonging to a past epoch as maintained by anti-Christian *Aufklärer* of every type. Yet on this basis it was not possible to refute the contention of Ludwig Feuerbach that the secret of theology is anthropology.[6] For on this view the revelation which could establish and validate all others was found in the breast of man himself, in the structure of human consciousness. His self-certainty was the basis of the certainty of God and the legitimation of the specifically Christian certainty of God. The secret of God was in truth that of self-glorifying man speaking of God and extolling his own divinity. But in these circumstances the need of man, his adaptation for the goal of culture, could not fail to become the standard by which the traditional form of the Christian message was judged and what was temporally conditioned in the Bible and ecclesiastical dogma was separated from what is still valid, i.e., serviceable, to-day. But once this standard was adopted, it is hard to see where a line could be drawn, and it seems fairly obvious that what we have here are only last-ditch attempts to resist those who with greater resolution were prepared to consign the whole of Christianity to the historical past. As knowledge of other cultures increased, and particularly of the great religions of Asia, the argument that Christianity stands at the top of a ladder of

13

religious development had necessarily to give ground to a relativism which could recognise it as the supreme expression of religion only for our European civilisation. When one of our clearest theological thinkers, Ernst Troeltsch, came to see this, he was only being more consistent when in 1914 he moved to a philosophical chair. But the self-understanding of the Christian message as contained in the biblical writings stood in irreconcilable conflict with this integration into the religious history of humanity, with this understanding of a consciousness of God innate from the very first in man. The revelation of which Christian proclamation had to speak was a happening from above downwards in which man was measured by God's standard and which was directed against a thinking from below upwards, a grounding of the assertions of Christianity in human immanence.

The theological or religio-philosophical training of the young minister in Safenwil was thus quite unsuitable for the task with which he saw himself to be charged, especially when he had to preach. Unlike many others, however, he could have no further illusions as to his position. The son of a New Testament professor at Berne, Fritz Barth, who stood on the positive side, and the pupil of leading liberal theologians in Berlin and Marburg, he realised that the differences between the positive and liberal trends were of little account in face of their common features. The year 1914 saw the outbreak of a world war which educated circles in Europe had regarded as impossible and the enlistment of the vast majority of the adherents of these circles into the various propaganda fronts of this war. This new turn in events made it unmistakeably clear that the only alternatives were either to continue to build God on man and thus to move further and further away from the true starting-point of Christianity until finally humanity was lost as well as Christianity, as the war now revealed, or to make a new and resolute attempt to think in biblical terms and thus seriously to accept as such the revelation of God attested in the Bible, making it the measure of all things. "For me personally a day at the beginning of August in that year (1914) was the *dies ater* (the black day), when ninety-three German intellectuals published an endorsement of the military policy of Kaiser Wilhelm II

14

and his councillors, on which to my horror I found the names of almost all the theological teachers whom hitherto I had confidently respected. If they could be so mistaken in ethos, I noted that it was quite impossible for me to adhere any longer to their ethics or dogmatics, to their exposition of the Bible or presentation of history. So far as I was concerned, there was no more future for the theology of the 19th century." [7]

In those first weeks of the first world war some of the ministers in Aargau met for one of their usual conferences, and, shaken by the fury of war which they saw unleashed beyond the Swiss frontiers, the majority thought that they should postpone their discussion of theological questions until more peaceful times. The young Barth, however, took the opposite view that theological work was the most urgent imperative of the hour, and he set himself to examine the foundations hitherto accepted and to look for better. He has remained true to the conviction that the way must always lead from within outwards, from the centre to the periphery, and that reflection on this centre is thus the most relevant and promising of all undertakings in unsettled times. Hence he did not follow the example of many others like F. Naumann, Albert Schweitzer and the Christian Socialists, who, equally dissatisfied with contemporary theology and philosophy, turned to supposedly more practical tasks. Instead he remained faithful to his pastoral office and sought a new way out of the dilemma in which it involved him.

There now fell on fruitful soil a number of voices from the outer edges of the main ranks of Christianity which might have been heard before but thus far had spoken in vain—the voice of Kierkegaard, of the unique Dutch-Rhenish preacher H. F. Kohlbrügge, of the two Swabian preachers of the kingdom of God, the elder and the younger Blumhardt (whose influence is shown by the sequel, and particularly by the volumes on reconciliation, to be the most enduring), of the spiritually powerful Zurich pastor and philosopher Hermann Kutter, of the Basle Church historian Franz Overbeck and his merciless criticism of the contemporary Christianity of culture, of Dostoievski and above all of the newly articulate Reformers.[8] All these combined, however, to point to the particularity of

15

the biblical Word. It was not that recourse was had to the Bible because a traditional dogma demanded it, but that alongside other voices the Bible had also to be tested, as it were, in the search for a way out. In fact, however, the Bible came right into the forefront, and it is perhaps consonant with this experience that Barth has always refused to find a principial basis of the particular authority of the Bible in the Christian Church and has always regarded it as a sufficient basis that it does in fact impose and continually assert itself in a way which is unique and irreplaceable.

It soon became apparent how the Bible began to speak when consulted in this predicament. In 1918 there was published a small Swiss edition of an exposition of the Romans which in the months before and after the German collapse many who were seeking new guidance took up and then passed on to others. What they found here was Paul speaking in up-to-date terms, not of human cultural ideals but of the judgments of God, not in an attempt to find parallels but in demonstration of the antithesis between the Gospel and human striving, not on the basis of human need but of his commission vertically from above, not as a genius but as an apostle, triumphant only in brokenness. The prophetic force of this exposition fell on receptive ears, and it was quickly reissued by C. Kaiser of München. A volume of sermons followed in which Barth co-operated with his friend E. Thurneysen, who has always been his most loyal partner and whose contribution to the early work particularly cannot be ignored. These sermons show what a new and strange and stimulating sound preaching can still achieve. Fresh adherents were gained as the new or dialectical theology attracted younger men and found a focus in the journal *Zwischen den Zeiten*. With Barth and Thurneysen, Friedrich Gogarten, Emil Brunner, Georg Merz and then Rudolf Bultmann became the leaders of the new movement.

The sermons published by Barth and Thurneysen in 1924 under the title *Komm Schöpfer Geist* bear as a motto the saying of Calvin : *Deus in sua inscrutabili altitudine non est investigandus* (God is not to be sought out in His inscrutable loftiness). The pathos of distance was directed against the comfortable mysticism of Neo-Protestantism, against the notion of man bearing God within his own breast and knowing well the right way. All the things which had seemed to be self-evident were now shown not to be so at all : that man knows about God ; that human questioning finds a divine answer ; that God can be known ; that God hears and speaks ; that God is love ; that God is concerned about man ; that the address of God means life for man and not death. Barth's correspondence in 1923 with his former teacher A. von Harnack [9] should be read to understand how revolutionary, menacing and inhuman the contesting of these supposedly self-evident truths must have seemed to the older generation.

In the Preface of his second edition of the *Epistle to the Romans* Barth writes : " If I have a system it consists in the fact that I keep as consistently as possible before me the negative and positive significance·of what Kierkegaard has called the ' infinite qualitative distinction ' between time and eternity. ' God is in heaven, and thou on earth.' The relation of this God to this man, and this man to this God, is for me the theme of the Bible and the sum of philosophy." If we ask concerning the relationship between the earlier Barth and the later, we may say that the second of the two statements quoted is the one which has remained, whereas the first shows us the difference. The pathos of distance, the contesting of supposedly self-evident truths, the recognition of God as the Wholly Other whom to encounter is mortal judgment, the preaching of the *diastasis* of Christianity and culture, the exclusion of mysticism and ethicism, the questioning of all hyphens, the championing of exclusivism against inclusivism—all these were necessary if revelation was to be recognised and taken seriously as miracle, grace as a far from self-evident gift, the Gospel as something really new which man cannot tell himself, and the Christian message as a message which has its own self-grounded and unique quality. But this was not all that was required. There had to be a positive as well as a negative movement.[10] If Barth saw this more quickly than his fellow-workers, this is because he cannot rest content with a single insight and spend the rest of his days in its systematic development. His self-criticism is too great and his urge for total knowledge too strong to allow him to remain blind for

17

long to the inadequate, truncated and one-sided aspects of a given position. It is for him a practical and not just a theoretical truth that all theology is *theologia viatorum* or " broken thought and utterance to the extent that it can progress only in isolated thoughts and statements directed from different angles to the one subject. It can never form a system, comprehending and as it were ' seizing ' the object " (III, 3, p. 293). In his own practice this does not mean, however, that he can accept the most disparate elements or the most paradoxical propositions as though paradox were an indication of truth. It means that he is committed to an unceasing movement from what is known to what is not yet known, to an active pilgrimage. On the other hand, his thinking cannot consist in the development of axioms into a system. It is always stimulated from without. It has a partner outside itself. It has a theme which is continually given it by something else. For Christian theological thinking this other is in the first instance—and whatever else may have to be said on the subject—the Bible as the basic and canonical witness to revelation. For Barth this has meant in practice that there is for him no distinction between exegetical and systematic theology. He is constantly occupied in exegetical work. He has embarked on his fresh developments in and by means of exegesis. In contrast to the builder of systems, whose steps can always be foreseen, he sees himself and his readers constantly faced by surprises in virtue of it. Exegetical labours of acknowledged rank have thus led him on and forced upon him changes which have alienated many who previously made common cause with him.

The main change is that the pathos of distance has now been replaced by the pathos of the Gospel, of the glad tidings that the distance has been overcome, though the earlier insight is retained that this is not self-evident, so that there can be no return to the old equations, to thinking from below. " God is God." In 1921 this was a warning against the identification of God with what man thinks he can find in himself by way of the consciousness of God. Thirty years later it is a grateful confession of the condescension of God, of His grace and self-offering on the cross. The titles " dialectical theology " and " theology of crisis " vanished even before the group thus designated was rent by the material differences which emerged between Barth and some of the others, but the title " Theology of the Word " is still apposite, and the concept Word has been increasingly filled out by the concrete name of Jesus Christ.

This main change has taken some twenty years, and three points may be noted : the publication of the *Christian Dogmatics in Outline* in 1927, which offended many because the prophet had now turned dogmatician ; the publication of the first volume of the *Church Dogmatics* in 1932, with its almost complete obliteration of the earlier outline ; and the publication of the essay *Justification and Law* in 1938. The way from the *Epistle to the Romans* to the *Dogmatics* was necessary and unavoidable if the antithesis formulated against Neo-Protestantism was not to remain in the framework of basic Neo-Protestant concepts but to be a real antithesis. How else could the new preaching of God as the Wholly Other, of the crisis of everything temporal in relation to eternity etc., be more than the articulation of a new facet of the consciousness of the age or the expression of a distinctive religious mentality no less justified than others but with no claim to exclusive justification ? How far was it not merely a religious possibility but a Christian necessity ? How far was it to be taken seriously that the " essence of Christianity " does not consist in ideas and ideals but in a concrete person Jesus of Nazareth, as is undoubtedly the view of the whole of the New Testament ? What was the result of taking this seriously ? In relation to this question everything that is merely an expression of the mood of the age, or that rests on a generally philosophical foundation, or that has recourse to a general dialectic of the infinite and the finite, is consistently rejected in favour of a persistent concern to bring all the essential statements of the Christian faith back to their christological basis, and thus to clarify their content and show them to be specifically Christian, i.e., to show how they are made possible but also necessary by the manifestation of Jesus Christ, and how it is only in relation to Him that they take on their own significance but also their impregnable certainty. There is thus achieved a christological concentration unparalleled in the history

19

of Christian thought, a focusing upon this one central human fact, which is not, however, a measurable fact but a Word which comprehends and reveals the whole history between God and man. This being the case, there can be no weighing of its significance without participation. When it speaks of this Word, language necessarily loses the character of academic neutrality and constantly reveals that it speaks in the presence of this subject, taking the form of worship and confession as is so often the case—though without sentimentality or vehemence—in the *Church Dogmatics*.

The essay *Justification and Law* (1938) brought to light, although naturally not without preparation,[11] an implication of the christological concentration which still occupies us to-day, namely, the political relevance of the Christian message. What we have thus far expounded can never be regarded merely as the movement of an individual thinker. The attention claimed by Barth since the *Epistle to the Romans* and the inner necessity of his understanding of the Gospel produced an inward correspondence of the history of his thinking to that of German Protestantism between the two world wars. When German Evangelical Christianity was confronted in 1933 by the demand that it should view National Socialism as a divine revelation, purge the Christian tradition according to the norm of a supposed German consciousness of God, and place preaching in the service of national renewal as Hitler understood it, and when it seemed for the most part inclined willingly to comply with this demand, it was of providential significance that the theological work associated with the name of Barth, though not, of course, prosecuted by him in isolation, disclosed and brought into even sharper focus the difference between Christian revelation and everything else that might claim to be revelation, the critical freedom of the Gospel in relation to all human claims and aspirations, and the exclusive authority of the Word of God over the action of the Church. Hence Barth's polemical work *Theologische Existenz heute* in the summer of 1933 was a basic document of the Confessing Church then in process of formation, and the Declaration of the Confessional Synod of Barmen of May, 1934, which still serves to direct the Evangelical Church, derived in all its main essentials from him.[12]

Although as a Swiss he was hampered in his participation and often hindered, he, too, was initially of the opinion that there should be a careful separation between the ecclesiastical opposition to National Socialism and the political. In view of the weighty reasons for this view only ill-wishers or fools can reproach him for it, as sometimes happens. But as the true nature of National Socialism emerged, he realised that the separation could not be maintained, and the theological work which he still prosecuted for all his participation in current events also served to force him into a more radical position. For the idea of separation presupposed an ultimate distinction between the religious and political spheres which reflection on the universal significance of the manifestation of Jesus Christ necessarily called in question. That there is an essential relevance of Christianity in politics, and that the Christian as such is charged with political responsibility, had always been recognised by Barth. For him the Gospel had always struck a revolutionary rather than a conservative note. It had always seemed to call for the alteration and amelioration of the *status quo* rather than its legitimation. For this reason he had supported Social Democracy in Switzerland from as early as 1915. But now he attained to theological clarity and understanding in the matter through his recognition that grace is commitment. To be graciously blessed is not merely to be spared punishment or loaded with benefits ; it is to be commissioned for active service. Already in the second edition of the *Epistle to the Romans* (p. 414) we read : " Admonition is the assertion of grace as demand." Grace demands, and for those who are graciously blessed by God there is no other demand than that which derives from grace. Hence the commands of God are not divorced from His grace ; they are its orders and applications to life. In political life this means that the Christian as a citizen stands under no other command than that of his Lord, and that in his political action he cannot be obedient to an autonomous decree of the state as a final authority, but must understand and test it as an answer to the grace of his Lord addressed not only to himself and his nation but to all men. The positions adopted by Barth, which have been much contested and misunderstood and cannot be more precisely indicated in the present context, are his own attempts to put this into practice. Those who do not merely attack them on the basis of passing hearsay, but attentively study them, can hardly fail to see both his loving concern for the ways and destiny of the German people to whom he is so closely related and his consistency in spite of every difference in detail, especially in relation to National Socialism and Communism. There is no question of any interest in the domination or self-preservation of the Church, nor in the execution of a programme deduced from the articles of the Christian faith. This would be to change the Gospel into an ideology. The concern is always for a daily answer to the lordship of grace of Jesus Christ. This is worked out in an answering of political questions which cannot be laid down in advance after the manner of casuistry, but which is guided by the recognition that politics must serve the life of the man saved by Christ, and that no man is excluded from His saving act.

Many difficult decisions have to be made in attempting a small selection from the *Church Dogmatics*. The work is a cosmos with no dead or isolated sections. Art consists in omission according to Liebermann, but what can we omit from the *Dogmatics* without hurt ? If we choose only passages which are accessible without prior knowledge or which appeal to those whose interest is only superficial, the real content of the work is left undisclosed and many statements even in the selected passages are rendered incomprehensible. On the other hand, if we introduce the leading trains of thought by assembling decisive portions, there is the danger that such a mosaic will demand no less and perhaps more of the receptivity of the ordinary reader than the original itself. Yet I have decided for the latter method on the assumption that such a collection will better serve the reader than a few choice morsels, since it will not only bring out the originality of Barth but also provide an outstanding example of the work of theology generally. Limitation of space naturally means that many indispensable expositions have had to be omitted. Thus the doctrine of the Trinity and the important new conception of the doctrine of predestination appear only on the margin, and there are no sections on the doctrine of the Church, on the doctrine of angels, on the eschatology already visible in outline in the present volumes, or on the significance of the people of Israel, whose election and destiny have been more highly evaluated in Barth than in any previous Christian theology, so that a new basis is here provided for discussion between the Church and the Synagogue. But if a reading of this selection gives rise to questions which are not answered, the reader will perhaps blame the fact that it is a selection and be stimulated to investigate the works of Barth himself.

THE " CHURCH DOGMATICS "

In its totality the *Church Dogmatics* is planned in five volumes, and thus far (1961) a single part of Volume IV has still to appear and the whole of Volume V on the doctrine of redemption (eschatology). The interrelationship of the existing parts, all of which are now available in English, is as follows.

Volumes I, 1 and I, 2 contain the prolegomena to the dogmatics, i.e., an attempt to understand the task, theme, presuppositions, methods and modes of knowledge both of theology in general and dogmatics in particular. Included are expositions of the doctrine of the Trinity, Christology and the doctrine of Holy Scripture.

Volumes II, 1 and II, 2 deal with the so-called doctrine of God in the narrower sense, i.e., in II, 1 the question of the possibility of the knowledge of God and the doctrine of the attributes of God (love, freedom, omnipotence, wisdom, presence etc.), and in II, 2 the doctrine of the election of grace (predestination) and basic definitions in relation to the commanding of God and therefore the foundation of Christian ethics.

Volume III deals with the doctrine of creation under the following heads :

III, 1, the basis in a great meditation on the creation stories of Genesis 1 and 2 ;

III, 2, the Christian view of man (theological anthropology) ;

III, 3, the doctrines of providence, nothingness and angels ; and

III, 4, the ethical questions raised by the creatureliness

of man, namely, his relationship to animals, his sexuality (male and female, marriage), parents and children, nation and humanity, respect for life (e.g., suicide, sickness, capital punishment and war), work, calling, honour etc.

Volume IV contains the doctrine of the reconciliation of God and man in Jesus Christ, as told in three great movements in the parts thus far completed.

IV, 1, Jesus Christ is the condescension of the Son of God as Judge to solidarity with the man who has fallen victim to judgment, the Lord becoming a servant (the high-priestly office of Christ), sin being unmasked as pride and opposed by the divine verdict which effects man's justification, and reconciliation being actualised on man's side by the work of the Holy Spirit in the gathering of the community and the awakening of individual faith ;

IV, 2, Jesus Christ is the restitution of man from the fall to life with and for God, the servant becoming Lord (the kingly office of Christ), sin being unmasked as sloth and opposed by the divine direction which effects man's sanctification, and reconciliation being actualised on man's side by the work of the Holy Spirit in the upbuilling of the community and the awakening of individual love ;

IV, 3, Jesus Christ the God-man is the victorious revelation of the accomplished reconciliation (the prophetic office of Christ), sin being unmasked as falsehood and opposed by the divine promise which effects man's vocation, and reconciliation being actualised on man's side by the work of the Holy Spirit in the calling of the community and the awakening of individual hope.

Help to an understanding of the whole work may be found in the so-called *Introductory Report* to the *Dogmatics* by Otto Weber (Verlag der Buchhandlung des Erziehungs-vereins Neukirchen, Kreis Mörs, 1950 ff., E.T., Lutterworth Press, 1953).

(Cf. the *Bibliographia Barthiana* of Charlotte von Kirschbaum in the "Festschrift" *Antwort* (1956), which lists 406 titles up to 1955.)

DOGMATIC WORKS

Credo (an exposition of the Apostles' Creed), München, 1935.
Gotteserkenntnis und Gottesdienst (an exposition of the *Scots Confession*), Zürich, 1938. E.T., *The Knowledge of God and the Service of God*, Hodder and Stoughton, 1938.
Dogmatik im Grundriss, München, 1947. E.T., *Dogmatics in Outline*, S.C.M. and Harpers, 1949.
Die Christliche Lehre nach dem Heidelberger Katechismus, München, 1949.

EXEGETICAL WRITINGS

Römerbrief, 2nd edit., München, 1921. E.T., *Epistle to the Romans* (6th ed.), O.U.P., 1950.
Die Auferstehung der Toten (I Kor), München, 1924. E.T., *The Resurrection of the Dead*, F. H. Revell, 1933.
Erklärung des Philipperbriefes, München, 1927.
Kurze Auslegung des Römerbriefes, München, 1956. E.T., *A Shorter Commentary on Romans*, S.C.M. and John Knox, 1959.

SERMONS

Suchet Gott, so werdet ihr leben (with E. Thurneysen), Bern, 1917, 2nd edit., München, 1928.
Komm Schöpfer Geist (with E. Thurneysen), München, 1924. E.T., *Come Holy Spirit*, Round Table Press and T. & T. Clark, 1933.
Die grosse Barmherzigkeit (with E. Thurneysen), München, 1935. Cf. E.T., *God's Search for Man*, Round Table Press and T. & T. Clark, 1935.
Fürchte dich nicht, München, 1949.
"*Fides quaerens intellectum.*" *Anselms Beweis der Existenz Gottes*, München, 1931. E.T., S.C.M. and John Knox, 1960.

Die protestantische Theologie im 19 *Jahrhundert. Ihre Vorgeschichte und Geschichte,* Zürich, 1947. E.T., *Protestant Thought from Rousseau to Ritschl,* S.C.M. and Harpers, 1959.

ESSAYS

Das Wort Gottes und die Theologie, München, 1924. E.T., *The Word of God and the Word of Man,* Hodder and Stoughton, 1928.
Die Theologie und die Kirche, München, 1928.
Eine Schweizer Stimme, 1938–1945, Zürich, 1945.
Karl Barth zum Kirchenkampf (Theologische Existenz heute, N.F., No. 49), München, 1956.
Theologische Fragen und Antworten, Zürich, 1957.

Many essays and articles by Barth have appeared in the two series *Theologische Existenz heute* (edited by Barth until 1936 and since then by K. G. Steck and G. Eichholz, München, Kaiser-Verlag), and *Theol. Studien* (edited by Karl Barth and Max Geiger, Evangelischer Verlag, Zürich-Zollikon). All the monographs of Barth have been published by the Verlag C. Kaiser, München, and the Evangelischer Verlag, Zürich-Zollikon (German edition, C. Kaiser).

LITERATURE ON KARL BARTH

This constitutes already a small library. One of the remarkable signs of the theological situation is that after a lively discussion of his earlier work German Protestantism has nothing to say about the *Church Dogmatics.* The fullest monographs concerning the *Dogmatics* in German are by two Swiss Roman Catholics and a Dutch Reformed, and all three are worth noting in virtue of their knowledge and discussion of the theme. They are :
Hans Urs von Balthasar, *Karl Barth, Darstellung und Deutung seiner Theologie* (Verlag J. Hegner, Köln, 1951) ;
Hans Küng, *Rechtfertigung, Die Lehre Karl Barths und eine katholische Besinnung. Mit einem Geleitbrief von Karl Barth* (Johannes-Verlag, Einsiedeln, 1957) ;

G. C. Berkouwer, *Der Triumph der Gnade in der Theologie Karl Barths* (Verlag der Buchhandlung des Erziehungsvereins, Neukirchen bei Mörs, 1957). E.T., *The Triumph of Grace in the Theology of Karl Barth*, Paternoster Press, 1956.

The great extent of Barthian work is made strikingly clear in the Festschrift prepared by his friends and pupils for his 70th birthday under the title *Antwort* (edited by E. Wolf, Evang. Verlag, Zürich-Zollikon, 1956). Among English works which call for notice are the two volumes prepared for Barth's 60th and 70th birthdays under the titles *Reformation Old and New* (edited by F. W. Camfield, Lutterworth Press, 1947) and *Essays in Christology for Karl Barth* (edited by T. H. L. Parker, Lutterworth Press, 1956).

NOTES

(1) Hans Urs von Balthasar, *Karl Barth. Darstellung und Deutung seiner Theologie*, Verlag J. Hegner, Köln, 1951, p. 35 f.

(2) *Theologische Aufsätze, Karl Barth zum 50. Geburtstag*, München, 1936.

(3) *Die protestantische Theologie im 19. Jahrhundert*, Zürich, 1947; cf. his article *Evangelische Theologie im 19. Jahrhundert*, Zürich, 1957.

(4) The title of his book on Anselm : " *Fides quaerens intellectum*," *Anselms Beweis der Existenz Gottes*, München, 1931.

(5) In the essay " Not und Verheissung der christlichen Verkündigung " (1922) in *Das Wort Gottes und die Theologie*, München, 1924, p. 99.

(6) Cf. Barth's essays on L. Feuerbach in *Die Theologie und die Kirche*, 1928, pp. 212–239, and *Die protestantische Theologie im 19. Jahrhundert*, pp. 484–489.

(7) K. Barth, *Evangelische Theologie im 19. Jahrhundert*, 1957, p. 6.

(8) On Blumhardt : E. Thurneysen : *Chr. Blumhardt*, München, 1926 ; on Overbeck : K. Barth : *Unerledigte Anfragen an die heutige Theologie* (1920), now in *Die Theologie und die Kirche*, pp. 1–25 ; on Dostoievski : E. Thurneysen : *Dostojewskij*, München, 1922 ; on the whole mood and development of the period 1914–1921 cf. E. Thurneysen's essay " Die Anfänge K. Barths Theologie der Frühzeit " in the Festschrift *Antwort*, 1956, pp. 831–864.

(9) Now in K. Barth : *Theologische Fragen und Antworten*, Zürich, 1957, pp. 7–31.

(10) This is Barth's own retrospective judgment on his own earlier period in the essay *Die Menschlichkeit Gottes*, Zürich, 1956.

(11) The most important preparatory work is to be found in the

article *Evangelium und Gesetz* (now in the series *Theologische Existenz heute*, N.F., No. 50, 1956).

(12) Barth's utterances during the Church conflict in Germany have now been collected in *K. Barth zum Kirchenkampf* (*Theologische Existenz heute*, N.F., No. 49, 1956), and, with his pronouncements during the second world war, in *Eine Schweizer Stimme* 1938–1945, Zürich, 1945.

I. REVELATION

1. God

The whole world speaks of God. Human history is a history of the relationship of men to their gods. Does Christian utterance concerning God mean the same as the rest of the world when it speaks of God, the gods and the divine ? Is it a particular result of the rich religious production of humanity and its unceasing reflection on the ultimate bases of human existence ? Barth perceives that what the biblical authors say about God is opposed to any such integration. His concern, then, is to work out the distinction. In Christian parlance the word God is used only to denote the One who has revealed Himself as the Lord of all being by His concrete intervention in His address to Israel and the manifestation of Jesus Christ.

[1] Who God is and what it is to be divine is something we have to learn where God has revealed Himself and His nature, the essence of the divine.   [IV, 1, p. 186]

[2] God is indeed the genuine Counterpart which alone can finally and primarily satisfy man and all creation as such. Far too often, however, this has been said in so general and therefore unconvincing a manner that we cannot be content to make the word " God " our final, or perhaps even our basic, term. Far too often this word is used simply as a pseudonym for the limitation of all human understanding, whether of self or the world. Far too often what is meant by it is something quite different, namely, the unsubstantial, unprofitable and fundamentally very tedious magnitude known as transcendence, not as a genuine counterpart, nor a true other, nor a real outside and beyond, but as an illusory reflection of human freedom, as its projection into the vacuum of utter abstraction. And it is characteristic of this transcendence that it neither has a specific will, nor accomplishes a specific act, nor speaks a specific word, nor exercises a specific power and authority. It can neither bind man effectively nor effectively liberate him. It can neither justify him nor satisfy him. It cannot be for his life either a clear meaning or a distinct purpose.

Its high-priests and prophets usually interrupt those who dare to say such things, telling them that it is only in the form of " mythologisation " that we can say anything definite, i.e., that we can ascribe to it a person and form, an ability to act and speak, or even specific words and acts, so that we are better advised not to make any attempts in this direction. Transcendence as they see it cannot mean anything more than that behind and above and before all human action there is this open sphere, this abyss as it were, into which every man is destined to plunge headlong, whether wise or foolish, whether blessed or judged, whether to salvation or perdition. And the only sure and certain result which accrues from contemplating this spectre seems to be the rather barren law of toleration, i.e., of refraining from absolutising, and therefore in fact of avoiding all positive statements concerning its binding content and direction. In the present context we need not join issue with this standpoint and its representatives on this aspect. We must certainly insist, however, that when we ourselves introduce the term " God " at this point, we necessarily have something very different in view.

The introduction of the term " God " is not an abuse of this name, but meaningful and helpful, if in respect of it we think of what is attested by Holy Scripture concerning God's speech and action. God is the One whose name and cause are borne by Jesus Christ. Hence there is no question of divinity in the abstract as suprahuman and supra-cosmic being. Holy Scripture knows nothing of this divinity. To be sure, the God of Holy Scripture is superior to man and the world as the Lord. But He has also bound Himself to man and the world in creating them. God is here introduced to us in the action in which He is engaged, not merely in His superiority over the creature, but also in His relationship to it. What is presented to us is the faithfulness of this God and His living approach to the creature. There is set before us His specific coming, acting and speaking in the creaturely world with the intention of asserting, protecting and restoring His right to the creature, and therefore the creature's own right and honour.   [III, 4, p. 479 f.]

[3] When Holy Scripture speaks of God, it does not

permit us to let our attention or thoughts wander at random until at this or that level they set up a being which is furnished with utter sovereignty and all other perfections, and which as such is the Lord, the Law-giver, the Judge and the Saviour of man and men. When Holy Scripture speaks of God it concentrates our attention and thoughts upon one single point and what is to be known at that point. And what is to be known there is quite simple. It is the God who in the first person singular addressed the patriarchs and Moses, the prophets and later the apostles. It is the God who in this " I " is and has and reveals sovereignty and all other perfections. It is the God who wills to be known and worshipped and reverenced as such. It is the God who created His people Israel by His Word, and separated them from all other peoples, and later separated the Church from Israel. It is the God who exercises His rule in what He wills and does with this people, the people first called Israel and later the Church. It is He, this God, who as the Lord and Shepherd of that people is also, of course, the World-ruler, the Creator of all things, the Controller of all events, both great and small. But in every way His government of the world is only the extension, the application and the development of His government in this one particular sphere. He does the general for the sake of the particular. Or to put it in another way, He does the general through the particular, and in and with it. That is God according to His self-revelation.

We may look closer and ask : Who and what is the God who is to be known at the point upon which Holy Scripture concentrates our attention and thoughts? Who and what is the God who rules and feeds His people, creating and maintaining the whole world for its benefit, and guiding it according to His own good-pleasure—according to the good-pleasure of His will as it is directed towards this people ? If in this way we ask further concerning the one point upon which, according to Scripture, our attention and thoughts should and must be concentrated, then from first to last the Bible directs us to the name of Jesus Christ. It is in this name that we discern the divine decision in favour of the movement towards this people, the self-determination of God as Lord and

Shepherd of this people, and the determination of this people as " his people, and the sheep of his pasture " (Ps. 100³). And in this name we may now discern the divine decision as an event in human history and therefore as the substance of all the preceding history of Israel and the hope of all the succeeding history of the Church. What happened was this, that under this name God Himself became man, that He became this particular man, and as such the Representative of the whole people that hastens towards this man and derives from Him. What happened was this, that under this name God Himself realised in time, and therefore as an object of human perception, the self-giving of Himself as the Covenant-partner of the people determined by Him from and to all eternity. What happened was this, that it became a true fact that under this name God Himself possesses this people : possesses it no less than He does Himself ; swears towards it the same fidelity as He exercises with Himself ; directs upon it a love no less than that with which in the person of the Son He loves Himself ; fulfilling His will upon earth as in the eternal decree which precedes everything temporal it is already fulfilled in heaven. What happened was this, that under this name God Himself established and equipped the people which bears the name to be " a light of the Gentiles," the hope, the promise, the invitation and the summoning of all peoples, and at the same time, of course, the question, the demand and the judgment set over the whole of humanity and every individual man. As all these things happened under this name, the will of God was done. And according to God's self-revelation attested in Scripture, it is wholly and utterly in these happenings that we are to know what really is the good-pleasure of His will, what is, therefore, His being, and the purpose and orientation of His work, as Creator of the world and Controller of history. There is no greater depth in God's being and work than that revealed in these happenings and under this name. For in these happenings and under this name He has revealed Himself. According to Scripture the One who bears this name is the One who in His own " I " introduces the concept of sovereignty and every perfection. When the bearer of this name becomes the object of our attention and thoughts, when they are directed to Jesus

Christ, then we see God, and our thoughts are fixed on
Him.   [II, 2, p. 52 f.]

[4] The King of Israel is the God who rules all things.

At its simplest, this is the definition with which we have
to fill out our hitherto formal consideration. And again,
we can elucidate the definition most clearly and simply by
saying that the God of Israel, and therefore the God who
rules all things, is the Subject whose speaking and acting
is the source and also the object and content of the witness
of the Old and New Testaments. To put it in another
way : The King of Israel is the One who according to the
witness of the Old and New Testaments spoke the " I am,"
and in speaking it actualised it for seeing eyes and
hearing ears by acts of power within the created cosmos and human history. The concrete name " the King
of Israel " covers both the Old Testament and New Testament forms of the spoken and actualised " I am " in
which we have to do with the Subject of the divine world-
governance.

It may be noted that with this definition and its elucidation the idea of the divine world-governance, whatever
may be our attitude towards it, does at least cease to be a
mere idea and is related to a reality. The form of the idea
acquires concrete substance. The colourless idea takes on
colour. And this takes place when it is seen that in the
idea of the divine world-governance the Subject God
bears this concrete name. To apprehend and affirm the
idea we have to think of definite periods in human history
as this name leads us. And we have to think of definite
places—the land of Canaan, Egypt, the wilderness of
Sinai, Canaan again, the land on the two sides of Jordan,
Jerusalem, Samaria, the towns and villages of Judaea and
Galilee, the various places beyond in Syria, Asia Minor
and Greece, and finally Rome. We have to think of
definite events and series of events which according to the
witness of the Old and New Testaments actually took
place at these periods and in these places, relating them
always to the spoken and actualised " I am." And then
necessarily we have to think of the concrete Scripture
which bears witness to these events, the text of the Old
and New Testaments. And if we cannot apprehend and
affirm the idea of the divine world-governance, then quite

concretely this means that we stand in a negative relationship to these events which took place at definite periods and in definite places, to this reality, and to this concrete Scripture. Belief or unbelief in the divine world-governance, whether we do or do not apprehend and confess it, is no longer a matter of the right or wrong development of the idea, but of the right or wrong relationship to this reality to which the idea has reterence, and therefore to these definite events as according to the equally definite witness of the Old and New Testament Scriptures they took place at definite periods and in definite places. For the Subject who speaks and actualises the " I am " in these events, the King of Israel, is the God who rules the world.

Thomas Aquinas (*S. theol.*, I, *qu.* 103, *art.* 2) postulates and in his own fashion tries to prove that the Subject that rules the world and directs it to Himself as the one supreme end and goal is necessarily *aliquid extra mundum*, a *bonum* or *principium extrinsecum a toto universo*. We can and must accept this postulate. For if the Subject that rules the world is not recognisable and actually recognised as something distinct from the world, how can it really be a Subject that rules the world and posits itself as the goal of all world-occurrence, and how can it be recognisable or recognised as such ? But we may question whether this quite justifiable postulate ought to be filled out by the particular concept of God which Thomas presupposes and uses in his own demonstration. For this concept of God, the concept of a being in Himself, quite independent of all other being and to that extent absolutely superior to it, is indeed an attempt to point away beyond the world. But the reality of this supramundane being cannot be reached by an attempt of this kind. For the only reality that we can point to in this concept is that of the world as it attempts to transcend itself, so that even in such an attempt it is still the world and not this *principium extrinsecum* which might as such be the Ruler of the world and recognisable and recognised as such. We thus have a concept of God which demands proof of the existence of God. If it is to be recognisable and recognised as a being which is different from the world and therefore qualified to be its Ruler, something more is needed and something more must be perceived than the attempt of the world to

34

transcend itself in this concept. What is needed is that the being itself should transcend the limit and self-knowledge of the world, and thereby demonstrate itself. For the idea of the world-governance of such a being can only have substance, the power postulated by Thomas, if by its own initiative and activity and revelation it actualises and makes perceptible the reality of its supramundane being over against the world, thereby demonstrating itself in the midst of the world. This supramundane being can make itself present in the world only by free grace. And it is the source and object and content of the biblical witness that this did actually occur. Of course, this witness does not refer us to the so-called natural proofs of God's existence in which Thomas found support at this critical point. It witnesses to the very intramundane and temporal and spatial " I am " as the work and revelation of grace in which the *principium extrinsecum*, which can as such be the World-ruler, has actually demonstrated itself to be such ; intramundane and temporal and spatial as opposed to the concept of God as an extramundane reality.

This is why in the biblical witness the divine world-governance is related to the King of Israel. From a philosophical standpoint the naivety with which it does this is highly objectionable. But it is in this naivety that its real strength lies. For it does not find any difficulty in the counter-question whether this supramundane being who as such can rule the world really exists. No second postulate is needed to fill out the first. No resort to natural proofs is needed to fill out the second postulate, and by means of the second the first. The outfilling is itself the starting-point. The basis is the intramundane self-demonstration of the extramundane God and World-ruler. And dogmatics has to take over this naivety and strength in its own thinking and utterance. There is no alternative if it is to be Christian thinking and utterance. If we are really to have a world-ruler, one who is capable of world-dominion as a *principium extrinsecum*, we have to relate the matter to the King of Israel. . . .

[III, 3, p. 177 f.]

[5] God Himself is the nearest to hand, as the absolutely simple must be, and at the same time the most distant, as the absolutely simple must also be. God Himself is the

irresolvable and at the same time that which fills and embraces everything else. God Himself in His being for Himself is the one being which stands in need of nothing else and at the same time the one being by which everything else came into being and exists. God Himself is the beginning in which everything begins, with which we must and can always begin with confidence and without need of excuse. And at the same time He is the end in which everything legitimately and necessarily ends, with which we must end with confidence and without need of excuse. God Himself is simple, so simple that in all His glory He can be near to the simplest perception and also laugh at the most profound or acute thinking—so simple that He reduces everyone to silence, and then allows and requires everyone boldly to make Him the object of their thought and speech. He is so simple that to think and speak correctly of Him and to live correctly before Him does not in fact require any special human complexities or for that matter any special human simplicities, so that occasionally and according to our need He may permit and require both human complexity and human simplicity, and occasionally they may both be forbidden us. . . .

Who and what is God Himself? We must not now go back and give an answer which declares what we think the conception of God ought to be, what God must be to be God according to all necessary postulates and ideas in respect of the concept of deity. God Himself is in fact simply the One of whom all prophets and apostles explained that they had heard His voice and had to obey Him, executing the messages and tasks He laid on them, and bearing witness of His will and work to others. In a remarkable way they also recognised His voice in the testimony of each other, at least to the extent that, in a long unbroken chain, admittedly in quite different ways, but in ways which at this point involved no contradiction, they all aimed to be servants and messengers of one and the same God. This One is God Himself, described by the unanimous testimony of prophets and apostles as the Subject of creation, reconciliation and redemption, the Lord. And as they describe and explain these works of His and His dignity, they characterise Him as the One who is gracious and holy, merciful and righteous, patient and wise, but also omnipresent, constant, omnipotent, eternal and glorious. [II, 1, p. 458]

[6] Knowledge of this God brings those who partake of it under a claim that is total and unlimited as regards what is divine. It isolates them unescapably. It confronts them with an exclusive demand that nothing can soften. In respect of God it sets bounds for them which they can break only by giving up the knowledge of this God. In this they experience God's love as grace, mercy and patience. They experience it as God's election in virtue of His freedom, an election in which God not only chooses them for Himself, but in doing so chooses Himself for them, and marks Himself out as the one, true and therefore unique God. They experience His love as an election in which a final decision is reached at every point regarding what is and what is not divine. The decision is reached that this God, who chooses them, is God alone, and that all other so-called or would-be gods are not what they claim to be. He alone is God, because all that He is and does has its significance and power and stands or falls by the fact that He is it and does it in an incomparable and unique way. There is no other like Him. He does not have to face any competition, either hostile or friendly. His Word does not need to fear any contradiction or His work any opposition, nor of course do they stand in need or are they capable of any assistance, supplementation or authorisation from any other source. . . .

Knowledge of God in the sense of the New Testament message, the knowledge of the triune God as contrasted with the whole world of religions in the first centuries, signified, and still signifies, the most radical " twilight of the gods," the very thing which Schiller so movingly deplored as the de-divinisation of the " lovely world." It was no mere fabrication when the Early Church was accused by the world around it of atheism, and it would have been wiser for its apologists not to have defended themselves so keenly against this charge. There is a real basis for the feeling, current to this day, that every genuine proclamation of the Christian faith is a force disturbing to, even destructive of, the advance of religion, its life and richness and peace. It is bound to be so. Olympus and Valhalla decrease in population when the message of the

37

God who is the one and only God is really known and believed. The figures of every religious culture are necessarily secularised and recede. They can keep themselves alive only as ideas, symbols, and ghosts, and finally as comic figures. And in the end even in this form they sink into oblivion. No sentence is more dangerous or revolutionary than that God is One and there is no other like Him. All the permanencies of the world draw their life from ideologies and mythologies, from open or disguised religions, and to this extent from all possible forms of deity and divinity. It was on the truth of the sentence that God is One that the " Third Reich " of Adolf Hitler made shipwreck. Let this sentence be uttered in such a way that it is heard and grasped, and at once 450 prophets of Baal are always in fear of their lives. There is no more room now for what the recent past called toleration. Beside God there are only His creatures or false gods, and beside faith in Him there are religions only as religions of superstition, error and finally irreligion.   [II, 1, p. 443 f.]

2. The Knowledge of God

The knowledge of God in the Christian sense is the result of an event which took place once and once for all. " The Word was made flesh " (Jn. 1¹⁴). God as Creator confronts the creature as an object (His primary objectivity), and He declares Himself as such by means of certain earthly realities, the reality of Jesus Christ and the witness to Him effected through Him and made efficacious by the power of His Spirit (His secondary objectivity). On the human side the corresponding factor is faith, i.e., an indirect knowledge of God which begins with the grateful recognition of this divine mode of revelation and keeps to the realities chosen by God.

[7] What God is as God, the divine individuality and characteristics, the *essentia* or " essence " of God, is something which we shall encounter either at the place where God deals with us as Lord and Saviour, or not at all. The act of revelation as such carries with it the fact that God has not withheld Himself from men as true being, but that He has given no less than Himself to men as the overcoming of their need, and light in their darkness—Himself as the Father in His own Son by the Holy Spirit. The act of God's revelation also carries with it the fact that man,

38

as a sinner who of himself can only take wrong roads, is called back from all his own attempts to answer the question of true being, and is bound to the answer to the question given by God Himself. And finally the act of God's revelation carries with it the fact that by the Word of God in the Holy Spirit, with no other confidence but this unconquerable confidence, man allows being to the One in whom true being itself seeks and finds, and who meets him here as the source of his life, as comfort and command, as the power over him and over all things.

[II, 1, p. 261 f.]

[8] The revelation of God, in which man's fulfilment of the true knowledge of God takes place, is the disposition of God in which He acts towards us as the same triune God that He is in Himself, and in such a way that, although we are men and not God, we receive a share in the truth of His knowledge of Himself. Certainly it is the share which He thinks proper and which is therefore suitable for us. But in this share we have the reality of the true knowledge of Himself. This share is given as God unveils Himself to us in that other, second objectivity, that is to say, in the objectivity of His works and signs in our creaturely sphere, before the eyes and ears and in the hearts which as such and of themselves alone are quite incapable of knowing Him. But the heart of it all is that it is He Himself, the one, supreme and true Lord, who thus unveils Himself to us ; that in revelation we have to do with His action as the triune God, and therefore with Himself in every creaturely work and sign that He uses. On this basis and only on this basis can there be real knowledge of God.

[II, 1, p. 51]

[9] In its subjective reality God's revelation consists of definite signs of its objective reality which are given by God. Among the signs of the objective reality of revelation we have to understand certain definite events and relations and orders within the world in which revelation is an objective reality, and therefore within the world which is also our world, the world of our nature and history. The special determination of these events and relations and orders is that along with what they are and mean within this world, in themselves, and from the standpoint of immanence, they also have another nature and meaning

39

from the side of the objective reality of revelation, i.e., from the side of the incarnation of the Word. Their nature and meaning from this transcendent standpoint is that by them the Word which entered the world objectively in revelation, which was spoken once for all into the world, now wills to speak further in the world, i.e., to be received and heard in further areas and ages of this world. By them it will have " free course " in this world. They are the instruments by which it aims at becoming a Word which is apprehended by men and therefore a Word which justifies and sanctifies men, by which it aims at executing upon men the grace of God which is its content. And their instrumental function is to veil the objective of revelation under a creaturely reality ; and yet to unveil it, i.e., in the actual form of such creaturely reality to bring it close to men, who are themselves also a creaturely reality. They point to revelation. They attest it. No, the Word of God made flesh attests by them that it was not made flesh in vain, that it was spoken once for all, that it is the valid and effective Word.   [I, 2, p. 223]

[10] He unveils Himself as the One He is by veiling Himself in a form which He Himself is not. He uses this form distinct from Himself, He uses its work and sign, in order to be objective in, with and under this form, and therefore to give Himself to us to be known. Revelation means the giving of signs. We can say quite simply that revelation means sacrament, i.e., the self-witness of God, the representation of His truth, and therefore of the truth in which He knows Himself, in the form of creaturely objectivity and therefore in a form which is adapted to our creaturely knowledge.   [II, 1, p. 52]

[11] At bottom, knowledge of God in faith is always this indirect knowledge of God, knowledge of God in His works, and in these particular works—in the determining and using of certain creaturely realities to bear witness to the divine objectivity. What distinguishes faith from unbelief, erroneous faith and superstition is that it is content with this indirect knowledge of God. It does not think that the knowledge of God in His works is insufficient. On the contrary, it is grateful really to know the real God in His works. It really lets itself be shown the objectivity of God by their objectivity. But it also holds fast to the

particularity of these works. It does not arbitrarily choose objects to set up as signs, in that way inventing a knowledge of God at its own good-pleasure. It knows God by means of the objects chosen by God Himself. It recognises and acknowledges God's choice and sanctification in the operation of this knowledge. And, for its part, it uses these special works of God as they ought to be used—as means of the knowledge of God. It lets their objectivity become a witness—yet only a witness—to the objectivity of God. Where the worship of God is made possible and necessary by God Himself, it does not establish an idol worship. Faith, and therefore the knowledge of God, stands or falls with all these determinations of the clothed objectivity of God. It is under these determinations that God is spoken about and heard in the Church of Jesus Christ. Not a single one of them can be set aside or altered without radically injuring the life of the Church.

[II, 1, p. 17 f.]

[12] In opposition to that we have to set first Ex. 33$^{11-23}$. We can hardly understand this except as a confirmation of Luther's general rule, and it forms a background for the understanding of all the rest. It says there of Moses that the Lord spake with him face to face, as a man speaks with his friend (v. 11). What does that mean ? We read in what follows that Moses called upon God in consequence of God saying to him : " I know thee by name, and thou hast also found grace in my sight." Thereupon Moses wished to know of God's " ways "—that is, to " know " Him (v. 13) as the One who would " go up with them " in the move from Sinai to Canaan which He had commanded. " If thy presence go not with me, carry us not up hence. For wherein shall it be known here that I and thy people have found grace in thy sight ? is it not in that thou goest with us ? so shall we be separated, I and thy people, from all the people that are upon the face of the earth " (v. 15 f.). God replies that this very thing shall take place. Moses insists that he would see the glory of the Lord (v. 18). And not even this request meets with a blank refusal. No ; God will make to pass before him " all his glory," and he shall hear the name of the Lord : " I will be gracious to whom I will be gracious, and will shew mercy on whom I will shew mercy " (v. 19). But it

41

is precisely in the passing before of God that Moses is to hear His name. " Thou canst not see my face : for there shall no man see me, and live " (v. 20). This " passing before " obviously means that His prayed and awaited going with them had begun, that God actually does go before him and the people. And in this " passing before " God will place him in the cleft of a rock and spread His hand over him so that he can only see Him from the back (and hence in the process of that passing before and going with and going before). It is in this way and not in any other that he can and shall see the glory of God. It is in this way that God speaks with Moses " face to face, as a man speaketh with his friend." God really speaks with him. Moses hears God's name. He is really encouraged and given directions by God Himself. He knows God, as he has prayed—God in His extremest objectivity. But all this comes to pass in God's passing before and going before, in God's work and action, in which he does not see God's face but in which he can only follow God with his eyes. In this case, more than that would not only be less, but even nothing at all—indeed, something negative. Man cannot see God's face, God's naked objectivity, without exposing himself to the annihilating wrath of God. It would indeed have to be a second God who could see God directly. How could man escape destruction by God ? Hence God shows Moses a twofold mercy : not only does He actually receive him according to His promise ; but also He does it in a way that is adapted to him as a creature, and speaks to him through the sign of His work. We can hardly presuppose that any of the other scriptural passages and references that should be considered in this context teach anything in opposition to this indirect knowledge of God. Rather we shall have to assume that, even in those passages where means and signs of God's appearance or speaking are not expressly mentioned, they are nevertheless taken for granted by the biblical writers. They always mean the God who is present and revealed to man in His secondary objectivity, in His work. . . .

Moreover, the message of the New Testament is nothing but the proclamation of the name of God on the ground of His gracious " passing before." And it is given in the form of a continual explanation of a definite historical event—of the same historical event that began with the Exodus, even with the call of Abraham, even with the covenant with Noah. But now its concrete aim and its totality become quite clear. The Messiah, the promised Son of Abraham and David, the Servant of Yahweh, the Prophet, Priest and King, has appeared ; and not only as sent by God, but Himself God's Son. Yet the Word does not appear in His eternal objectivity as the Son who alone dwells in the bosom of the Father. No ; the Word became flesh. God gives Himself to be known, and is known, in the substance of secondary objectivity, in the sign of all signs, in the work of God which all the other works of God serve to prepare, accompany and continue, in the manhood which He takes to Himself, to which He humbles Himself and which He raises through Himself. " We say his glory " now means : we say this One in His humanity, the humanity of the Son of God, on His way to death, which was the way to His resurrection. Hence, it is again an indirect encounter with God in which the apostles, as the witnesses of the New Testament, find themselves. They, too, stand before a veil, a sign, a work of God. In the crib of Bethlehem and at the cross of Golgotha the event takes place in which God gives Himself to them to be known and in which they know God. The fact that they see this in the light of the resurrection, and that in the forty days they see it as what it really is, God's own presence and action, does not alter the fact that in the forty days they do see this unambiguously secondary objectivity, and in it as such, and attested by it, they know the primary objectivity and hence God Himself. The fact that the God-manhood of the Mediator Jesus Christ is the fulfilment of the revelation and reconciliation proclaimed in the New Testament is equivalent to the fact that the knowledge of faith in the New Testament is indirect (and for that very reason real !) knowledge of God.

And it is precisely this knowledge of faith, attested in the Old and New Testaments as the knowledge of God from His works, which is now the content of knowledge in the Church of Jesus Christ. Since this message is the Gospel of its Lord and therefore of the God-man, the Mediator, it stands in explicit contrast to any message having the pure and naked objectivity of God Himself as its object. It is the Gospel of faith and the summons to faith in that it proclaims God—really God Himself—in His mediability, in the sign of His work, in His clothed objectivity. And it is this just because it does not leave the realm of indirect knowledge of God, but keeps to the fact that in this very realm God Himself—and therefore all things—is to be sought and found, and that this indirect knowledge is the right and true knowledge of God because it is chosen and ordained by God Himself. Letting this be enough for oneself is not resignation but the humility and boldness of the man who really stands before God in faith, and in faith alone. The Gospel of the Church of God is therefore of necessity a defined, circumscribed and limited message. It does not contain and say anything and everything. Its content is not the ἄπειρον, the boundless and groundless that human presumption would like to make God out to be. It does not destroy perception ; it integrates it. It does not oppose a definite and concrete view ; it establishes it. It does not teach thought to lose itself in an unthinkable one and all ; it forms it to very definite concepts, affirming this and denying that, including this and excluding that. It contains the veritable Gospel, the Gospel of Jesus Christ, the Messiah of Israel, the true God who became also true man in His own time and place. It explains, not an idea of God, but His name revealed in His deeds. And in correspondence with its content it is itself objective in form—visible Church, audible preaching, operative sacrament. These constitute an area of objectivity among and alongside so many other areas of objectivity ; but this is grounded on the witness of the apostles and prophets which must be shown and proved objectively. Nor is it ashamed of this witness ; on the contrary, it boasts of it as just one book among many others. Christian faith as knowledge of the true God lets itself be included in this area of objectivity, and allows itself to be kept in this area, which in itself and as such is certainly not identical with the objectivity of God. But in it God's work takes place, and hence God's own objectivity gives itself to be known and is to be known, and this on the strength of the choice and sanctification of His free grace. We shall have to destroy the very roots of the Church of Jesus Christ and annihilate faith itself if we want to deny and put an end to the area of secondary objectivity ; if, to reach a supposedly better knowledge of God, we want to disregard and pass over the veil, the sign, the work in which He gives Himself to be known by man without diminution but rather by manifestation of His glory as the One He is. Faith either lives in this sphere, or it is not faith at all. And just the same thing is also true of the knowlege of God through faith.

[II, 1, pp. 18 ff.]

[13] He exists, not only inconceivably as God, but also conceivably as a man ; not only above the world, but also in the world, and of the world ; not only in a heavenly and invisible, but in an earthly and visible form. He becomes and is, He exists—we cannot avoid this statement ; to do so would be the worst kind of Docetism— with objective actuality. Does this mean, then, that He exists as one thing amongst others, and that as such He can be perceived and may be known like other things ? Well, we cannot deny that He is a thing like this, and can be perceived and known as such, if He was and is a man in the world, with an earthly and visible form. But, of course, a man is not merely a thing or object. As a man among men he is a human Thou, and as such distinct from all mere things. Now as a Thou man is not merely an existential determination of the I, but the sum of all the objective reality of the world. And in Jesus Christ God becomes and is man, the fellow-man of all men. As God He is not merely one of many such fellow-men, nor is He merely the idea of fellow-humanity. We are speaking of " the Father's Son, by nature God." He became and is man, the fellow-man of all men ; and therefore Thou, not merely in a simple, but in a supremely objective reality, *the* human Thou, which as such is also directly the Thou of the one eternal God. It is not that a man has rightly or wrongly taken it upon himself to be the objective reality of this human Thou, and has been grasped and understood and interpreted by others as the objective reality of this Thou. The fact is rather that God Himself, in His deep mercy and its great power, has taken it upon Himself to exist also in human being and essence in His Son, and therefore to become and be a man, and therefore this incomparable Thou. God Himself is in the world,

45

earthly, conceivable and visible, as He is this man. We have to do with God Himself as we have to do with this man. God Himself speaks when this man speaks in human speech. God Himself speaks when this man speaks in human speech. God Himself acts and suffers when this man acts and suffers as a man. God Himself triumphs when this One triumphs as a man. The human speaking and acting and suffering and triumphing of this one man directly concerns us all, and His history is our history of salvation which changes the whole human situation, just because God Himself is its human subject in His Son, just because God Himself has assumed and made His own our human nature and kind in His Son, just because God Himself came into this world in His Son, and as one of us " a guest this world of ours He trod." [IV, 2, p. 50 f.]

[14] If the fact that the Son of God became and is also the Son of Man may be known as such among all the other facts of world-occurrence, how else can it be but by His self-revelation ? Which of all the forms of contemplation and thought that we know and use for the perception of other subjects can be of any avail in this connexion ? What physics or metaphysics can even lead us to this subject, let alone enable us to know it—to know it, that is, in a way that permits us, as in theology, to see and handle it materially as a basis, and formally as an axiom, of all subsequent reflection ? What authority, even if it is that of an infallible Church or the apostles, can guarantee it if it does not guarantee itself in their witness ? If it is in fact guaranteed, it is by itself, because and as it is revealed in the sense described. Otherwise it is not guaranteed. Otherwise we will be forced to admit that we have only hazarded a hypothesis—a bold and profound hypothesis perhaps, but only a hypothesis. We have only *made* an assumption, and we will have to rely on the fact that we have made it consistently, and that it may be relevant and fruitful. But at bottom we will not really know. We will only suspect. And the whole Church will rest on this hypothesis. It will not really know, but only suspect, where and on what it really stands. If it does know, if we know, it is only on the ground that this fact is not merely a fact, but that as such it speaks for itself, that it makes that self-disclosure, that from its maintained

objectivity there springs the fact that it makes itself known, that it therefore includes in itself a subject which knows it as such. It is better not to conceal the truth that there can be no sure knowledge of it at all except—in this sense—from itself. [IV, 2, p. 123]

[15] The presupposition of this knowledge of the man Jesus is the participation of the knowing subject in the new thing which makes this One this man within the cosmos. And the presupposition of this participation is that the ground of being of this One penetrates and transcends of itself the limits of the sphere of what we can see and interpret and know, that it discloses and declares and attests and reveals itself in this sphere. But this means that in the power and mercy of the same divine act of majesty which is the ground of His being the man Jesus speaks for Himself, expounds Himself and gives Himself to be known, so that He is no longer just confessed in a way, but known and recognised as the One He is. This means that in and with His self-disclosure He induces and initiates the human seeing and interpreting which attaches itself to the divine act of majesty in and by which He has His being, following and accompanying it, repeating the being which He has on this basis, and therefore becoming and being a relevant human seeing and interpreting (as that which is mastered by Him). The essence of the knowledge of this One is that the divine act of majesty in and by and from which the man Jesus has His being should be reflected and repeated in the human seeing and interpreting which is awakened and controlled by Him and therefore corresponds to Him. [IV, 2, p. 39]

[16] The Holy Spirit is the coming of the man Jesus, who is the Son of God, to other men who are not this but with whom He still associates. And the witness of the Holy Spirit is the disclosure to these men, and therefore their discovery, of the fact that because they are associated with Him they can be called what they are certainly not called of themselves, and be what they can certainly never become or be of themselves—children of God, children of light who in the midst of death are freed from the fear of death because as sinners they are freed from the curse of sin, and as such messengers to all those who, because they do not see the light, are still in darkness, but are not to

remain in this darkness. And as and because the Holy Spirit is the coming of Jesus Christ Himself, and His witness this disclosure to men concerning themselves, He and His witness are in fact the self-revelation of Jesus Christ and as such the basis of the knowledge of Jesus Christ.   [IV, 2, p. 128]

[17] We have to realise that God's revealedness for us is God's own person and God's own work. All the comfort, all the power, all the truth of this revealedness depends upon the fact that it is with God that we are dealing. All our understanding of this revealedness depends upon the fact that we identify it with God Himself, ruling out all other possibilities but God's possibility. We have therefore to realise that as the recipient of revelation man is brought under God's judgment. It is only because of this that he is brought under God's promise. It is only because of this that God meets him as the One who intercedes for him, who undertakes and directs his cause, who does not therefore quench his own ability and will and accomplishment but subordinates it to His own, since man must always be subordinated to God, if God's glory is to triumph and man is to be helped. We are to understand, therefore, that for God to be revealed involves the dislodging of man from the estimation of his own freedom, and his enrichment with the freedom of the children of God. This negation, the negation of man through God's eternal grace and mercy, is only the obverse of his position as a child of God, as a member of the covenant between God and man. But this obviously means that the negation of man cannot be put into effect any more than his position as a child of God except through God's own action. Thus God's possibility triumphs over the very imprisonment in which we are involved, where we only fulfil our own possibilities and only believe in our own possibilities. The self-enclosed uniqueness of man, who only has and knows his own freedom, is overarched and enclosed and finally relativised through the uniqueness of God and His freedom, the freedom in which He is resolved to have fellowship with this man and once and for all to be his Lord. How could man ever foresee this triumph and the wonder of it ? How could he ever anticipate this triumph or prepare himself for it ? It is God's triumph. It is a state or position in which

man may very well find himself, but only with amazement, only with gratitude, only in humble recognition of an accomplished fact, without any opportunity to think how it might come to pass, without possessing any need or capacity to derive it from his earlier state or to indicate the way which led from the one to the other.

[I, 2, p. 259 f.]

[18] Knowledge of God is obedience to God. Observe that we do not say that knowledge of God may also be obedience, or that of necessity it has obedience attached to it, or that it is followed by obedience. No ; knowledge of God as knowledge of faith is in itself and of essential necessity obedience. It is an act of human decision corresponding to the act of divine decision ; corresponding to the act of the divine being as the living Lord ; corresponding to the act of grace in which faith is grounded and continually grounded again in God. In this act God posits Himself as our object and ourselves as those who know Him. But the fact that He does so means that our knowing God can consist only in our following this act, in ourselves becoming a correspondence of this act, in ourselves and our whole existence and therefore our considering and conceiving becoming the human act corresponding to the divine act. This is obedience, the obedience of faith. Precisely—and only—as this act of obedience, is the knowledge of God knowledge of faith and therefore real knowledge of God. Were it something else, did it not spring from obedience and therefore from faith, it would miss God and would certainly not be knowledge of God. For God will be known as the One He is. But precisely as the One He is, He acts. It is as this One who acts, however, that He will be known. [II, 1, p. 26]

3. THE QUESTION OF NATURAL THEOLOGY

By the natural knowledge of God (natural theology or general revelation) there has always been understood in Christian theology the knowledge of God which man has thought he could receive apart from the concrete divine act of revelation and on the basis of general human utterance concerning the gods and the divine. Barth thinks that the linking of Christian thought about God with this supposed general knowledge is a fateful error, because important characteristics are imparted by what man thinks he knows of himself. Revelation seeks to rescue man from his own imaginings concerning the divine. Hence there can be no concord but only conflict between religion (as the knowledge of God possible to man) and the Gospel. Historic Christianity itself is religion, and must constantly come under the criticism of the Gospel. This was for Barth the real issue in the German Church conflict after 1933, as recognised in the *Barmen Declaration* of 1934, which was essentially composed by him.

[19] When we spoke of the original and basic will of God, of His " first act " fulfilled in and with creation but transcending creation, we did not speak of an " original revelation " which we must differentiate from Jesus Christ because it is in fact different from Him. We did not speak in the light of the results of any self-knowledge or self-estimate of human reason or existence. We did not speak with reference to any observations and conclusions in respect of the laws and ordinances which rule in nature and human history. We certainly did not speak in relation to any religious disposition which is supposed to be or actually is proper to man. There is only one revelation. That revelation is the revelation of the covenant, of the original and basic will of God. How else could this be revealed to us ? The concept of an " original revelation " which must be differentiated from the revelation in Jesus Christ because it is actually different from it is a purely empty concept, or one that can be filled only by illusions.

In a word, the covenant of grace which is from the beginning, the presupposition of the atonement, is not a discovery and conclusion of " natural theology." Apart from and without Jesus Christ we can say nothing at all about God and man and their relationship one with another. Least of all can we say that their relationship can be presupposed as that of a covenant of grace. Just because it is a covenant of grace, it cannot be discovered by man, nor can it be demonstrated by man. As the covenant of grace it is not amenable to any kind of human reflection or to any questions asked by man concerning the meaning and basis of the cosmos or history. Grace is inaccessible to us : how else can it be grace ? Grace can only make itself accessible. Grace can never be recalled. To remember grace is itself the work of grace. The perception of grace is itself grace.   [IV, 1, p. 45]

[20] Natural theology is the doctrine of a union of man with God existing outside God's revelation in Jesus Christ. It works out the knowledge of God that is possible and real on the basis of this independent union with God, and its consequences for the whole relationship of God, world and man. It is a necessary undertaking in the sphere of man as such—presupposing that there is such a sphere and that it can therefore be the object of serious consideration. Whatever we may think of its character as reality or illusion, this sphere arises and exists in the fact that man depends on himself over against God. But this means that in actual fact God becomes unknowable to him and he makes himself equal to God. For the man who refuses his grace God becomes the substance of the highest that he himself can see, choose, create and be. It is of this that he gives an account in natural theology He must do it, because this is the self-exposition and self-justification of the being of man in this sphere.

[II, 1, p. 168]

[21] This " coming to us " of the truth is revelation. It does not reach us in a neutral condition, but in an action which stands to it, as the coming of truth, in a very definite, indeed a determinate relationship. That is to say, it reaches us as religious men ; i.e., it reaches us in the attempt to know God from our standpoint. It does not reach us, therefore, in the activity which corresponds to it. The activity which corresponds to revelation would have to be faith ; the recognition of the self-offering and self-manifestation of God. We need to see that in view of God all our activity is in vain even in the best life ; i.e., that of ourselves we are not in a position to apprehend the truth, to let God be God and our Lord. We need to renounce all attempts even to try to apprehend this truth. We need to be ready and resolved simply to let the truth be told us and therefore to be apprehended by it. But that is the very thing for which we are not resolved and ready. The man to whom the truth has really come will concede that he was not at all ready and resolved to let it speak to him. The genuine believer will not say that he came to faith from faith, but—from unbelief, even though

51

the attitude and activity with which he met revelation, and still meets it, is religion. For in faith, man's religion as such is shown by revelation to be resistance to it. From the standpoint of revelation religion is clearly seen to be a human attempt to anticipate what God in His revelation wills to do and does do. It is the attempted replacement of the divine work by a human manufacture. The divine reality offered and manifested to us in revelation, is replaced by a concept of God arbitrarily and wilfully evolved by man.   [I, 2, p. 301 f.]

[22] We begin by stating that religion is unbelief. It is a concern, indeed, we must say that it is the one great concern, of godless man. . . .

In the light of what we have already said, this proposition is not in any sense a negative value-judgment. It is not a judgment of religious science or philosophy based upon some prior negative judgment concerned with the nature of religion. It does not affect only other men with their religion. Above all it affects ourselves also as adherents of the Christian religion. It formulates the judgment of divine revelation upon all religion. It can be explained and expounded, but it cannot be derived from any higher principle than revelation, nor can it be proved by any phenomenology or history of religion. Since it aims only to repeat the judgment of God, it does not involve any human renunciation of human values, any contesting of the true and the good and the beautiful which a closer inspection will reveal in almost all religions, and which we naturally expect to find in abundant measure in our own religion, if we hold to it with any conviction. What happens is simply that man is taken by God and judged and condemned by God. That means, of course, that we are struck to the very roots, to the heart. Our whole existence is called in question. But where that is the case there can be no place for sad and pitiful laments at the non-recognition of relative human greatness.

That is why we must not omit to add by way of warning that we have not to become Philistines or Christian icono-clasts in face of human greatness as it meets us so strikingly in this very sphere of religion. Of course it is inevitable and not without meaning that in times of strong Christian feeling heathen temples should be levelled to the earth,

idols and pictures of saints destroyed, stained glass smashed,
organs removed : to the great distress of aesthetes everywhere. But irony usually had it that Christian churches
were built on the very sites of these temples and with
materials taken from their pillars and furnishings. And
after a time the storm of iconoclasm was succeeded by a
fresh form of artistic decoration. This goes to show that
while the devaluation and negation of what is human may
occasionally have a practical and symbolical significance
in detail, it can never have any basic or general significance.
And it must not, either. We cannot, as it were, translate
the divine judgment that religion is unbelief into human
terms, into the form of definite devaluations and negations.
From time to time it has to be manifested in the form of
definite devaluations and negations. But we must still
accept it as God's judgment upon all that is human. It
can be heard and understood, strictly and exactly as
intended, only by those who do not despair of the human
element as such, who regard it as something worth while,
who have some inkling of what it means really to abandon
the world of Greek or Indian gods, China's world of wisdom,
or even the world of Roman Catholicism, or our own
Protestant world of faith as such, in the thoroughgoing
sense of the divine judgment. In this sense the divine
judgment, which we have to hear and receive, can actually
be described as a safeguard against all forms of ignorance
and Philistinism. It does not challenge us to a venal and
childish resignation in face of what is humanly great, but
to an adult awareness of its real and ultimate limits, which
do not have to be fixed by us but are already fixed. In
the sphere of reverence before God, there must always be
a place for reverence for human greatness. It does not lie
under our judgment, but under the judgment of God.

[I, 2, p. 299 f.]

[23] It (religion) is a feeble but defiant, an arrogant but
hopeless, attempt to create something which man could
do, but now cannot do, or can do only because and if God
Himself creates it for him : the knowledge of the truth,
the knowledge of God. We cannot, therefore, interpret the
attempt as a harmonious co-operating of man with the
revelation of God, as though religion were a kind of out-
stretched hand which is filled by God in His revelation.

53

Again, we cannot say of the evident religious capacity of man that it is, so to speak, the general form of human knowledge, which acquires its true and proper content in the shape of revelation. On the contrary, we have here an exclusive contradiction. In religion man bolts and bars himself against revelation by providing a substitute, by taking away in advance the very thing which has to be given by God.

He has, of course, the power to do this. But what he achieves and acquires in virtue of this power is never the knowledge of God as Lord and God. It is never the truth. It is a complete fiction, which has not only little but no relation to God. It is an anti-God who has first to be known as such and discarded when the truth comes to him. But it can be known as such, as a fiction, only as the truth does come to him. [I, 2, p. 303]

[24] We will conclude with a short historical commentary on the first article of the *Theological Declaration* of the Synod of Barmen on May 31st, 1934. The text is as follows :

" I am the way, the truth, and the life : no man cometh unto the Father, but by me " (Jn. 14⁶).

" Verily, verily, I say unto you, He that entereth not by the door into the sheepfold, but climbeth up some other way, the same is a thief and a robber. . . . I am the door : by me if any man enter in, he shall be saved " (Jn. 10¹, ⁹).

Jesus Christ, as He is attested to us in Holy Scripture, is the one Word of God, whom we have to hear and whom we have to trust and obey in life and in death.

We condemn the false doctrine that the Church can and must recognise as God's revelation other events and powers, forms and truths, apart from and alongside this one Word of God.

This text is important and apposite because it represents the first confessional document in which the Evangelical Church has tacked the problem of natural theology. The theology as well as the confessional writings of the age of the Reformation left the question open, and it has actually become acute only in recent centuries because natural theology has threatened to turn from a latent into an increasingly manifest standard and content of Church proclamation and theology. The question became a burning one at the moment when the Evangelical Church in Germany was unambiguously and consistently confronted by a definite and new form of natural theology, namely, by the demand to recognise in the political events of the year 1933, and especially in the form of the God-sent Adolf Hitler, a source of specific new revelation of God, which, demanding obedience and trust, took its place beside the revelation attested in Holy Scripture, claiming that it should be acknowledged by Christian proclamation and theology as equally binding and obligatory. When this demand was made, and a certain audience was given to it, there began, as is well known, the so-called German Church conflict. It has since become clear that behind this first demand stood quite another. According to the dynamic of the political movement, what was already intended, although only obscurely outlined, in 1933 was the proclamation of this new revelation as the only revelation, and therefore the transformation of the Christian Church into the temple of the German nature- and history-myth.

The same had already been the case in the developments of the preceding centuries. There can be no doubt that not merely a part but the whole had been intended and claimed when it had been demanded that side by side with its attestation in Jesus Christ and therefore in Holy Scripture the Church should also recognise and proclaim God's revelation in reason, in conscience, in the emotions, in history, in nature, and in culture and its achievements and developments. The history of the proclamation and theology of these centuries is simply a history of the wearisome conflict of the Church with the fact that the " also " demanded and to some extent acknowledged by it really meant an " only." The conflict was bound to be wearisome and even hopeless because, on the inclined plane on which this " also " gravitated into " only," it could not supply any inner check apart from the apprehension, inconsistency and inertia of all interested parties. Actually in these centuries too the Church was —as always miraculously—saved because the Bible remained in face of the " also " of invading natural theology and it secret " only." For it threw its own " only " into the scales, and in this way—not without the co-operation of that

55

human apprehension, inconsistency and inertia—did at least maintain the point that for their part God's revelation in Jesus Christ and faith and obedience to Him are " also " not actually to be reduced to silence and oblivion. Thus things were not carried as far as the logic of the matter really demands. The logic of the matter demands that, even if we only lend our little finger to natural theology, there necessarily follows the denial of the revelation of God in Jesus Christ. A natural theology which does not strive to be the only master is not a natural theology. And to give it place at all is to put oneself, even if un-wittingly, on the way which leads to this sole sovereignty. But during the developments of these centuries this whole state of affairs was almost entirely hidden, particularly from the eyes of those who wanted in good faith to defend the validity and value of the biblical revelation. It is noteworthy that it was conservative movements within the Church, like those inspired by Abraham Kuyper and Adolf Stöcker, which acted most naively. But the naivety reigned at every point. The concept of revelation and that of reason, history or humanity were usually linked by the copulative particle " and," and the most superficial provisos were regarded as sufficient protection against all the possible dangers of such combinations. Happy little hyphens were used between, say, the words " modern " and " positive," or " religious " and " social," or " German " and " Evangelical," as if the meaning then became self-evident.' The fact was overlooked that all this pointed to the presence of a trojan horse within which the superior enemy was already drawn into the city. For in the long run the fundamentally peaceful acknowledg-ment of the combination came to be accepted as the true orthodoxy, as the basis of theology (especially of Church governments). The resistance occasionally offered to it necessarily came under suspicion as fanatical one-sidedness and exaggeration.

This was how matters stood when the Church was con-fronted with the myth of the new totalitarian state of 1933—a myth at first lightly masked, but unmasked soon enough. It need not be said that at first the Church stood entirely defenceless before this matter and simply had to succumb to it for the time being. Once again, as so often for two hundred years—or so it seemed—the representative of a new trend and movement of the human spirit knocked at the door of the Church. Its petition was very understandable in the light of every precedent. It asked simply that its ideas and ideals should be allowed into the Church like those of all earlier times and phases. Its argument was that they constituted a more timely form, a new historical hinterland, a point of contact given by God Himself, *rebus sic stantibus*, for the proclamation of the Gospel, which in itself, of course, would remain unaltered. Exactly the same thing had happened at the beginning of the 18th century with the reviving humanism of the Stoa ; or a century later with idealism ; or, in its train, with Romanticism ; and then with the positivism of the bourgeois society and scholarship of the 19th century ; and the nationalism of the same period ; and a little later socialism : they had all wanted to have their say in the Church. And in face of these clear precedents there could be no basic reason for silencing this new nationalism of race. Whether it was as worthy as its predecessors to be heard and to have its say in the Church is a matter on which there might be different opinions outside Germany. A negative answer would normally be given where the phenomenon of race nationalism is unknown or known only from a distance, and a different political and philosophical position causes it to be regarded with repugnance. But we must not fail to realise that inside Germany an affirmative answer could be given with what is basically just the same right. If it was admissible and right and perhaps even orthodox to combine the knowability of God in Jesus Christ with His knowability in nature, reason and history, the proclamation of the Gospel with all kinds of other proclamations—and this had been the case, not only in Germany, but in the Church in all lands for a long time— it is hard to see why the German Church should not be allowed to make its own particular use of the procedure. And the fact that it did with its customary German thoroughness is not really a ground of reproach. What the " German Christians " wanted and did was obviously along a line which had for long enough been acknowledged and trodden by the Church of the whole world : the line of the Enlightenment and Pietism, of Schleiermacher,

Richard Rothe and Ritschl. And there were so many parallels to it in England and America, in Holland and Switzerland, in Denmark and the Scandinavian countries, that no one outside really had the right to cast a stone at Germany because the new combination of Christian and natural theology effected there involved a combination with the race nationalism which happened to be rather uncongenial to the rest of the world, and because this combination was now carried through with a thoroughness which was so astonishing to other nations. Now that so many other combinations had been allowed to pass uncontradicted, and had even been affectionately nurtured, it was about two hundred years too late to make any well-founded objection, and in Germany there were at first good reasons to make a particularly forceful stand for this new combination. It had the merit of recommending itself especially to German Lutheranism as, so to say, its distinctive and perhaps definitive solution of the question of the relationship of Christian and natural theology and proclamation. It could seem like the powerful river in which the different separate streams of the older and oldest history of the German Church and religion might possibly unite. It seemed to promise the exponents of culture and fellowship the unexpected fulfilment of their deepest wishes. It seemed to raise like a tidal wave the ship of the Church, which many people felt had run aground, and at last, at long last to be trying to bear it back again to the high seas of the real life of the nation and therefore into the sphere of reality. Humanly speaking, it was inevitable that in 1933 the German Evangelical Church should accede to the demand made of it, to the new " also," and the " only " which lay behind it, with exactly the same abandon as it had done to so many other demands, and as the Church in other lands—wittingly or unwittingly— had continually done to so many other demands. The only question was whether the Bible, which was not at first to be suppressed, and the usual apprehension, inconsistency and inertia of all concerned, would not this time too act as a counter-weight and prevent matters being carried to extremes.

It was, therefore, an astonishing fact—and this is the significance of the first article of the Barmen *Declaration*—

that within Germany there arose an opposition to the new combination which was aimed not only at this particular combination, but basically at the long-accustomed process of combination, at the " and " which had become orthodox in Germany and in the whole world, at the little hyphen as such and therefore at no more and no less than the condominion of natural theology in the Church. For when in Barmen Jesus Christ as He is attested to us in Holy Scripture was designated as the one Word of God whom we have to trust and to obey in life and in death ; when the doctrine of a source of Church proclamation different from this one Word of God was repudiated as false doctrine ; and when, in the concluding article of the whole *Declaration*, the acknowledgment of this truth and the repudiation of this error were declared to be the indispensable theological foundation of the German Evangelical Church—an assertion was made (far above the heads of the poor " German Christians " and far beyond the whole momentary position of the Church in Germany) which, if it was taken seriously, contained in itself a purifying of the Church not only from the concretely new point at issue, but from all natural theology. The German Christians were contradicted by the contradiction of the whole development at whose end they stood. The protest—this was expressed with blunt words at Barmen by Hans Asmussen, who had to explain the whole proposal—was " against the same phenomenon which for more than two hundred years had slowly prepared the devastation of the Church." The protest was without doubt directed against Schleiermacher and Ritschl. The protest was directed against the basic tendencies of the whole 18th and 19th centuries and therefore against the hallowed traditions of all other Churches as well. And it must be noticed that this protest was formulated in a contemporary application of the confession of the Reformation yet without the possibility of appealing to any express formula in that confession. In the unity of faith with the fathers something was expressed which they had not yet expressed in that way. The venture had to be made, even at the risk of the suspicion and later the actual charge of innovation in the Church. It was under the sign of this protest that the German Church conflict continued from this point.

59

All its individual and practical problems were and still are directly and indirectly connected with the first article of Barmen. The Church was the " confessional " Church precisely in the measure that it took this decision seriously in all its aspects. The conclusions of the Synod of Dahlem in November, 1934 clarified its position in relation to Church law. But this clarification was dependent upon the dogmatic clarification of Barmen and could be carried through only in conjunction with it. The accumulated errors and vacillations in the Confessional Church are connected with the fact that the insight expressed at Barmen—Jesus Christ is the one Word of God whom we have to trust and to obey—did not at first correspond to the flesh and blood reality of the Church but contradicted it, and had still to be repeated, attained and practised in a wearisome struggle. Where this did not happen, no other attitude could be reached in practice than that of continual partial retreats and compromises. Where it did happen, it carried with it automatically the will and the power to resist. The German Confessional Church has either the power of the ecumenical gift and task which it received and accepted at Barmen, or it has no power. It fights either for the purification of which the Evangelical Church has long been in need and is everywhere in need, or in reality it does not fight at all. Had it been concerned simply with the German error of 1933, or with certain fatal consequent manifestations of this error, its conflict would have had no less but also no more meaning than the different reactions within the great modern disorder which had never been entirely lacking earlier and are not entirely lacking elsewhere. It would then not have been a real and serious conflict. It is a real and serious conflict so far as it is concerned with the matter as a whole ; and not merely because what is at issue is obviously the opponent natural theology in its newest form, but because it is this time a question of the Church itself in its repudiation of natural theology as a whole, because it is a question of its own fundamental purification. But the very thing which (in what is best described as a cry of need and of joy) is expressed in the first article of the Barmen *Declaration* is that this is at issue. The fact that in 1934 the basic opposition could be made which is laid down in this article, and that, in spite

60

of all uncertainty and reverses, this opposition could since prove and maintain itself as the nerve of the whole attitude of the Confessional Church in a position of the severest tribulation, is something which, however things may develop, we can already describe as one of the most notable events in modern Church history.

It was not the new political totalitarianism, nor was it the methods of beleaguerment which precipitated this event. And it is naive in the extreme to find in " Calvinism " or the activity of this or that professor of theology the effectual power of salvation (or corruption) in this affair. The fact is that, when nothing else was left for the Church, the one Word of God who is called Jesus Christ remained. The fact is that it could not let itself fall into the abyss, as was demanded, but that it could take and had to take a new stand. The fact is that this time the logic of the case worked irresistibly on the other side and therefore this time it was arrested in the Church. And all this has to be appraised spiritually or it cannot be appraised at all. What might have been expected was that, having so often blunted the temptation in its earlier, finer forms, the Church would now be tired and its eyes blurred and it would be inwardly exhausted, so that it would succumb all the more easily and this time for good to the assault of the blatant temptation. But the fact is that this did not happen. The Word of God still remained, in spite of everything, in the same Church in which it had been so often denied and betrayed. Men could still be so terrified by the spectre of the terrible form of the new god and his messiah as not to give way to it. They could still come to the position of knowing that there is another possibility than that of crashing into the abyss. In spite of every weakness they could still reach after this other possibility, reading the Bible again, confessing again its clear assertions, and therefore uttering the cry of need and of joy from Barmen. And they could at once stand and hold their position on this ground after all other grounds had crumbled under their feet. That this could be the case certainly has its spiritual-historical, theological and political presuppositions and determinations. But all the same it was impossible, and in the end a miracle, in the eyes of those who saw it at close quarters. And so the first article of Barmen was not merely a pretty little discovery of the theologians. The position in the spring of 1933 was not one in which a fortune could be made in Germany with little theological discoveries. Basically it was quite simply a public statement of the very miracle that against all expectation had once again happened to the Church. When it had lost all its counsellor and helpers, in the one Word of God, who is called Jesus Christ, it still had God for its comfort. Things being as they were, to whom else could it give its trust and obedience ; to what other source of its proclamation could it and should it cling ? *Rebus sic stantibus*, any other source could only be myth and therefore the end of all things and certainly the end of the Church. But from this very end the Church now saw itself pulled back and guarded by the Word of God in contemporaneous self-attestation. What option had it but to confess this Word of God alone ? If we want really to understand the genesis of Barmen, we shall be obliged to look finally neither to the Confessional Church as such nor to its opponents. For there is not much to be seen here. The Confessional Church was, so to speak, only the witness of a situation in which simultaneously there took place a remarkable revelation, as there had not been for a long time, of the beast out of the abyss, and a fresh confirmation of the one old revelation of God in Jesus Christ. It was only a witness of this event. Indeed, it was often a most inconspicuous and inconvenient witness. But it was a witness. It was obliged to notice what was going to be seen on this occasion—that Satan had fallen from heaven like lightning and that the Lord is mighty over all gods. What it noticed on this occasion was the fact of the unique validity of Jesus Christ as the Word of God spoken to us for life and death. The repudiation of natural theology was only the self-evident reverse side of this notice. It has no independent significance. It affirms only that there is no other help—that is, in temptation— when it is a question of the being or not being of the Church. What helps, when every other helper fails, is only the miracle, power and comfort of the one Word of God. The Confessional Church began to live at the hand of this notice and at its hand it lives to this day. And it is this notice which it has to exhibit to other Churches as the testimony which it has received and which is now laid upon it as a commission. It will be lost if it forgets this testimony, or no longer understands it, or no longer takes it seriously ; the power against which it stands is too great for it to meet it otherwise than with the weapon of this testimony. But it will also be lost if it does not understand and keep to the fact that this testimony is not entrusted to it simply for its own use, but at the same time as a message for the world-wide Church. And it may well be decisive for other Churches in the world, for their existence as the one, ecumenical Church of Jesus Christ, whether they on their side are able to hear and willing to accept the message of the Confessional Church in Germany.

For the understanding of what the first article of Barmen has to say in detail, it is perhaps advisable not to pass over the preceding verses from Jn. 14 and Jn. 10, but to understand everything from them as a starting-point. The emphasis of everything said previously lies in the fact that Jesus Christ has said something, and, what is more, has said it about Himself : I myself am the way, the truth, and the life. I myself am the door. The Church lives by the fact that it hears the voice of this " I " and lays hold of the promise which, according to this voice, is contained in this " I " alone ; and therefore it chooses the way, knows the truth, lives the life, goes through the door, which is Jesus Christ Himself alone. Moreover, it is not on its own authority, or in the execution of its own security programme, but on the basis of the necessity in which Jesus Christ Himself has said that no man comes to the Father but by Him, and that any by-passing of Him means theft and robbery, that the Church makes its exclusive claim, negating every other way or truth or life or door apart from Him. The negation has no independent significance. It depends entirely on the affirmation. It can make itself known only as the affirmation makes itself known. But in and with the affirmation it does and must make itself known. For this reason the positive assertion has precedence even in what follows, and for this reason the resulting critical assertion can be understood only as its converse and unambiguous elucidation. The Church lives by the fact that it hears the Word of God to which it can give

63

entire trust and entire obedience, and that in life and in death—that is, in the certainty that it will be sustained in this trust and obedience for time and eternity. Precisely because it is allowed and invited to entire trust and obedience, it knows that the Word said to it is the one Word of God by which it is bound but in which it is also free, alongside whose Gospel there is no alien law and alongside whose Law there is no alien gospel, alongside or behind or above which we do not have to honour and fear any other power as way, truth, life or door. And this one Word is not first to be found, but has already given itself to be found : in Him who has the power and the right to call Himself the way, the truth, the life and the door because He is these things. This one Word means Jesus Christ from eternity to eternity. In this form it is attested in the Holy Scriptures of the Old and New Testaments. In this form it has founded the Church ; and upholds and renews and rules, and continually saves the Church. In this form it is comfort and direction in life and in death. In this form and not in any other ! It is of the " not in any other " that the concluding critical article speaks. We may notice that it does not deny the existence of other events and powers, forms and truths alongside the one Word of God, and that therefore throughout it does not deny the possibility of a natural theology as such. On the contrary, it presupposes that there are such things. But it does deny and designate as false doctrine the assertion that all these things can be the source of Church proclamation, a second source alongside and apart from the one Word of God. It excludes natural theology from Church proclamation. Its intention is not to destroy it in itself and as such, but to affirm that, when it comes to saying whom we have to trust and obey in life and in death, it can have no sense and existence alongside and apart from the Word of God. Whatever else they may be and mean, the entities to which natural theology is accustomed to relate itself cannot come into consideration as God's revelation, as the norm and content of the message delivered in the name of God. When the Church proclaims God's revelation, it does not speak on the basis of a view of the reality of the world and of man, however deep and believing ; it does not give an exegesis of these events and powers,

64

forms and truths, but bound to its commission, and made free by the promise received with it, it reads and explains the Word which is called Jesus Christ and therefore the book which bears witness to Him. It is, and remains, grateful for the knowledge of God in which He has given Himself to us by giving us His Son.   [II, 1, pp. 172 ff.]

THE GOSPEL AND THE BIBLE

By the Gospel, i.e., the glad tidings of the enacted revelation of God, men are brought into the presence of this revelation. The messenger to whom this message is committed is the Church. The basic and therefore the normative form of the witness with which the Church is charged is the Bible. This is a human witness historically conditioned, yet by the concentration of its gaze on revelation it is also the standard or Canon for all further witness. The true understanding of the relationship between the Word of God and the word of man is a main theme in all Christian theology and therefore in the *Church Dogmatics*. The historico-critical investigation of the Bible as pursued for the last two centuries is affirmed by Barth as a legitimate consequence of its humanity and does not contradict its recognition as the Canon.

[25] (3) The third point to be mentioned is what we might call the *opus proprium* of the community, namely, its commission to preach the Gospel to the world. It is in this wider, deeper and more material sense that it is a missionary community. It is for this purpose that it must expand in the world, that it wills to renew itself by admission of men from the world. Through increasing and ever new witnesses the world must be given the intimation that God has espoused its cause, that God has aided it, that it is not a world left to itself but a world which He has loved and saved and which He preserves and rules and conducts to its salvation, and that everything that takes place in it, the whole of human life in all its confusion and affliction and sin and guilt and trouble, indeed, the whole of creaturely life in its subjection, hastens to meet the revelation of what God has accomplished in its favour. The community has to proclaim to the world the free grace of God and the hope which this carries with it. It has to declare to it that Jesus Christ, very God and very man, has come as its Saviour and will come again. This is the announcement of

the kingdom of God. This is the Gospel. The Christian community does not exist for itself ; it exists for the Gospel. It has accepted the primary fact that in Jesus Christ God has put matters right, securing once and for all His own glory as Creator but also the glory of His creature. It has seen that this first thing will also be the last. It has perceived that every happening has in it both its beginning and its end, deriving from it and hastening back to it. It has seen that time and all that is in it is lovingly, patiently, mercifully and helpfully included in it. Having perceived this, it lives among those who have not, at the heart of their great attempt to live without God, in the midst of their countless small attempts to help, justify, sanctify and glorify themselves, within the evils which they thereby inflict on themselves, in the misery which they bring upon themselves and in all the resultant excitement, anxiety and care in which they must exist. The Christian community knows that all this is unnecessary. It sees that No has already been said to it. This is what it has to say to men on the basis of what it has perceived. To be sure, it cannot conceal from them the fact that their great attempt is wrong and futile, that it is outmoded from the very outset, that it can be made only in new sin and with the prospect of new corruption, and therefore that all the small attempts in which the great is revealed and presented are radically overthrown. It cannot approve nor tolerate the way and ways of the world. It has to indicate a very different path. On the other hand, its decisive task is not to confront men with this objection, criticism and negation, nor with a programme, plan or law in the performance of which men must abandon that great attempt to live without God, counterbalancing it by the opposite attempt to return to God and with His help to make everything different and better. This is what the Synagogue does. This is what Freemasonry does. This is what Moral Rearmament does. But this is not what the Church of Jesus Christ does. It has no right to make proposals to men as though they could now help, justify, sanctify and glorify themselves more thoroughly and successfully than hitherto. It cannot set before them any better men, any sinless men, any innocent men, any men who escape the confusion and sorrow of the world. It has no such men to hold out as examples to follow, as though others had only to imitate them to extricate themselves from the quagmire and hell in which they live. It realises indeed that men, belonging to God as His creatures, know deep down the perversity and futility of their attempt and attempts. It knows that at the true and final core of their being is a great weariness and sorrow which they can only conceal and suppress with all their running and clamouring and fighting. It knows that they are all in God's hand, that they cannot escape it, that they inflict so much sorrow on themselves only by continually trying to resist and oppose it. It knows, therefore, that it cannot help them by confirming their true state in the form of accusation. It knows that of themselves men certainly will not overcome and remove this opposition. It knows also that it cannot do it for them. It knows that it does not even say anything new, let alone give real aid, if it can do no more than propose the best and latest plans, programmes and laws, for the elimination of the suffering which results from this opposition, and of its underlying causes. It knows above all that it, too, stands under judgment with all others, that the same opposition is also to be found among Christians, that the community also, the Church in all its forms and enterprises, participates fully and very concretely in the perversity and futility of all human efforts, and that it is therefore useless from the very outset for it to offer or commend either itself or the Christians united within it as a salutary example. No, its great and simple but very different commission is that of declaring to them the kingdom of God, and not therefore a means to help them to do something, but the one truth that God has already begun to do something for them and that He will also complete it in spite of their opposition, outbidding all the attempts which spring from this opposition, overlooking and bypassing all their perversity and futility. What it has to attest to them is neither the divine No nor an improved and Christian Yes, but the divine Yes which does, of course, include a No, i.e., the divine judgment, and which also evokes and entails a new human Yes, but which over and above all is the wise and intrinsically powerful Yes which God has spoken to His creature and which He will finally execute and reveal. The presence of this divine Yes is the new and glorious message which is entrusted to

67

the Christian community and which it is commissioned to deliver on earth. It need neither ask nor worry what the result will be, what success it will either enjoy or not enjoy, so long as it is obedient in this service. The power, fruitfulness, blessing and true help of the Word of God is God's own work, and He has His own varied and very secret ways to accomplish this work. All that the community can and should do is to attest this Word. It does not live by its own triumphs over the world, nor in order to be able to achieve and celebrate such triumphs. It does not live by its numerical growth, nor by asserting itself in the world. It lives by its commission. Its task is simply to see to it that the comfort and exhortation of the divine Yes are declared, and that they are declared as clearly and forcibly and impressively and universally as possible. It has simply to scatter the seed as it is, not on any account mixing with it its own ideas either in criticism of the world or for its amelioration. Nevertheless it must not be faint-hearted. It must be confident that just as it is this seed is the good seed which will bear fruit a hundredfold, sixtyfold or thirtyfold, possibly in very different ways from what it imagines, but all the same real fruit. It must be only the community of the Gospel, content to be no more. Whatever may be enterprised against it cannot prevent it from being the community of the Gospel, let alone destroy it as such. And whatever may have to be said against either it or its members cannot hinder it from being the community of the Gospel. The Word which it has to declare will always place it first under judgment in a far more serious manner than anything that may be said against it from without or that it may have to allege against itself. But the Word which it has to declare will always uphold it. As the community of the Word it may always and supremely live by the Gospel, accepting the divine Yes, taking to heart both its admonition and its consolation, and therefore, notwithstanding all its weakness and all the perversity and futility of human action in which it shares, being fundamentally sure of its cause and therefore undaunted.

[III, 4, pp. 506–508]

[26] In the Church which is charged with this ministry the commitment of the member is beyond computation. There is no possible place for idleness, indifference or luke-

warmness. No appeal can be made to human imperfection where the claim is directed to the very man whose incapacity and unworthiness for this ministry is known and admitted even when he is charged with it, without altering the fact that he really is charged with it. If there is no escape in arrogance, there is no escape in pusillanimity or indolence. He can entertain no illusions, but he has no excuse for diffidence or nonchalance. He can only address himself to the task without pretensions and without reservations. This is what the qualifications and elucidations imply. But they can never become arguments against the positive truth that the members of the Church in all their humanity are invited to share in God's own work of proclaiming His Word. They can never be obstacles to our believing in this positive truth and therefore to our accepting the vocation it implies and holding ourselves in readiness for the service it involves. If they do become obstacles for us, this only shows our failure to understand them, that they are not the great attack of God upon us, from which they derive when they have power. They are the accusations of a kind of scepticism in the guise of piety. We are making them ourselves, not as members of the Church, but in assertion of the arrogance and diffidence of those who wish to evade the power of the resurrection of Jesus Christ and the power of the Holy Spirit. The only power they can have is that of accusations which we ourselves can make. They cannot have real power unless they arise from the realisation that the Son of God has come in the flesh, that His Holy Ghost has been poured out upon the Church, and that the duty of speaking about God has been laid on the Church. They cannot have real power unless they arise, not from unbelief, but from faith. And the power which they then have will be not the power of destruction, paralysis and discouragement, but in a two-fold sense, directed against both our pride and our diffidence, the power of salutary criticism. And behind and above this criticism will stand the transformation which was wrought at the cross and on Easter Day. As members of the Church we share in this transformation (which we ourselves certainly cannot effect either in reality or in thought) in so far as we accept its reality in faith. But that means that we do not escape but accept the salutary

69

criticism and the great assault. And to accept this transformation means to recognise and confess : " He is present with us, in the power of His Spirit and gifts." To accept it means, in all our reflection about the humanity of the Church and ourselves, to look beyond it, and beyond all its incapacity and unworthiness, to the foundation and beginning of the Church and to its existence in Jesus Christ. There, in Him, it is not unworthy and not incapable of speaking about God. There it is all that it has to be for this purpose. There it has everything that it needs for it. There it is justified and sanctified, blessed and authorised in its action. There the miracle has already happened which has to happen to a man if he is to speak about God— really speak about God. The Church looks to Jesus Christ. It allows Him to be its own life, and therefore its consolation. It does not cling to its own humanity—either in arrogance or diffidence—but to the task imposed upon it in its humanity. And as it does so, it can confess, but with a final certainty, that as it speaks about God in human words, it proclaims God's own Word. [I, 2, p. 756 f.]

[27] We have stated that we are told such and such in the New Testament. We are, in fact, told these things. That is where we must begin. And, as we have put it, we for our part must let ourselves be told these things, whether or not they seem either illuminating or acceptable. It is quite indispensable that we should let ourselves be told these things, whatever may be the outcome. But these stiff and cold and non-committal expressions are not the end of the matter. For what the New Testament tells us, at the very heart and centre which is our present concern, it tells us in a specific and distinctive way which addresses and summons us, applying what it says to ourselves and claiming us for it. It tells it to us as witness : witness to a person, to Jesus Christ, to the whole nexus and history of reality and truth bound up in this name, as it is given by those who have the necessary information ; but also witness addressed to persons, to us, who can also acquire this information by receiving the witness, and who are already claimed in anticipation as those whom it concerns. What we have said about the objective content of truth of the reality of Jesus Christ, which includes our own reality, presses in upon us, from its objectivity to our subjectivity,

in order that there should be in us a correspondence. We have already seen this from what we find in its human attestation as it concerns us in the New Testament. It has its historical form in the existence of the New Testament. It becomes a historical event in the encounter between this witness and us. In the name and commission of the reality and truth of Jesus Christ we are concretely seized, whether we like it or not, in the course of this address and summons and application and claim. It is not with aloof detachment, but seizing us in this way, that the New Testament tells us what it has to tell us and what we have to let ourselves be told : who and what is real and true, Jesus Christ as the Lord and we as His ; who and what is also active and effective and reaches and affects us. This is not told us merely as an imparting of information, but as that which lays claim on us for what is imparted. In relation to all generations, and therefore to us, the New Testament has always come with this demand. It has always dared to claim man in this way. It has always dared to lay hold of him, for the impartation of its content, in order that he should receive it and at once become a new witness of its message. Thus to allow ourselves to be told what it tells us means rather more than is at first suggested by this formula. It is to be exposed to this attack which takes place in the New Testament. It is to be involved in the wrestling with this demand. When the New Testament encounters us, we are not at all the " we " that we think (but only think) we know so well, and that so boldly try to control themselves, in all their neutrality and with all their reservations and question-marks and pretexts and caprices and individual activities. But when its witness reaches us, when we are confronted by its witnesses, we are already in the circle of the validity of what they say to us, and are no longer the same in the sense that we are now marked, like trees for cutting, for the fulfilment of our own actual acknowledgment of its validity. This is how the prophets saw and treated their contemporaries, as did also the apostles, both Jews and Gentiles. They confronted them, and the world, with the very sober and not at all enthusiastic presupposition that they belonged to Jesus Christ, and were therefore ordained to hear the news concerning Him. By their very existence these witnesses are never present in vain for the rest, for the world around, for us. To hear them is to hear Him, and to hear Him is to be placed directly before and in the altered world situation, before one's Lord who is the Lord over all. The only thing is that we must not imagine that we are still somewhere alongside or outside the Word that God has spoken through these witnesses. We stand already under the Word.

[IV, 2, p. 303 f.]

[28] The attitude of the biblical witnesses is decided by the fact that, whatever else may rightly or wrongly be said about their other attitudes, they are in the position and are called to give information upon a question put to them from without. They are called by God in the face of all other men to be witnesses of His own action. They can and must attest, before all the world and so that every one may hear, that God has spoken and acted and how He has spoken and acted in Jesus Christ and to His people. Their starting-point is this speaking and acting of God in its determinate reality, and they think and speak before the face of the same God, who now as Judge asks of them nothing but the truth concerning this reality, concerning His own speaking and acting which has taken place once for all. They speak under this twofold pre-supposition, with the weight of it, and therefore with the unchecked flow of a headlong mountain stream. Of course, they also describe, narrate, reflect and argue. How can any witness speak without to some extent doing these things too ? But these things do not make him a witness. Nor did they make the prophets and apostles witnesses of God's revelation. What makes them its witnesses is the fact that they speak under this twofold presupposition : they believe and therefore speak.   [I, 2, p. 817]

[29] The Church is apostolic and therefore catholic when it exists on the basis of Scripture and in conformity with it, i.e., in the orientation which it accepts when it looks only in the direction indicated by the witness which speaks to it in Scripture, with no glances aside in any other direction. The Bible itself cannot do this merely as a sacred but closed book. As such it belongs to the very constitution of all supposed or actual, more or less Christian Churches. But this does not of itself make them true

Churches. What counts is that the Bible speaks and is heard. Again, the Bible cannot do it merely as the book of the law of the Church's faith and order. To the degree that it is treated as such, it is, in fact, controlled. Like the apostles, it does not will to rule but to serve. And it is where it is allowed to serve that it really rules ; that it is not betrayed to any human control. It is not a prescript either for doctrine or for life. It is a witness, and as such it demands attention, respect and obedience—the obedience of the heart, the free and only genuine obedience. What it wants from the Church, what it impels the Church towards—and it is the Holy Spirit moving in it who does this—is agreement with the direction in which it looks itself. And the direction in which it looks is to the living Jesus Christ. As Scripture stirs up and invites and summons and impels the Church to look in this same direction there takes place the work of the Spirit of Scripture who is the Holy Spirit. Scripture then works in the service of its Lord, and the Church becomes and is apostolic and therefore the true Church. [IV, 1, p. 722 f.]

[30] By recognising the existence of a Canon, the Church declares that particularly in its proclamation it realises that it is not left to its own devices, but that the commission which underlies its proclamation, the object of its proclamation, the judgment to which it is subject and its actual eventuation must all come from another source, and that they must do so concretely in the utter externality of the concrete Canon as an imperative which is categorical yet also historical, being issued in time. And by acknowledging that this Canon is actually identical with the Bible of the Old and New Testaments, with the word of the prophets and apostles, it declares that this connexion of its proclamation with something external and concrete is not a general principle, nor a mere determination of form the content of which might be totally different, but that this connexion is completely determined in content, that it is an order received, an obligation imposed, that this piece of past occurrence composed of definite texts constitutes its working instructions, its marching orders, by which itself as well as its preaching stands or falls, so that in no circumstances, not even hypothetically, can they be thought away, or thought to be replaced by

73

others, if proclamation and the Church itself are not to be thought away. [I, 1, p. 113 f.]

[31] In every age, therefore, the Evangelical decision will have to be a decision for Holy Scripture as such. As such, of course, it is only a sign. Indeed, it is the sign of a sign, i.e., of the prophetic-apostolic witness of revelation as the primary sign of Jesus Christ. Of course, the Church can only read Scripture to hear the prophets and apostles, just as it can only hear the latter to see Jesus Christ with them, and to find in Him, and properly, ultimately and decisively only in Him, the prior direct and material and absolute authority from which its authority depends, on which it is founded and by which it is everywhere and always measured. But again, it can distinguish between seeing Jesus Christ, hearing His prophets and apostles and reading their Scriptures, and yet it cannot separate these things, it cannot try to have the one without the other. It cannot see without hearing and it cannot hear without reading. Therefore if it would see Jesus Christ, it is directed and bound to His primary sign and therefore to the sign of this sign—if it would see Jesus Christ, it is directed and bound to Holy Scripture. In it His authority acquires and has that concreteness as an authority higher than the Church which arrests the apparently irresistible revulsion of obedience to self-government. We can appropriate God and Jesus and the Holy Ghost and even the prophetic-apostolic witness in general, and then exalt the authority of the Church under the name and in the guise of their divine authority. But in the form of Holy Scripture God and Jesus Christ and the Holy Ghost and the prophets and apostles resist this change. In this form their divine authority resists the attack which the Church and its authority is always making upon it. Whenever this attack is made and seems to have succeeded, it again escapes it. Rightly or wrongly, in loyalty or disloyalty, the Church may say a thousand things expounding and applying Scripture. But Scripture is always autonomous and independent of all that is said. It can always find new and from its own standpoint better readers, and obedience in these readers, even in a Church which has perhaps to a large extent become self-governing, and by these readers a point of entry to reform and renew the whole Church and to bring it back from self-government

to obedience. If the Reformation of the 16th century means the decision for Holy Scripture, conversely we must also say that for every age of the Church the decision for Holy Scripture means the decision for the reformation of the Church : for its reformation by its Lord Himself through the prophetic-apostolic witness which He established and the force of which is revealed and effective because it is written. Let the Church go away from Scripture as such. Let it replace it by its traditions, its own indefinite consciousness of its origins and nature, its own pretended direct faith in Jesus Christ and the Holy Ghost, its own exposition and application of the word of the prophets and apostles. In the proportion in which it does this, it will prevent that entry upon which its whole life and salvation rests, and therefore at bottom refuse to be reformed. All kinds of " life," evolutions and revolutions will be possible in the Church. It can include conservative and progressive thinking in their constant action and reaction. There can be undeniable tensions and party conflicts like those between Catholicism and Neo-Protestantism, or like the internal Catholic battles between Realists and Nominalists, Episcopalians and Curialists, Benedictines and Jesuits, or the internal Neo-Protestant between Orthodox and Pietists, " Positives " and " Liberals." And these may give the deceptive appearance that the Church is really alive. But it does not live in the inner movement of these tensions. In them we see rather the process of decay to which the Church is at once subject when it ceases to live by the Word of God, which means by Holy Scripture. What is ultimately at issue in these tensions is the very secular antithesis of various human principles which can all be reduced easily to the denominator of this or that philosophical dialectic, and which ultimately reflect only the deep disunity of man with himself. And in these tensions the Church is obviously only disputing with itself. And in this debate properly both partners are right and both wrong. According to the circumstance of the age the debate may end with a victory for this side or that, but neither party, not even the victor, can say Amen with an ultimate certainty and responsibility, because neither way is it or can it be a matter of confession, i.e., of responsibility to a higher tribunal confronting both partners with concrete authority. These debates in the Church are conducted in the absence of the Lord of the Church. But are they then really conducted in the Church ? Has the Church not ceased to be the Church the moment it wants to be alone with itself ? And does it not want to be alone with itself, if it will not stand with its authority under the Word in the concrete sense of the concept, and therefore under Holy Scripture ?

It is here that we come to the final positive meaning of the Evangelical decision : it is taken in the thankful recognition that the Church is not alone, that it is not left to its own discussions and especially that it is not left to itself. It would be the moment its authority ceased to be confronted by that divine authority. For then clothed with divine dignity the Church would have to stand and live by itself like God. And however grand it might seem to be in its godlikeness, for the creature which is distinct from God that means only misery, the misery of sin and death. From this misery of the solitariness of the creature fallen in sin and death the Church is snatched away by the fact that God in Jesus Christ is present and gracious to it in concrete authority, which means in an authority which is different from and superior to its own. It is the Word of God as Holy Scripture which puts an end to this misery. Because Holy Scripture is the authority of Jesus Christ in His Church, the Church does not need to smooth out its own anxieties and needs and questions, it does not need to burden itself with the impossible task of wanting to govern itself, it can obey without having to bear the responsibility for the goal and the result. [I, 2, p. 583 ff.]

[32] 1. The history of Holy Scripture. We are thinking now of its origin and transmission, and its exegesis and influence in the course of history generally. Certainly we cannot say that from this standpoint it sheds any compelling, universal, direct or necessary light upon its content, i.e., the occurrence of that particular and sacred history, and therefore the King of Israel as the Lord of world-occurrence. For there is no doubt that these aspects can be considered and explained as simply the result of a particular epoch in the religious development of mankind, or even as the result of certain peculiar superstitions and delusions, or it may be of the most serious and profound

experiences and insights of the human race, according to the standpoint of the individual observer. And this certainly does not mean that they can be regarded as the result of a demonstration of the world-governance of the One concerning whom this Scripture speaks. We cannot say more than that the history of Holy Scripture can also be considered quite differently from this standpoint. But this we can say. We can take up the position which man necessarily occupies according to the content of this Scripture. And then we can receive and accept its witness, and the Old and New Testament message of the Word and work of God to which it bears testimony. It can then be the case that as we encounter this witness we encounter God Himself and His gracious and compelling existence, and that we are claimed and liberated and captivated by it. It can then be the case that in consequence we are men in whose lives the governance of this God—far from being the governance of a particular god in his own sphere, or the power of a particular idea—has actually shown itself to be the governance of the world. Clearly, the history of Holy Scripture can be considered from quite a different angle on this presupposition, and we may think that on this presupposition it has to be considered from this quite different angle.

We can see this already in relation to its origin. If we accept the witness of Holy Scripture, then implicitly we accept the fact that, quite irrespective of the way in which they were humanly and historically conditioned, its authors were objectively true, reliable and trustworthy witnesses. It is not merely that we recognise their opinions to be good and pious, or appreciate their part and significance in religious history. We perceive rather that it pleased God the King of Israel, to whom the power of their witness is pledged as to the Lord, to raise up these true witnesses by His Word and work. In this fact, at the very beginning of the history of Scripture, and at the heart of world-occurrence, even while the fact itself is a moment in occurrence generally, what we see is not merely a moment in occurrence generally, and in religious occurrence in particular, but a trace of the governance of God as the one and only true God, a trace of this God as the Lord of all world-occurrence.

And this is what we also see in the continuation of this history, the rise, completion and transmission of the Canon of the Old and New Testaments. Certainly it is not a history which is apart from the developments and complications which affect all human history. Certainly it is not a history which is preserved inwardly from the follies and errors and oddities of all human history. It is a history which is not accidental but necessary in its whole course and sequence. It is a true history, not a perverted history. It is a history whose necessity and truth have constantly to be recognised, understood, tested, and actualised. And as such it is a history which can be interpreted in many different ways at different times. But however it is considered and interpreted, it is a history whose meaning persists and maintains itself. It is a history which gives rise to constant questioning, but which constantly puts more important questions on its own account. From this angle again, what we see is not a trace of creaturely occurrence but of the plan and will which rule this occurrence—the plan and will of the One whose Word and work are the subject of the Scripture whose peculiarity is so much emphasised.

And this is also what we can and must see in the history of exegesis which begins already with the history of the text and Canon and necessarily returns again and again to this history. Here, too, we are not outside the sphere of world-occurrence generally, but inside it. Here, too, we see the powerful and far-reaching effect of the various languages and racial characteristics, the politics, economics, philosophy, scholarship, artistic sense, faith, heresy and superstition of the different ages, the individual talents of the various individual readers and exegetes. And here, too, we must give sober consideration to all these factors : how it was all a help or a hindrance ; how it was that such singular honour came to be paid to the Old and New Testaments, and what they had to put up with ; to what extent men faithfully reproduced the teaching of Scripture, and to what extent they wilfully read their own teaching into it ; how again and again Scripture was continually discovered and forgotten, esteemed and despised ; how at all times it was continually understood and misunderstood. Should our estimate of this history be an optimistic or a pessimistic one ? If our attitude to the content of the texts which we are considering is the attitude of that original freedom and constraint, there can be no doubt at least that we shall always see in that history a history of their own self-exegesis. And this means that we shall never look upon the prophets and apostles as merely objects for the study and assessment of later readers ; they will always be living, acting, speaking subjects on their own account. The fact that they have spoken once does not mean that they have now ceased to speak. On the contrary, they take up and deliver the Word afresh in every age and to every people, at every cultural level and to every individual. And they do it in such a way that what they have to say is far more acute and relevant than what may be said or thought about them. What are all the commentaries and other expositions of the Bible but a strong or feeble echo of their voice ? If we are in that direct relationship to the Bible, then in the last and decisive analysis we shall not consider the history of biblical exegesis in the light of what took place outwardly. On the contrary, we shall consider the history of its outward experiences in the light of its own continually renewed and for that reason always surprising action, as a history of its self-declaration and self-explanation in the midst of that general occurrence to which it belongs and within which it constitutes its own life-centre and origin in virtue of its affinity with the divine Word and work to which it testifies. It was not merely a rhetorical flourish when at the time of the Reformation Scripture was gladly described and magnified as *dux* and *magistra*, or even as *regina*. The fact is—and it does not make the slightest difference whether it is recognised or not—that in all ages Scripture has been the subject of its own history, the guiding, teaching, ruling subject, not under men but over men, over all the men who in so many ways, and with such continual oddities and contradictions, have applied themselves to its exposition. And for this reason its history is in this respect too—those who have eyes to see, let them see—a trace of the ruling God whom it declares. It has a concealed but not a completely hidden part in His kingly rule.

And finally, we have to consider the history of its influence or effects. What happened to that witness ? What is happening to it now ? What does it actually accomplish in the world in which it is spoken and transmitted and continually expounded ? In this respect, too, we have to consider it in the sequence of all the other factors of world-occurrence and their effects. Let us take as an illustration the well-known theory that what we call Western Christendom is a hybrid product deriving from biblical Christianity on the one hand and Graeco-Roman antiquity on the other. But how many other causes do we have to mention side by side with the Bible, some of them oriental and some occidental, some of them spiritual and some very strongly material ? If we have not already done so, we shall have to accustom ourselves to thinking of the historical effect of the biblical witness as one effect among many others. And when we do this, we cannot be too serious in reckoning with the fact that what we have to do with here—we need only think of what we call Western Christendom—is a historical effect which is very much diluted and distorted, and which in addition is always restricted in power, and constantly threatened with extinction. In a genuinely historical investigation it can even be asked whether one day this force will not be exhausted and lost like so many others. But what is this force, the influence of the Bible in world history ? If we consider it in the light of the influence which we know as an event in our own lives, then we know it as a wonderful election and calling which we cannot explain merely as a possibility of our own. To our own astonishment we find that we are added to the people, the Church, the community of the King of Israel. We find this particular influence of the biblical witness in the quite extraordinary existence of this community and its commission in the world. And in face of this influence we can only be amazed, first that we are not excluded from it, that we can be aware of it in our own lives, and then that we are not alone in this experience, but can publicly share it with so many others both past and present, both far and near. It claims our whole attention to take this influence seriously, and gratefully to do justice to it. And this means that we have neither the time nor the energy for general historical considerations. We have a prior claim and commission within and in face of all other occurrence. And

80

we shall not experience any surprise at the way in which the influence of the biblical witness is necessarily diluted and distorted and threatened as seen against world-occurrence generally. This fact will not cause us any anxiety or despair. We shall be well enough aware of it from the way in which this influence is diluted and distorted and threatened in our own lives as members of the people of God both individually and corporately. Far from despairing, we shall be ashamed, and do penance, and pray, and work, not only for ourselves, but for the whole people of God. And we shall remember that it would be something far more strange if this high and solemn thing were something triumphant in the midst of world-occurrence, if it were an enormous and undiluted and unequivocal success, if it were something popular. We know that all the influence of the biblical witness can itself have only the form of a witness, the witness of most inadequate creatures. By our commission and its execution we shall not cease to aim at what the Church either is accomplishing or could accomplish by means of it. And there can be no mistake as to the influence which—with all the ambiguity and weakness of that which results from it—the biblical witness does actually have, and always has had, and always will have, in the fact that new witnesses are called out and new confessing communities are assembled by this witness. In the vast ocean of other influences we shall be aware of the fact that at all times and in all places this calling out and assembling has taken place and still does take place. And we shall not look at this influence merely as one among many. We shall not weigh and evaluate it optimistically or pessimistically in relation to the others. In this influence, in the power of the prophetic and apostolic witness at all times and in all places to call out and assemble, we shall again find traces of the One with whom that witness has to do, of the One who is manifestly present as King not only in this influence, but everywhere and always.

[III, 3, pp. 200–204]

5. THEOLOGY

Like all knowledge of God, theology is an impossible enterprise from the human standpoint and can never escape the limitations of humanity. Yet it is both possible and necessary. It is possible because God's revelation is such that it does not exclude the action of man but enlists it into service, the human understanding thus being given a proper role. It is necessary because it can never be taken for granted that the men called to service, i.e., the Church, will give true service and therefore critical testing is constantly demanded. The work of theology is thus wholly related to the task of the Church which is that of every Christian. Whether we can call theology a science depends on what we mean by science. If we do not mean a systematic world-view, but strict objectivity and method, then theology must also, though not exclusively, be pursued in scientific terms.

[33] All theology is *theologia viatorum*. It can never satisfy the natural aspiration of human thought and utterance for completeness and compactness. It does not exhibit its object but can only indicate it, and in so doing it owes the truth to the self-witness of the theme and not to its own resources. It is broken thought and utterance to the extent that it can progress only in isolated thoughts and statements directed from different angles to the one object. It can never form a system, comprehending and as it were " seizing " the object. [III, 3, p. 293]

[34] But the claim is issued—and in this it shews itself to be a true claim—in spite of our powerlessness. It is disclosed to us that we do not view and think of God, that we cannot speak of Him ; and because this is disclosed to us, it is brought home to us that this is the very thing which has to happen no matter what the circumstances, that we must not fail to do it. It is the one characteristic of the revelation of God attested in the Bible that when it is issued it is impossible for man not to proceed to think of God, or to be silent about God. When it is issued, man is convicted of his inability to think of God and to speak of God. And when it is issued, it is required of man that in spite of his inability, and even in his inability, he should still do both. On the ground of this requirement, thanks to the truth of God in it, there is a true knowledge of God on the part of man. The human knowledge of God is true in so far as it does not evade this requirement, but fulfils it in obedience. [II, 1, p. 212]

[35] But the authorisation given us by God's revelation demands our trust and its command our obedience. In its consequences it is nothing more nor less than a denial of Jesus Christ and blasphemy against the Holy Spirit,

resembling the act of the servant who took and hid the one talent entrusted to him, if we try to value our incapacity more highly than the capacity which God Himself in His revelation confers upon our incapacity ; using the appeal to it, and the resigned complaint that God is a hard Master, to justify our failure to attempt to view and conceive Him, and our resort to the way of mystical theology. As God encounters us visibly and conceivably in the witness of His revelation, in the creaturely form of a historical occurrence or a succession of such occurrences, and in the relationships of our own life to these occurrences, we are invited and summoned to know Him as the One who acts and rules in these occurrences and relationships. But this means that our human viewing and conceiving are claimed within their natural limits. They are, of course, claimed by God's revelation of Himself in these visible occurrences and relationships—of God Himself, who as such neither is nor becomes visible.   [II, 1, p. 201]

[36] In this sober exuberance there takes place the true human knowledge of God and the undertaking to view and conceive God humanly and to speak of Him in human words. It is not the undertaking of a slave but of a child. It is childlike even in the restrictive sense of the term, but in such a way that the very limitation of that which is childlike is also the earmark of the peculiar freedom here bestowed upon man. In this exuberance, which has nothing to do with conceit and presumption, in the exuberance of the worship of God in the heart and mouth of the sinful creature, human knowledge of God is an act of gratitude and therefore partakes of the veracity of the revelation of God.   [II, 1, p. 219]

[37] We say awe, having previously said thanksgiving, and having referred finally to the necessary joyfulness of the knowledge that participates in the veracity of the revelation of God. But as in the case of thanksgiving, and therefore joyfulness, we have to say awe of necessity. Awe refers to the distance between our work and its object. This distance is certainly overcome. But it is still a distance which is overcome only by God's grace, the distance between here and there, below and above. In awe we gratefully let grace be grace, and always receive it as such. We never let reception become a taking. Our knowledge of God is always compelled to be a prayer of thanksgiving,

83

penitence and intercession. It is only in this way that there is knowledge of God in participation in the veracity of the revelation of God. [II, 1, p. 223]

[38] Theology can, of course, be sheer vanity. It is this when it is not pertinent, and that simply means—not humble. The pertinence of theology consists in making the exposition of revelation its exclusive task. How can it fail to be humble in the execution of this programme, when it has no control over revelation, but has constantly to find it, or rather be found by it ? If we presuppose this happening—and we can, of course, presuppose it only as we pray and work—theology is as little vanity as the " old wife's " stammering. If she may stammer, surely theology may also try to speak. The attempt may and must be made, within the limits of human cognition, to ask about the truth, to distinguish the true from the false, and continually to carry the " approximation " further—although always knowing that the goal as such is attainable only to faith and not to our viewing and conceiving as such. This means, to seek after better human views and concepts in closer correspondence with their object, and therefore, so far as we are able, to make the witness to the reality of God more complete and clear. If this presupposition is valid—as it can and will be valid—theology can be pursued in the confidence which is not forbidden but commanded us against the background of the hiddenness of God, without any pretensions, but also without any false shame, so much the more so because it is not an arbitrary undertaking, but one which is necessary to the task of the Church's proclamation. If this presupposition is valid, theology is on firm ground for its undertaking—indeed, on disproportionately firmer ground than all other sciences. [II, 1, p. 203 f.]

[39] As a theological discipline dogmatics is the scientific self-examination of the Christian Church with respect to the content of its distinctive utterance concerning God.
[I, 1, p. 1 ; thesis of § 1]

[40] The Church produces theology in this special and peculiar sense by subjecting itself to self-examination. It puts to itself the question of truth, i.e., it measures its action, its utterance concerning God, by its being as the Church. Thus theology exists in this special and peculiar sense because before it and apart from it there is in the

84

Church utterance concerning God. Theology follows the utterance of the Church to the extent that in its question as to the correctness of this utterance it does not measure it by an alien standard but by its own source and object. Theology guides the utterance of the Church to the extent that it concretely reminds it that in all circumstances it is fallible human work which in the matter of relevance or irrelevance lies in the balance and must be obedience to grace if it is to be well done. Theology accompanies the utterance of the Church to the extent that it is itself no more than human " utterance concerning God," so that with this utterance it stands under the judgment that begins at the house of God and lives by the promise given to the Church. [I, 1, p. 2 f.]

[41] To participate in this, and therefore to accompany even the work of erudite theology in the stricter sense, is the task of the community and therefore of each individual member. The Christian is not free to adopt any current religious idea, to espouse his own private philosophy, and then to urge this upon the community. On the other hand, he is both free and yet also summoned and obliged to reflect on the Word which underlies the community and is to be declared by it, and to give responsible expression to his reflections. No one will do this obediently unless he is prepared to let himself be stimulated, advised and guided by others, including professional theologians. No one will do it obediently if he is not in dialogue not only with God but also with his fellow-men and fellow-Christians. The freedom at issue is freedom in the community and not a foolish freedom on one's own responsibility and on the basis of hopeful or defiant private inspirations. No one, however, can be content at this point to be a mere " layman," to be indolent, to be no more than a passive spectator or reader. No one is excused the task of asking questions or the more difficult task of providing and assessing answers. Preaching in the congregation, and the theology which serves its preparation, can be faithful to its theme and therefore relevant and adapted to the circumstances and edifying to the community, only if it is surrounded, sustained and constantly stimulated and fructified by the questions and answers of the community. With his own questions and answers in matters of right understanding

85

and doctrine, each individual Christian thus participates in what the community is commanded to do. If he holds aloof, or slackens, or allows himself to sleep, or wanders into speculation and error, he must not be surprised if sooner or later the same will have to be said about the community as such and particularly about its more responsible members. How many complaints about the "Church" would never be made if only those who make them were to realise that we ourselves are the Church, so that what it has or has not to say stands or falls with us. There can be no doubt that all the great errors which have overtaken the preaching and theology of the community in the course of its history have had their true origin, not so much in the studies of the well-known errorists and heretics who have merely blabbed them out, but rather in the secret inattention and neglect, the private drowsing and wandering and erring, of innumerable nameless Christians who were not prepared to regard the listening of the community to the Word as their own concern, who wanted privacy in their thinking, and who thus created the atmosphere in which heresy and error became possible and even inevitable in the community. Conversely, there can be no doubt that the revivals and quickenings continually granted to the preaching and theology of the community have had their basis, not so much in the bearers of the great names which have come down to us in Church history as representatives of these movements, but effectively, if secretly, in the community from which they sprang, by which they were surrounded and as the mouthpiece of which they spoke, and therefore again in the innumerable nameless Christians for whom the question of correct doctrine was a burning one which they tried to address to the right quarter, and who then quietly if inarticulately found and espoused the relevant new and better answers until someone was found to bring them to expression. In this matter of co-operation in the service of the community, each must consider whether and in what sense he has thus far participated in the service of the Word which is so central for its inner life. Each must remember that as a Christian he is fully responsible, either directly or indirectly. Each must see to it that he begins to take this responsibility seriously, or more seriously than previously.   [III, 4, p. 498 f.]

II. JESUS CHRIST

1. THE CHRISTOLOGICAL BASIS

The statements of Christian proclamation must be statements of certainty, not of conjecture or private opinion. They are such when they derive from the basis which Christian faith recognises and acknowledges as the sum of certainty, as the truth itself. A Christian faith which did not say this of Jesus Christ would not be Christian faith. Hence Barth seeks to anchor to this place of certainty all the declarations of theology, whether concerning God or —and here he is an innovator—concerning man and his nature and action. Man does not know himself of himself, but has to be told about himself through the manifestation of Jesus Christ.

[42] But the voice which reigns, the voice by which we were taught by God Himself concerning God, was the voice of Jesus Christ. Along all the path now behind us we could not take a single step without stumbling again and again across that name. And " across that name " does not mean across an empty title. It does not mean across a form or figure in which God could declare Himself to us or exist for us and yet be quite different in and by Himself. It does not mean across a name which is only a means or medium, and which God could ultimately discard, because ultimately it is not the real name of God, but only of a divine arrangement which in the last analysis is quite different from God Himself. The truth is that we continuously stumbled across that name in matter and substance. We stumbled across it necessarily. For as we proceeded along that path, we found that that name was the very subject, the very matter, with which we had to deal. In avoiding the different sources of error, we saw that they had one feature in common : the negligence or arbitrariness with which even in the Church the attempt was made to go past or to go beyond Jesus Christ in the consideration and conception and definition of God, and in speech about God. But when theology allows itself on any pretext to be jostled away from that name, God is inevitably crowded out by a hypostatised image of man. Theology must begin with Jesus Christ, and not with general principles, however

better, or, at any rate, more relevant and illuminating, they may appear to be : as though He were a continuation of the knowledge and Word of God, and not its root and origin, not indeed the very Word of God itself. Theology must also end with Him, and not with supposedly self-evident general conclusions from what is particularly enclosed and disclosed in Him : as though the fruits could be shaken from this tree ; as though in the things of God there were anything general which we could know and designate in addition to and even independently of this particular. The obscurities and ambiguities of our way were illuminated in the measure that we held fast to that name and in the measure that we let Him be the first and the last, according to the testimony of Holy Scripture. Against all the imaginations and errors in which we seem to be so hopelessly entangled when we try to speak of God, God will indeed maintain Himself if we will only allow the name of Jesus Christ to be maintained in our thinking as the beginning and the end of all our thoughts.

[II, 2, p. 4 f.]

[43] This name is the answer to our earlier question. In the Christian " God with us " there is no question of any other source and object than that indicated by this name. Other than in this name—as on the basis of the necessity and power of its conceptual context—it cannot be truth, either on the lips of those who speak it or in the ears and hearts of those who receive it. Without this name it is left insecure and unprotected. It is exposed to the suspicion that it might be only a postulate, a pure speculation, a myth. It is truth as it derives from this name and as it points to it, and only so. Where is it that the men stand who declare this message ? The answer is that they stand in the sphere of the lordship of the One who bears this name, in the light and under the impelling power of His Spirit, in the community assembled and maintained and overruled by Him. They have not placed themselves there but He has placed them there, and it is as they stand there by Him that their report is a report of actuality. Again, where will those others stand to whom they address their report and witness, who both receive it and then, on their own responsibility, spread it further ? The answer is that they too stand in the sphere of the

lordship, which has now claimed them, of the One who bears this name, of His Spirit, of the call to His community which has now come to them. They too have not placed themselves there. And those who said to them " God with us " have not brought it about. But, again, it is He Himself who bears this name that has called and led and drawn them, and it is as that happens that it is given to them, too, to pass on to others their report of actuality as such. Therefore the One who shows and persuades and convinces and reveals and communicates from man to man that it is so, " God with us," is the One who bears this name, Jesus Christ, no other, and nothing else. That is what the message of the Christian community intends when at its heart it declares this name. If it were a principle and not a name indicating a person, we should have to describe it as the epistemological principle of the message. Where between man and man there is real communication of the report of what took place in Him and through Him, He Himself is there and at work, He Himself makes Himself to be recognised and acknowledged. The Christian message about Him—and without this it is not the Christian message—is established on the certainty that He is responsible for it, that He as the truth speaks through it and is received in it, that as it serves Him He Himself is present as actuality, as His own witness. He Himself by His Spirit is its guarantor. He Himself is the One who establishes and maintains and directs the community which has received it and upon which it is laid. He Himself is the strength of its defence and its offensive. He Himself is the hope of freedom and enlightenment for the many who have not yet received and accepted it. He Himself above all is the comfort, and the restlessness, and yet also the uplifting power in the weakness of its service. In a word : the Christian message lives as such by and to the One who at its heart bears the name of Jesus Christ. It becomes weak and obscure to the extent that it thinks it ought to live on other resources. And it becomes strong and clear when it is established solely in confidence in His controlling work exercised by His Spirit ; to the extent that it abandons every other conceivable support or impulse, and is content to rest on His command and commission as its strength and pledge. He, Jesus Christ, is Emmanuel, " God with us." How else can He be proclaimed except as the One who proclaims Himself ? And how else can human activity and speech and hearing be effective in His service except in the prayer and expectation that He will constantly do it ?   [IV, 1, p. 17 f.]

[44] But the Christian message does say something individual, new and substantial because it speaks concretely, not mythically, because it does not know and proclaim anything side by side with or apart from Jesus Christ, because it knows and proclaims all things only as His things. It does not know and proclaim Him, therefore, merely as the representative and exponent of something other. For it, there is no something other side by side with or apart from Him. For it, there is nothing worthy of mention that is not as such His. Everything that it knows and proclaims as worthy of mention, it does so as His.

It is not, therefore, doing Him a mere courtesy when it names the name of Jesus Christ. It does not use this name as a symbol or sign which has a certain necessity on historical grounds, and a certain purpose on psychological and pedagogic grounds, to which that which it really means and has to say may be attached, which it is desirable to expound for the sake of clarity. For it, this name is not merely a cipher, under which that which it really means and has to say leads its own life and has its own truth and actuality and would be worth proclaiming for its own sake, a cipher which can at any time be omitted without affecting that which is really meant and said, or which in other ages or climes or circumstances can be replaced by some other cipher. When it speaks concretely, when it names the name of Jesus Christ, the Christian message is not referring simply to the specific form of something general, a form which as such is interchangeable : in the phrase of Lessing, a " contingent fact of history " which is the " vehicle " of an " eternal truth of reason." The peace between God and man and the salvation which comes to us men is not something general, but the specific thing itself : that concrete thing which is indicated by the name of Jesus Christ and not by any other name. For He who bears this name is Himself the peace and salvation. The peace and salvation can be

90

known, therefore, only in Him, and proclaimed only in His
name.   [IV, 1, p. 21]

[45]   If the freedom of divine immanence is sought and
supposedly found apart from Jesus Christ, it can signify
in practice only our enslavement to a false god.   For this
reason Jesus Christ alone must be preached to the heathen
as the immanent God, and the Church must be severely
vigilant to see that it expects everything from *Jesus
Christ*, and from Jesus Christ *everything* ; that He is
unceasingly recognised as the way, the truth, and the life
(Jn. 14[6]).   This attitude does not imply Christian absolu-
tism or ecclesiastical narrowmindedness because it is
precisely in Jesus Christ, but also exclusively in Him, that
the abundance and plenitude of divine immanence is
included and revealed.   If we do not have Christ, we do
not have at all, but utterly lack, the fulness of God's presence.   If we separate ourselves from Him, we are not
even on the way to this richness, but are slipping back
into an impoverishment in which the omnipresent God is
not known. . . .

The legitimacy of every theory concerning the relationship of God and man or God and the world can be tested
by considering whether it can be understood also as an
interpretation of the relationship and fellowship created
and sustained in Jesus Christ.   Is it capable of adaptation
to the fundamental insights of the Church concerning the
person and work of Jesus Christ—the *analogia fidei* ?   Or
does it stand in isolation from Christ's person and work,
so that it can be brought into connexion with these insights
only as an introduction or an appendix, neither deriving
from them nor leading back to them.   There are strictly
speaking no Christian themes independent of Christology,
and the Church must insist on this in its message to the
world.   It is at all events impossible to assert the contrary with reference to God and His freedom.   If we
appeal to God and His freedom, in the last resort, directly
or indirectly, we can expound and elucidate only this one
theme.   [II, 1, p. 319 f.]

[46]   Eliminate this name and the religion is blunted
and weakened.   As a " Christianity without Christ " it
can only vegetate.   It has lost its only *raison d'être*.   Like
other religions, for other reasons, it can look only for a

speedy dissolution. It we try to look away from the name of Jesus Christ even momentarily, the Christian Church loses the substance in virtue of which it can assert itself in and against the state and society as an entity of a special order. Christian piety (no matter whether it vaunts itself as a piety of head or heart or action) loses the substance in virtue of which it can be something distinctive alongside morals, art and science. Christian theology loses the substance in virtue of which it is not philosophy, or philology, or historical science, but sacred learning. Christian worship loses the sacrificial and sacramental substance in virtue of which it is more than a solemn, half insolent and half superfluous pastime—its substance, and therefore its right to live, and at the same time its capacity to live. The Christian religion is the predicate to the subject of the name of Jesus Christ. Without Him it is not merely something different. It is nothing at all, a fact which cannot be hidden for long. It was and is and shall be only in virtue of the act of creation indicated by this name. And it is because of this act of creation that along with its existence it also receives its truth. Because it was and is and shall be through the name of Jesus Christ, it was and is and shall be the true religion : the knowledge of God, and the worship of God, and the service of God, in which man is not alone in defiance of God, but walks before God in peace with God. [I, 2, p. 347]

2. " THE WORD WAS MADE FLESH "

The dogmatic definitions of the Early Church concerning the relationship of deity and humanity in the person of Jesus Christ, or the divine and human natures of Christ, are not regarded by Barth as the result of a distortion of primitive Christianity by Greek metaphysics, but as an irreplaceable introduction to the proper understanding of the New Testament statements about Christ. To guard against the misconception that these definitions refer to a strange and marvellous God-man, Barth interprets them as the description, not of a static essence, but of an action of God which takes place in Jesus Christ and is the determinative centre of cosmic and human destiny. The person and work of Jesus Christ are one, and cannot be separated even for the purpose of study. All that He is, is also His work for men ; He is man for other men. It is of a piece with the relating of all Barth's thinking to the manifestation of Jesus Christ that his ability to light up the biblical narrative is at its peak in respect of the New Testament tradition of the life and work of Jesus, as illustrated by a long extract from the sub-section " The Royal Man " (IV, 2, pp. 171–180). In Barth's exposition of the cross and resurrection of Jesus it is to be noted (1) how the understanding of the reconciliation of God and man is freed from the widespread notion of the placation of an angry God by innocent sacrifice, atonement being an undertaking of the love of God exposing Himself for us to the flames of His own wrath, the burning wrath of His love ; (2) how the same is true in relation to human sin as to the knowledge of God and the true reality of man, its nature and gravity being known only from its conquest and therefore from the history of Jesus Christ ; and (3) how the resurrection of Jesus is understood as God's confession of the self-sacrificing obedience of Jesus.

[47] A. Harnack opened his lectures on " What is Christianity ? " (1900) by recalling the dictum of John Stuart Mill that humanity cannot be reminded too often of the fact that there was once a man named Socrates ; and he added a sentence which is worth pondering, that although Mill was right it is even more important continually to remind humanity that there once stood in its midst a man named Jesus Christ. We may differ from Harnack as to the way in which we should remember this man. But we can agree that we cannot be reminded too often that this man once dwelt in the midst of humanity. In Him we have the central human factor.

[III, 2, p. 160]

[48] This same is God : " Christ Jesus is his name, The Lord Sabaoth's Son ; He, and no other one, Shall conquer in the battle." There we have the clearest expression of the Christian faith in the divine world-governance. And the Christian idea of the matter is not an empty idea, or an idea which can be filled out in a variety of ways. When we think of the divine governance we are not thinking of an empty form, of a general and overriding order and teleology in all occurrence. We are not looking either up above or down below. We are simply looking at the Old and New Testaments ; at the One whom Scripture calls God ; at the events which Scripture attests in their relationships the one to the other ; at the incursion of the supremacy of free grace which Scripture records ; at the Subject who is active in this incursion ; at His inconceivable but manifest act of election ; at the faithfulness

93

which He demonstrates and maintains ; and, at the very heart of these events, at Jesus Christ on the cross ; at the One who was not crucified alone, but two thieves with Him, the one on the right hand and the other on the left (Mt. 27^{38}) ; at the One who accepted solidarity with all thieves both Jew and Gentile ; at the One who is King over them all and on behalf of them all. It is from this point, and in this sense, and according to this purpose as it is active and revealed in these events, that the world is ruled, heaven and earth and all that therein is. This is the Christian belief in the divine world-governance. The history of salvation attested in the Bible cannot be considered or understood simply in and for itself. It is related to world history as a whole. It is the centre and key to all events. But again, world history cannot be considered or understood simply in and for itself. It is related to the history of salvation. It is the circumference around that centre, the lock to which that key belongs and is necessary.

[III, 3, p. 186]

[49] There is no discernible stratum of the New Testament in which—always presupposing His genuine humanity—Jesus is in practice seen in any other way or—whatever terms may be used—judged in any other way than as the One who is qualitatively different and stands in an indissoluble antithesis to His disciples and all other men, indeed, to the whole cosmos. There is no discernible stratum which does not in some way witness that it was felt that there should be given to this man, not merely a human confidence, but that trust, that respect, that obedience, that faith which can properly be offered only to God. Allowing for every difference in viewpoint and concept, the heavenly Father, His kingdom which has come on earth, and the person of Jesus of Nazareth are not quantities which can be placed side by side, or which cut across each other, or which can be opposed to each other, but they are practically and in effect identical. This would still be true even if it could be proved and not merely suspected that Jesus Himself did not expressly speak of His majesty, His Messiahship, His divine Sonship. In the context of what we know of the disciples and the community in the New Testament there is no ground for even suspecting the existence of disciples or a community

94

which could be practically related to Him except on the presupposition of His majesty.

So, then, we can speak of this and that title being " conferred " on Jesus only with the reservation that this conferring is not represented as something arbitrary which we might omit or handle otherwise. This conferring, and the valuation and estimation and judgment which underlies it, has nothing whatever to do with the free apotheosis of a man. In spite of all the mitigations of later Judaism this would have been an unprecedented thing in the original Palestinian community, in the direct sphere of the Old Testament concept of God. And since there has never been a Christian community without the Old Testament, it could not possibly have been carried through in Hellenistic Christianity (or only *per nefas*). The exaltation of a man as a cult-god, or his investiture with the dignity of a gnostic hypostasis, was not at all easy on this presupposition. We do not understand either the practical attitude to Jesus discernible on all levels of the New Testament tradition, or the titles of majesty conferred upon Him, if we do not at least hazard the hypothesis that the peculiar place and function of the man Jesus for New Testament Christians was not a hypothesis, that the practice and theory of their relationship to Him was not a religious experiment—however earnest and sincere—against the background of an " as though " which secretly left the question open. Their estimation and judgment of Jesus is as such something secondary, a necessary consequence. It is not itself their theme, the subject-matter of their preaching. They are occupied with Jesus Himself. They aim to be His witnesses. They answer His question. They give an account of His existence. He has placed them in this attitude. He has put these titles of majesty on their lips. They do not try to crown Him in this way, but they recognise Him as the One who is already crowned, to whom these titles belong. . . .

It is clear that we can reject this New Testament witness concerning the man Jesus. It has been rejected again and again—even within the community. But there can be no disputing the fact that, in the sense of those who gave it, this witness is to the simple effect that, prior to any attitudes of others to Him or statements of others about

95

Him, the man Jesus did in fact occupy this place and function, that, prior to any knowledge of His being or temporally conditioned confession of it, He actually was and is and will be what He is represented in the reflection of this witness, the Son of the Heavenly Father, the King of His kingdom, and therefore " by nature God." We have to let go the whole New Testament witness step by step and turn it into its opposite if we read it as a documentation of " religious valuations," if we do not see and admit that step by step it relates to the being and revelation of this man in the unprecedented and quite unique determination of His existence. It is not a Christian conception of Him, and to that extent not the Christian *kerygma*, but He Himself in His revelation and being, who according to the New Testament builds His community and calls the world to decision : He Himself in the power of His resurrection, the Lord who is the Spirit. Only when this is seen and admitted do we know what we are doing when we either accept or reject the New Testament witness.

[IV, 1, pp. 161–3]

[50] Jesus was not in any sense a reformer championing new orders against the old ones, contesting the latter in order to replace them by the former. He did not range Himself and His disciples with any of the existing parties. One of these, and not the worst, was that of the Pharisees. But Jesus did not identify Himself with them. Nor did He set up against them an opposing party. He did not represent or defend or champion any programme—whether political, economic, moral or religious, whether conservative or progressive. He was equally suspected and disliked by the representatives of all such programmes, although He did not particularly attack any of them. Why His existence was so unsettling on every side was that He set all programmes and principles in question. And He did this simply because He enjoyed and displayed, in relation to all the orders positively or negatively contested around Him, a remarkable freedom which again we can only describe as royal. He had need of none of them in the sense of an absolute authority which was vitally necessary for Him, and which He could prescribe and defend as vitally necessary for others because it was an absolute authority. On the other hand, He had no need consistently to break any

96

of them, to try to overthrow them altogether, to work for their replacement or amendment. He could live in these orders. He could seriously acknowledge in practice that the temple of God was in Jerusalem, and that the doctors of the Law were to be found in this temple, and that their disciples the scribes were scattered throughout the land, with the Pharisees as their most zealous rivals. He could also acknowledge that the Romans were in the land with their native satellites, and that the emperor in Rome bore supreme rule even over the land and people of the divine covenant. He could grant that there were families, and rich and poor. He never said that these things ought not to be. He did not oppose other " systems " to these. He did not make common cause with the Essene reforming movement. He simply revealed the limit and frontier of all these things—the freedom of the kingdom of God. He simply existed in this freedom and summoned to it. He simply made use of this freedom to cut right across all these systems both in His own case and in that of His disciples, interpreting and accepting them in His own way and in His own sense, in the light shed upon them all from that frontier. It was just that He Himself was the light which was shed upon all these orders from that frontier. Inevitably, then, He clashed with these orders in the interpretation commonly placed on them in the world in which He lived. Inevitably their provisional and relative character, the ways in which they were humanly conditioned, their secret fallibility, were all occasionally disclosed —not in principle, only occasionally, but on these occasions quite unmistakeably—in His attitude toward them and His assessment of their significance. But it was not these incidental disclosures of the freedom of God which made Him a revolutionary far more radical than any that came either before or after Him. It was the freedom itself, which could not even be classified from the standpoint of these orders. For where are these orders when He expresses both in word and deed that abasement of all that is high and exaltation of all that is low ? Do they not all presuppose that the high is high and the low low ? Was not the axe really laid at the root of all these trees in and by His existence ? In the last resort, it was again conformity with God Himself which constituted the secret of the character of Jesus on this side too. This is the relationship of God Himself to all the orders of life and value which, as long as there is history at all, enjoy a transitory validity in the history of every human place. This is how God gives them their times and spheres, but without being bound to any of them, without giving any of them His own divine authority, without allotting to any of them a binding validity for all men even beyond their own time and sphere, without granting that they are vitally necessary and absolutely authoritative even for their own time and sphere. In this way God Himself is their limit and frontier. An alien light is thus shed on them by God Himself as on that which He has limited. This is how He Himself deals with them, not in principle, not in the execution of a programme, but for this reason in a way which is all the more revolutionary, as the One who breaks all bonds asunder, in new historical developments and situations each of which is for those who can see and hear—only a sign, but an unmistakeable sign, of His freedom and kingdom and overruling of history.

Attention should first be paid to what we might call the passive conservatism of Jesus. Rather curiously, Jesus accepts and allows many things which we imagine He ought to have attacked and set aside both in principle and practice and which the community in which the Gospels arose had to a very large extent outgrown. It did not—and obviously could not—find it a source of vexation to have to maintain this aspect of the traditional picture.

He accepted the temple as quite self-evidently the house of His Father (Lk. 2⁴⁹). Even the astonishing act of cleansing it of the traders and moneychangers presupposes (Mk. 11¹⁷) that it is for Him the house of God. As we see from Mt. 23¹⁶ᶠ·, He does not take it (or take the altar in it) less seriously but more seriously than the scribes and Pharisees. He assumes that the pious Israelite will still go up to it to bring his sacrifices (Mt. 5²³ᶠ·). When He Himself comes to Jerusalem, He does not teach in the streets and market-places, but daily in its forecourt (Mk. 12³⁵, 14⁴⁹). It is there that the Pharisee and publican make their prayers in the parable which brings out so strongly the difference between Himself and those around Him (Lk. 18⁹ᶠ·). We may also note the description of the conduct of His disciples in the closing verse of St. Luke's Gospel : " And they were continually in the temple, praising and blessing God." We may also recall that after His crucifixion, resurrection and ascension they still continued " daily with one accord in the temple."

But respect may also be seen for the order of the family, for according to Lk. 2^{51} Jesus was at first subject to His parents in Nazareth. And in Mk. $7^{11f.}$ He insisted that the duty of caring for father and mother must take precedence of all cultic obligations. We may also remember, with reservations, the provision which He made for His mother even on the cross, according to the saying handed down in Jn. 19^{26}.

Again, at least at the beginning of His teaching activity, He did not separate Himself from the Galilean synagogues (Mk. 1^{21}, 3^1). Indeed, in Lk. $4^{17f.}$ we have an obvious description of the way in which He adapted Himself to current synagogue practice. As concerns the Law, He not only protests (Mt. $5^{17f.}$) that He has not come to destroy it and the prophets, but He maintains that He has come to fulfil it, that not one jot or tittle shall pass from it until heaven and earth pass away, and that only those can be great in the kingdom of heaven who practise and teach even its most minute regulations. In Mt. $23^{1f.}$ He concedes (even if ironically) that the scribes and Pharisees who expound the Law sit in Moses' seat, so that if the people and His disciples have to be warned against their example, they are also enjoined : " All therefore whatsoever they bid you observe, that observe and do." And if in Mt. $23^{23f.}$ He accused them of hypocritically tithing mint and anise and cummin and omitting the weightier matters of the Law, judgment, mercy and faith, He added as something self-evident : " These ought ye to have done, and not to leave the other undone." In Mt. 13^{52} again, He recognised the possibility of the scribe " instructed unto the kingdom of heaven " who " is like unto a householder, which bringeth forth out of his treasure things new and old "—the old as well as the new. The antithesis in Mt. $5^{21f.}$ (" Ye have heard that it was said by them of old time. . . . But I say unto you . . .") certainly implies a more radical understanding of the Ten Commandments, but this in turn involves a recognition. And the same is true of the more

99

precise exposition of the three traditional exercises of almsgiving, prayer and fasting in Mt. 6¹ᶠ·. Even to the sayings on the cross, the tradition likes to see Jesus speaking in direct or indirect quotations from the Old Testament, and it sets Him generally in the confines, not merely of the world of religion, but of the special religious promise given to His own people. In Jn. 4²² we even have the express saying that " salvation is of the Jews." The point is made so emphatically that it can be reported without any inhibitions that some of His more kindly-disposed contemporaries regarded Him merely as " a prophet, or as one of the prophets " (Mk. 6¹⁵), or perhaps a particularly " great " prophet (Lk. 7¹⁵). Similarly, in the later search for the so-called " historical Jesus " the suggestion could be made that He might be reduced to the figure of a (very outstanding) representative of a reformed and deepened Judaism.

It is also to be noted that we never see Him in direct conflict with the economic relationships and obligations of His time and background. We have only to think of the uncritical equanimity with which He accepted in the parables of the kingdom the existence of free employers of labour and employees dependent on their good will, of masters and servants and capital and interest, as though all these things were part of the legitimate *status quo*. In Lk. 16¹ᶠ· unqualified praise was given to the οἰκονόμος, not as a deceiver, but at least as one who knew how to act wisely within the current arrangement in relation to rents. To the man who asks Him to see that his brother divides the inheritance fairly He replies in Lk. 12¹³ᶠ· that it is not His office to judge and divide in such matters. In this request, at any rate in the context in which Luke reports it, He sees only the cry of covetousness and not at all a cry for justice. " Ye have the poor with you always " (Mk. 17⁴), is His answer to the disciples who would have preferred a corresponding almsgiving to the woman's lavish devotion. He thus takes it as almost axiomatic that there must always be poor people—a thought which has given an illusory comfort to many in subsequent periods. And then in Lk. 16⁹, ¹¹ we are told to make friends with mammon (even the unrighteous mammon), and that the true riches (ἀληθινόν) will not be entrusted to those

who are not " faithful " in relation to it. This was certainly
not an invitation to maintain and augment our financial
possessions as cleverly as possible—a process which later
came to be regarded almost as a specific Christian virtue
in certain parts of the Calvinistic world—but it is obviously
not a summons to socialism.

Traces of the same attitude may finally be discerned in
respect of political relationships and orders and disorders.
It is freely presupposed in Mt. 5$^{25f.}$ and elsewhere that
there are judges and officers and prisons. That there are
those who " think to rule over the nations " (the qualifying
δοκοῦντες is to be noted), and do in fact exercise dominion
and authority over them, is certainly described in Mk.
10$^{42f.}$ as a procedure which is not to have any place in the
community, but there is no direct criticism of it as such.
The God who does not allow His elect to cry to Him in vain
(Lk. 18$^{1f.}$) can appear in the guise of a notoriously unjust
judge who neither fears God nor has any respect for man.
It is expressly recognised by Jesus in Jn. 19^{11} that Pilate
has an authority even in relation to Himself, and that this
is given him from above. In Mt. 26^{52} He did not allow
Peter to put up any resistance to the Sanhedrin guard,
but ordered him to put up his sword into its sheath. We
do not find in the Gospels the slightest trace either of a
radical repudiation of the dominion of Rome or Herod, or,
for that matter, of any basic anti-imperialism or anti-
militarism.

It is quite evident, however, and we must not ignore
this aspect, that there is also no trace of any consistent
recognition in principle. We can describe the attitude of
Jesus as that of a passive conservatism in the further sense
that it never amounted to more than a provisional and
qualified respect (we might almost say toleration) in face
of existing and accepted orders. Jesus acknowledged them
and reckoned with them and subjected Himself to them
and advised His disciples to do the same ; but He was
always superior to them. And it was inevitable—we will
now turn to this aspect—that this superiority, the freedom
of the kingdom of God, should occasionally find concrete
expression in His words and actions, that an occasional
creaking should be unmistakeably heard in the timbers.

As regards the temple, He made it plain to the Pharisees

in Mt. 12⁶ that there is something greater than the temple. When He paid the temple tax for Peter and Himself in Mt. 17²⁴ᶠ·, He did not do so on the basis of an unqualified recognition which the disciple was to regard as binding, but " lest we should offend them." For : " What thinkest thou, Simon ? of whom do the kings of the earth take custom or tribute ? of their own children, or of strangers ? " And when Peter answered : " Of strangers. Jesus saith unto him, Then are the children free."

Again, it was an unmistakeable assault on the order of the family, which is so firmly stabilised by nature and custom, when in Mk. 3³¹ He gave to His mother and brethren, who had " sent unto him, calling him," the following answer : " Who is my mother, or my brethren ? " and then, " looking round about on them that sat about him " : " Behold, my mother and my brethren." And we need hardly refer to the even harsher saying in the story of the wedding at Cana : τί ἐμοὶ καὶ σοί, " What have we in common ? " (Jn. 2⁴). It also has a most destructive sound in this respect when He replied to the man who wanted to be His disciple, but only after he had buried his father : " Let the dead bury their dead : but go thou and preach the kingdom of God " (Lk. 9⁵⁹ᶠ·), and to the other who asked if he might first make his farewells to those at home : " No man, having put his hand to the plough, and looking back, is fit for the kingdom of God " (Lk. 9⁶¹ᶠ·).

Again, there are breaches of the prevailing religious or cultic order. The accusation was made in Mk. 2¹⁸ᶠ· that His disciples did not fast like those of the Pharisees or even the Baptist. To those who raised this point He gave the puzzling answer : " Can the children of the bride-chamber fast, while the bridegroom is with them ? " There was also the complaint in Mk. 7¹ᶠ· that His disciples neglected the purifications prescribed for meals : " Why walk not thy disciples according to the tradition of the elders ? " In reply, Jesus explains that it is not what is without but what is within that really defiles a man—the evil thoughts and acts which come from the heart (Mk. 7¹⁴ᶠ·). Above all, there is His attitude to the sabbath, which allowed His disciples to satisfy their hunger by plucking ears of corn (Mk. 2²³ᶠ·) and Himself to heal on the sabbath (Mk. 3¹ᶠ· ; Jn. 5¹ᶠ·, 9¹ᶠ·). The offence which He gave and the reproaches which He incurred at this point were particularly severe. His answers were as follows : " Is it lawful to do good on the sabbath days, or to do evil ? to save life, or to kill ? But they held their peace " (Mk. 3⁴). " If a man on the sabbath day receive circumcision, that the law of Moses should not be broken ; are ye angry at me, because I have made a man every whit whole on the sabbath day ? " (Jn. 7²³). And above all : " The sabbath was made for man, and not man for the sabbath : therefore the Son of man is Lord also of the sabbath " (Mk. 2²⁷ᶠ·). As appears in Mk. 3⁶ and elsewhere, this breach was one of the most concrete things which made His destruction necessary in the eyes of His opponents.

Again, there are some striking breaches of the contemporary (and not only the contemporary) industrial and commercial and economic order. We may mention certain features in the parables which are definitely not taken from real life but are quite foreign to customary practice in these spheres. As Goethe pointed out, no sensible husbandman would ever sow as did the man in Mt. 13³ᶠ·, scattering his seed irrespectively over the path and stony ground and among thorns as well as on good ground. And what servants will ever be prepared to say that they are unprofitable when they have done all that they are required to do (Lk. 17¹⁰) ? What king will ever be so magnanimous as to pronounce unconditional freedom from punishment or guilt on the steward who has so obviously misappropriated that which was entrusted to him (Mt. 18²³ᶠ·) ? What owner of a vineyard will ever pay his workmen as did the owner of Mt. 20¹ᶠ· ? And what sense does it make that the man whose land has been fruitful and who therefore plans (in good and sensible fashion) to pull down his barns and build greater, hoping to enjoy a future in which he can take his ease and eat and drink and be merry, is described by God as a fool—simply because he has the unavoidable misfortune to die before his enterprise can be completed, and he can no longer call all these goods his own (Lk. 12¹⁶ᶠ·) ? Nor does Jesus seem to have a proper understanding of trade and commerce when we consider the story, recorded in all four Gospels, of the expulsion from the temple of those who changed money and sold doves. " A den of thieves " (Mk. 11¹⁷) is rather a harsh description for the honest, small-scale financial and commercial activities which had established themselves there. These detailed signals only give warning of the real threat and revolution which the kingdom of God and the man Jesus signify and involve in relation to this sphere, but they are signals which we ought not to overlook.

There are similar signals in the political sphere as well. Can we adduce in this respect the not very respectful way in which Jesus describes His own particular ruler, Herod, as a " fox " (Lk. 13^{32}) ? However that may be, the question and answer in Mk. 12$^{13f.}$ are certainly relevant. Ought tribute to be paid to Cæsar or not ? Well, the coin bears the image of Cæsar, and there can be no doubt that authority rests in his hands, so : " Render to Cæsar the things that are Cæsar's—precisely those things, and no more, is the obvious meaning—and to God the things that are God's." There is not a second kingdom of God outside and alongside the first. There is a human kingdom which is authoritative and can demand obedience only as such. And this kingdom is sharply delimited by the one kingdom of God. According to Jn. 19^{10} Pilate's power over Jesus is only the power to release Him or to crucify Him. When He asked : " Art thou the king of the Jews ? " Jesus did not owe him a defence which He never made—for although Pilate, like the high-priests, made a case against Him, Jesus did not conduct any case—but only the confession : " Thou sayest it." Even the more explicit statement recorded in Jn. 18$^{33f.}$ is only a paraphrase of this confession, this καλὴ ὁμολογία as it is called in 1 Tim. 6^{13}. With this confession as the one thing that He had to set against it He both honoured the imperial kingdom and yet at the same time drew unmistakeable attention to its limitations, setting it under a cloud and calling it in question. " Behold, I cast out devils, and I do cures to day and to morrow, and the third day I shall be perfected," was His answer when Herod threatened Him (Lk. 13^{32}). To the extent that it is another form of the same confession this saying is also relevant in this context.

But the crisis which broke on all human order in the man Jesis is more radical and comprehensive than may be gathered from all these individual indications. Our best starting-point for this deeper consideration is the comparison recorded by all the Synoptics in connexion with the question of fasting : " No man also seweth a piece of new cloth on an old garment : else the new piece that filled it up taketh away from the old, and the rent is made worse. And no man putteth new wine into old bottles : else the new wine doth burst the bottles, and the wine is spilled, and the bottles will be marred : but new wine must be put into new bottles " (Mk. 2²¹ᶠ·). For Jesus, and as seen in the light of Jesus, there can be no doubt that all human orders are this old garment or old bottles, which are in the last resort quite incompatible with the new cloth and the new wine of the kingdom of God. The new cloth can only destroy the old garment, and the old bottles can only burst when the new wine of the kingdom of God is poured into them. All true and serious conservatism, and all true and serious belief in progress, presupposes that there is a certain compatibility between the new and the old, and that they can stand in a certain neutrality the one to the other. But the new thing of Jesus is the invading kingdom of God revealed in its alienating antithesis to the world and all its orders. And in this respect, too, the dictum is true : *neutralitas non valet in regno Dei*. There is thus concealed and revealed, both in what we called the passive conservatism of Jesus and the individual signs and penetrations which question the world of human orders as such, the radical and indissoluble antithesis of the kingdom of God to all human kingdoms, the unanswerable question, the irremediable unsettlement introduced by the kingdom of God into all human kingdoms.

In Mk. 13¹ᶠ·, when His disciples were admiring the temple, Jesus answered them : " Seest thou these great buildings ? there shall not be left one stone upon another " —a saying that was brought against Him in Mk.14⁵⁸ (and again on the cross in Mk. 15²⁹) as implying that He Himself would destroy the temple made with hands and replace it in three days by another not made with hands. Mark and Matthew ascribed this version of the saying to false witnesses. But according to the version preserved in Jn. 2¹⁹, although He did not speak of Himself destroying the temple, He certainly spoke of its rebuilding in three days. The comment of John is that He spoke of the temple of

His body (Jn. 2²¹). Either way, while He honoured the temple as the house of God and was even jealous for its sanctity, He could not ascribe to it any permanent place or significance in the light of what He Himself brought and was. Unlike the Law in Mt. 5¹⁷ᶠ·, it was not to continue until heaven and earth passed away. The saying to the Samaritan woman is relevant in this connexion: "Woman, believe me, the hour cometh, when ye shall neither in this mountain, nor yet at Jerusalem, worship the Father" (Jn. 4²¹). And what is said about the heavenly Jerusalem in Rev. 21²² is like an echo of all these sayings: "And I saw no temple therein: for the Lord God Almighty and the Lamb are the temple thereof."

Everything else that we have to say concerning the radical antithesis of the new thing which was actualised and appeared in Jesus to the totality of the old order can be said only in relation to its complete ignoring and transcending of this order. We can merely attempt to see with what profundity He attacked it by this ignoring and transcending. He attacked it—in a way from which it can never recover—merely by the alien presence with which He confronted it in its own sphere. What was, in fact, this way in which He confronted it?

In the first place, He himself remained unmarried—no one has ever yet explained with what self-evident necessity. And in Mt. 19¹² He reckoned with the fact that there might be others who would remain unmarried for the sake of the kingdom of heaven. In this way He set against the whole sphere of the family (in addition to the sayings already adduced) the basic question of its right and permanence to which there could be given only a provisional and relative answer. "For when they shall rise from the dead, they neither marry, nor are given in marriage" (Mk. 12²⁵).

But above all we must take up again the question of His relationship to the economic order. It, too, was simply but radically called in question by the fact that neither He Himself nor His disciples accepted its basic presupposition by taking any part in the acquisition or holding of any possessions. It is as if the declaration and irruption of the kingdom of God had swept away the ground from under us in this respect. We have already mentioned the passage in the commissioning of the disciples in Mt. 10⁹ which refers to the total insecurity to which He abandons His disciples. Those who followed Him had left everything (Mt. 19²⁷), their nets and boats (Mk. 1¹⁸ᶠ·), their families and houses and lands (Mt. 19²⁹). " Lacked ye anything ? " He asks them, and their answer is : " Nothing " (Lk. 22³⁵). But this is not due to acquisition or possession. Those who came to Him, those who went through the narrow gate, were told : " Sell whatsoever thou hast, and give to the poor, and thou shalt have treasure in heaven " (Mk. 10²¹). Those who were sad and went away grieved when they came to this narrow gate (v. 22) did not come to Him. A dangerous alternative for all the economic attitudes and practices conceivable or serviceable to man ! As is well-known, in Ac. 2⁴⁴ we read of a bold attempt by the most primitive post-Pentecostal community to take up this basic challenge. " And all that believed were together, and had all things common ; and sold their possessions and goods, and parted them to all men, as every man had need." There is only one other direct mention of this attempt, in Ac. 5¹ᶠ· It has often been taken up since in different forms. But in whatever form can it ever have more than the significance of an attempt ? It is worth pondering that the venture was at least made. And it will always be inevitable that there should be impulses in this direction wherever the Gospel of Jesus is proclaimed and heard. But it has never happened—least of all in the modern system called " Communism "—that even in smaller circles the way which leads in this direction has been trodden to the end. And the proclamation in Mt. 6¹⁹ is even more dangerous : " Lay not up for yourselves treasures upon earth, where moth and rust doth corrupt, and where thieves break through and steal," and especially in Mt. 6²⁵ᶠ· : " Take no thought for your life, what ye shall eat, or what ye shall drink ; nor yet for your body, what ye shall put on. . . . Take therefore no thought for the morrow : for the morrow shall take thought for the things of itself." Surely there could be no sound or solid economy, either private or public, without this laying up and taking thought ? But this is what Jesus says in words which are strangely illuminating and pregnant and penetrating—who can escape

their truth and comfort and inspiration?—even though
they obviously do not give to the community in which the
Gospels arose any directions as to their practical realisation,
and have a final validity even though they are exposed
from the very outset to the accusation that they are
incapable of practical realisation. And how dangerous it
is when this laying up and taking thought are scorned as
" Gentile " and there is opposed to them the freedom of
the fowls of the air and the lilies of the field which neither
worry nor work ! How dangerous it is that the concept of
mammon, which seems to denote only the idea of material
possession, is used as a comprehensive term for the whole
of that dominion which is opposed to the kingdom of God,
the antithesis of the rich and the poor being adopted as a
basic *schema* for all the blessedness or otherwise of man !
Obviously this is to shake the basic pillars of all normal
human activity in relation to the clearest necessities of
life—and in the irritating form, not of the proclamation of
a better social order, but of the free and simple call to
freedom. This is indeed a new piece which cannot be
sewn on the old garment, new wine which cannot be put
into old bottles. Its relation to the old is that of something which is unmistakeably different and opposed, the
strident proclamation of its end and of a new beginning
beyond this end, a question and challenge and invitation
and demand which cannot as such be silenced. It was the
new thing—we must be content, for the moment, with the
simple affirmation—of the royal man Jesus penetrating to
the very foundations of economic life in defiance of every
reasonable and to that extent honourable objection.

It is exactly the same in relation to the juridical and
political sphere. Here, too, we have a questioning of the
very presuppositions which is all the more powerful in its
lack of any direct aggressiveness. What are all the attempts
at reform or revelation in which Jesus might have taken
part or which He might have instigated or directed compared with the revolution which He did actually accomplish in this sphere ? He did not oppose the evil which
He came to root out. He was the Judge and He did not
judge : except, perhaps, those who thought that they
could be the judges ; except by causing Himself to be
judged for these usurpers of judgment. His injunction to

His followers, not as a law, but as a free call to freedom, is of a piece with this. They are not to resist evil (Mt. 5[38f.]). They are to let themselves be smitten on the left cheek as well as the right. They are to give away their cloak if their coat is taken from them. They are to go two miles with those who compel them to go one. More than that, if they do not want to be judged, they are not to judge (Mt. 7[1f.]). More still, they are to love their enemies (Mt. 5[43f.]) and pray for their persecutors, as children of their Father in heaven who causes His sun to shine on the good and the bad and His rain to fall on the just and the unjust, and obviously as brothers of Jesus, who, when His enemies (really the enemies of God) did their worst against Him, prayed for them (Lk. 23[34]) : " Father, forgive them ; for they know not what they do." It is again clear—for what political thinking can do justice or satisfaction to this injunction and to the One who gives it ?—that this involves a shaking of every human foundation ; that the right of God is in irreconcilable conflict with every human right ; that the divine state is quite incompatible not merely with the wicked totalitarian state but with every conceivable human regime ; that the new thing cannot be used to patch or fill the old. It is evident that human order is here betrayed into the proximity of a final and supreme menace. The community has again and again stifled and denied and even forgotten this, so that it could also be forgotten by the world around. But in this dimension too it has never been able to free itself completely from the unsettlement which it has within itself—whether it accepts the fact or not—as the community of this royal man. Nor has it been able completely to hide it from the world around. For in so far as it has been present as the community of this man, it has been present as such for the world, and the confrontation of the old order with the incommensurable factor of the new has been inescapable in this respect too. From the very outset and continually— cost what it may—the presence of this man has meant always that the world must wrestle with this incommensurable factor.

In all these dimensions the world is concretely violated by God Himself in the fact that the man Jesus came into it and is now within it.

But we have not yet mentioned the decisive point at which the man Jesus is the image and reflection of God Himself. In all the matters that we have emphasised so far we have been protecting this point against any attempt to render it innocuous or trivial. We have been forestalling the opinion that what we have to call the decisive point is something that can be attained and conceived and controlled by men, and incorporated into the scale of known relationships of magnitude and value. That is why we have first had to set Jesus against man and his cosmos as the poor man who if He blessed and befriended any blessed and befriended the poor and not the rich, the incomparable revolutionary who laid the axe at the root of the trees, who pitilessly exposed the darkness of human order in the cosmos, questioning it in a way which is quite beyond our capacity to answer. We do not know God at all if we do not know Him as the One who is absolutely opposed to our whole world which has fallen away from Him and is therefore self-estranged ; as the Judge of our world ; as the One whose will is that it should be totally changed and renewed. If we think we know Him in any other way, what we really know (in a mild or wild transcendence) is only the world itself, ourselves, the old Adam. In the man Jesus, God has separated Himself from this misinterpretation. And we have had to copy this divine separation in all that we have said so far. But again, we do not really know Jesus (the Jesus of the New Testament) if we do not know Him as this poor man, as this (if we may risk the dangerous word) partisan of the poor, and finally as this revolutionary.

[IV, 2, pp. 171–180]

[51] The subject-matter, origin and content of the message received and proclaimed by the Christian community is at its heart the free act of the faithfulness of God in which He takes the lost cause of man, who has denied Him as Creator and in so doing ruined himself as creature, and makes it His own in Jesus Christ, carrying it through to its goal and in that way maintaining and manifesting His own glory in the world.

[IV, 1, p. 3 ; thesis of § 57]

[52] Between God and man there stands the person of Jesus Christ, Himself God and Himself man, and so medi-

ating between the two. In Him God reveals Himself to man. In Him man sees and knows God. In Him God stands before man and man stands before God, as is the eternal will of God, and the eternal ordination of man in accordance with this will. In Him God's plan for man is disclosed, God's judgment on man fulfilled, God's redemption of man accomplished, God's gift to man present in fulness, God's claim and promise to man declared. In Him God has joined Himself to man. And so man exists for His sake. It is by Him, Jesus Christ, and for Him and to Him, that the universe is created as a theatre for God's dealings with man and man's dealings with God. The being of God is His being, and similarly the being of man is originally His being. And there is nothing that is not from Him and by Him and to Him. He is the Word of God in whose truth everything is disclosed and whose truth cannot be over-reached or conditioned by any other word. He is the decree of God behind and above which there can be no earlier or higher decree and beside which there can be no other, since all others serve only the fulfilment of this decree. He is the beginning of God before which there is no other beginning apart from that of God within Himself. Except, then, for God Himself, nothing can derive from any other source or look back to any other starting-point. He is the election of God before which and without which and beside which God cannot make any other choices. Before Him and without Him and beside Him God does not, then, elect or will anything. And He is the election (and on that account the beginning and the decree and the Word) of the free grace of God. For it is God's free grace that in Him He elects to be man and to have dealings with man and to join Himself to man. [II, 2, p. 94 f.]

[53] " God with us " means more than God over or side by side with us, before or behind us. It means more than His divine being in even the most intimate active connexion with our human being otherwise peculiar to Him. At this point, at the heart of the Christian message and in relation to the event of which it speaks, it means that God has made Himself the One who fulfils His redemptive will. It means that He Himself in His own person— at His own cost but also on His own initiative—has become

the inconceivable Yet and Nevertheless of this event, and so
its clear and well-founded and legitimate, its true and holy
and righteous Therefore. It means that God has become
man in order as such, but in divine sovereignty, to take
up our case. What takes place in this work of inconceivable mercy is, therefore, the free overruling of God, but it
is not an arbitrary overlooking and ignoring, not an artificial bridging, covering-over or hiding, but a real closing
of the breach, gulf and abyss between God and us for
which we are responsible. At the very point where we
refuse and fail, offending and provoking God, making ourselves impossible before Him and in that way missing our
destiny, treading under foot our dignity, forfeiting our
right, losing our salvation and hopelessly compromising
our creaturely being—at that very point God Himself
intervenes as man. Because He is God He is able not
only to be God but also to be this man. Because He is
God it is necessary that He should be man in quite a
different way from all other men : that He should do what
we do not do and not do what we do. Because He is God
He puts forth His omnipotence to be this other man, to
be man quite differently, in our place and for our sake.
Because He is God He has and exercises the power as this
man to suffer for us the consequence of our transgression,
the wrath and penalty which necessarily fall on us, and
in that way to satisfy Himself in our regard. And again
because He is God, He has and exercises the power as this
man to be His own partner in our place, the One who in
free obedience accepts the ordination of man to salvation
which we resist, and in that way satisfies us, i.e., achieves
that which can positively satisfy us. That is the absolutely
unique being, attitude and activity of God to which the
" God with us " at the heart of the Christian message
refers. It speaks of the peace which God Himself in this
man has made between Himself and us. [IV, 1, p. 12 f.]

[54] But it is something very bold and profoundly
astonishing to presume to say without reservation or sub-
traction that God was truly and altogether in Christ, to
speak of His identity with this true man, which means
this man who was born like all of us in time, who lived
and thought and spoke, who could be tempted and suffer
and die and who was, in fact, tempted and suffered and

died. The statement of this identity cannot be merely a postulate. . . . It aims very high. In calling this man the Son or the eternal Word of God, in ascribing to this man in His unity with God a divine being and nature, it is not speaking only or even primarily of Him but of God. It tells us that God for His part is God in His unity with this creature, this man, in His human and creaturely nature —and this without ceasing to be God, without any alteration or diminution of His divine nature. But this statement concerning God is so bold that we dare not make it unless we consider seriously in what sense we can do so. It must not contain any blasphemy, however involuntary or well-meant, or however pious. That it does do this is to this very day the complaint of Judaism and Islam against the Christian confession of the deity of Christ. It cannot be taken lightly. It cannot be secured by a mere repetition of this confession. We must be able to answer for this confession and its statement about God with a good conscience and with good reason. We must be able to show that God is honoured and not dishonoured by this confession.   [IV, 1, p. 183 f.]

[55] We may believe that God can and must only be absolute in contrast to all that is relative, exalted in contrast to all that is lowly, active in contrast to all suffering, inviolable in contrast to all temptation, transcendent in contrast to all immanence, and therefore divine in contrast to everything human, in short that He can and must be only the " Wholly Other." But such beliefs are shown to be quite untenable, and corrupt and pagan, by the fact that God does in fact be and do this in Jesus Christ. We cannot make them the standard by which to measure what God can or cannot do, or the basis of the judgment that in doing this He brings Himself into self-contradiction. By doing this God proves to us that He can do it, that to do it is within His nature. And He shows Himself to be more great and rich and sovereign than we had ever imagined. And our ideas of His nature must be guided by this, and not *vice versa*.

We have to think something after the following fashion. As God was in Christ, far from being against Himself, or at disunity with Himself, He has put into effect the freedom of His divine love, the love in which He is divinely free.

He has therefore done and revealed that which corresponds
to His divine nature. His immutability does not stand in
the way of this. It must not be denied, but this possibility
is included in His unalterable being. He is absolute,
infinite, exalted, active, impassable, transcendent, but in
all this He is the One who loves in freedom, the One who
is free in His love, and therefore not His own prisoner.
He is all this as the Lord, and in such a way that He
embraces the opposites of these concepts even while He is
superior to them. He is all this as the Creator, who has
created the world as the reality distinct from Himself but
willed and affirmed by Him and therefore as His world, as
the world which belongs to Him, in relation to which He
can be God and act as God in an absolute way and also
a relative, in an infinite and also a finite, in an exalted and
also a lowly, in an active and also ·a passive, in a
transcendent and also an immanent, and finally, in a
divine and also a human—indeed, in relation to which He
Himself can become worldly, making His own both its
form, the *forma servi*, and also its cause ; and all without
giving up His own form, the *forma Dei*, and His own
glory, but adopting the form and cause of man into the
most perfect communion with His own, accepting solidarity
with the world. God can do this. And no limit is set to
His ability to do it by the contradiction of the creature
against Him. It does not escape Him by turning to that
which is not and losing itself in it, for, although He is not
the Creator of that which is not, He is its sovereign Lord.
It corresponds to and is grounded in His divine nature
that in free grace He should be faithful to the unfaithful
creature who has not deserved it and who would inevitably
perish without it, that in relation to it He should establish
that communion between His own form and cause and
that of the creature, that He should make His own its
being in contradiction and under the consequences of that
contradiction, that He should maintain His covenant in
relation to sinful man (not surrendering His deity, for how
could that help ? but giving up and sacrificing Himself),
and in that way supremely asserting Himself and His
deity. His particular, and highly particularised, presence
in grace, in which the eternal Word descended to the lowest
parts of the earth (Eph. 4⁹) and tabernacled in the man

Jesus (Jn. 1^{14}), dwelling in this one man in the fulness of His Godhead (Col. 2^9), is itself the demonstration and exercise of His omnipresence, i.e., of the perfection in which He has His own place which is superior to all the places created by Him, not excluding but including all other places. His omnipotence is that of a divine plenitude of power in the fact that (as opposed to any abstract omnipotence) it can assume the form of weakness and impotence and do so as omnipotence, triumphing in this form. The eternity in which He Himself is true time and the Creator of all time is revealed in the fact that, although our time is that of sin and death, He can enter it and Himself be temporal in it, yet without ceasing to be eternal, able rather to be the Eternal in time. His wisdom does not deny itself, but proclaims itself in what necessarily appears folly to the world ; His righteousness in ranging Himself with the unrighteous as one who is accused with them, as the first, and properly the only one to come under accusation ; His holiness in having mercy on man, in taking his misery to heart, in willing to share it with him in order to take it away from him. God does not have to dishonour Himself when He goes into the far country, and conceals His glory. For He is truly honoured in this concealment. This concealment, and therefore His condescension as such, is the image and reflection in which we see Him as He is. His glory is the freedom of the love which He exercises and reveals in all this. In this respect it differs from the unfree and loveless glory of all the gods imagined by man. Everything depends on our seeing it, and in it the true and majestic nature of God : not trying to construct it arbitrarily ; but deducing it from its revelation in the divine nature of Jesus Christ. From this we learn that the *forma Dei* consists in the grace in which God Himself assumes and makes His own the *forma servi*. We have to hold fast to this without being disturbed or confused by any pictures of false gods. It is this that we have to see and honour and worship as the mystery of the deity of Christ. [IV, 1, pp. 186–188]

[56] As applied to Jesus Christ we can legitimately call the term " Son of God " a true but inadequate and an inadequate but true insight and statement. This means that on the one side we can be sure that the term as applied in

this way does correspond to its object, that it does express it, that it is therefore true, that it tells us what Jesus Christ in fact is. We have no better term, and this one forces itself necessarily upon us. From the standpoint from which we have tried to understand Jesus Christ it is very suitable and indeed indispensable if we are to say what has to be said concerning His deity. It is quite right that it should have acquired its very particular importance and role in the New Testament and in the language of the later Church. It confesses the final thing that we have to confess of Him, and therefore necessarily it takes the first place. But it confesses it in the way that we men can confess the mystery to which it points. As a true description of Jesus Christ it goes far beyond anything that it can say in any other application. As applied to this " Son " it is in a certain sense burst wide open, it can be thought through to the end only as we bring into it meanings which it cannot have in any other use which we can make of it. As applied in this way it deserves our every confidence because it is true, but it must be used with great reserve because of its inadequacy. And is it not fitting that the true deity of the One who is obedient in humility, of the Son who is in this way the only begotten Son of the Father, wills to be known and can be known only in this way—with every confidence but also with great modesty ? For in this matter, as others, what can all our Christian statements be but a serious pointing away to the One who will Himself tell those who have ears to hear who He is ?   [IV, 1, p. 210]

[57] What does the man Jesus say in the midst of the cosmos and all other men ? If we are to put the matter in the simplest terms we must undoubtedly say—Himself. He speaks by the mere fact of his existence. By the very fact that He is, He is the Word of God. And the Word of God at its simplest is to the effect that He, this man Jesus, is. Thus His own existence is the content of the speech of this man. He speaks of the creaturely presence, action and revelation of God actualised in Himself ; of the saving action of God, and therefore of His kingdom, of the doing of His will, of His own creaturely being as wholly dedicated to this purpose, of God's lordship over Him, and therefore of His own freedom for this service. The

man Jesus Himself is in fact this act of salvation, His
doing of the will of God, this service, this sovereignty of
the Creator and freedom of the creature. And He also
speaks of it. He declares and shows that the created
cosmos, men and each individual man are not without
Him. He thus declares that what is needed to deliver the
creature from the evil of nothingness is about to be done.
He declares that the creature is not abandoned by its
Creator ; that it is not left to itself and its own defence-
lessness. He declares that the yawning abyss of non-
being will not be allowed to engulf its being. The Creator
of all being is beside it in person—He who knew, negated,
and rejected non-being as such, and by His wisdom, goodness and power imparted being to His creation, thus judg-
ing between light and darkness and separating the one
from the other. He makes Himself responsible for the
preservation of being, and in so doing He vindicates His
own honour as the Creator. If the creature as such is
endangered by its own impotence, the kingdom of the
Creator comes to it, and the will of the Creator is done in
regard to it. The very existence of Jesus tells us this.
He is thus the light of the divine election and mercy to
the creature. He is the utterance of the promise which
the creature is given and under which it can stand from
the very outset. He is the expression of the friendliness
with which God adopted it in creation. He also declares
the righteousness with which God resolved to maintain
and order it in creation. Creation is not to be undone or
to perish. It belongs to its Creator and to no one else.
This is what is declared by the man Jesus within it ; by
the man Jesus as the Word of God, and therefore as a
Word which is unassailable and irrevocable. And so the
world, and in particular the sphere of man, is not without
this Word. When we say " man " we have to remember
above all that there is one man among many who is this
Word, and in respect of the many that it is in their sphere
that this Word is to be found—the Word which is for
them, which is the Word of their hope, and which in
defiance of every threat promises them freedom, security
and life.   [III, 2, p. 148 f.]

[58] The Cross.

It cannot be ignored that many men have suffered

117

grievously, most grievously, in the course of world history. It might even be suggested that many men have perhaps suffered more grievously and longer and more bitterly than did this man in the limited events of a single day. Many who have suffered at the hands of men have been treated no less and perhaps more unjustly than this man. Many have been willing as He was to suffer in this way. Many in so doing have done something which, according to their intention and it may be in fact, was significant for others, perhaps many others, making a redemptive change in their life. And in face of any human suffering do we not have to think ultimately of the obscure but gracious control of divine providence and therefore of the goodwill of God which becomes act and event in it ? The suffering of man may be deserved or undeserved, voluntary or involuntary, heroic or not heroic, important for others or not important for others. But even if it is only the whimper of a sick child it has in it as such something which in its own way is infinitely outstanding and moving and in its human form and its more or less recognisable or even its hidden divine basis something which we can even describe as shattering. This is true of the passion of Jesus of Nazareth, but in so far as it is a human passion it is not true in a way which is basically different from that of any other human passion. If this is the scope of the Gospel story and the starting-point of Gospel proclamation, it was not the intention of the New Testament, nor was it seriously the intention of the Church as it understood itself in the light of the New Testament, that the fundamentally unique occurrence should be found in the human passion as such. If we single out this human passion above others, we may be able to see and to say something which is noteworthy as such, but we shall not be helped forward a single step towards an understanding of what this occurrence is all about. For this reason we have already had to look beyond the human story at every point.

The mystery of this passion, of the torture, crucifixion and death of this one Jew which took place at that place and time at the hands of the Romans, is to be found in the person and mission of the One who suffered there and was crucified and died. His person : it is the eternal God

Himself who has given Himself in His Son to be man, and as man to take upon Himself this human passion. His mission : it is the Judge who in this passion takes the place of those who ought to be judged, who in this passion allows Himself to be judged in their place. It is not, therefore, merely that God rules in and over this human occurrence simply as Creator and Lord. He does this, but He does more. He gives Himself to be the humanly acting and suffering person in this occurrence. He Himself is the Subject who in His own freedom becomes in this event the object acting or acted upon in it. It is not simply the humiliation and dishonouring of a creature, of a noble and relatively innocent man that we find here. The problem posed is not that of a theodicy : How can God will this or permit this in the world which He has created good ? It is a matter of the humiliation and dishonouring of God Himself, of the question which makes any question of a theodicy a complete anticlimax ; the question whether in willing to let this happen to Him He has not renounced and lost Himself as God, whether in capitulating to the folly and wickedness of His creature He has not abdicated from His deity (as did the Japanese Emperor in 1945), whether He can really die and be dead. And it is a matter of the answer to this question : that in this humiliation God is supremely God, that in this death He is supremely alive, that He has maintained and revealed His deity in the passion of this man as His eternal Son. Moreover, this human passion does not have just a significance and effect in its historical situation within humanity and the world. On the contrary, there is fulfilled in it the mission, the task, and the work of the Son of God : the reconciliation of the world with God. There takes place here the redemptive judgment of God on all men. To fulfil this judgment He took the place of all men, He took their place as sinners. In this passion there is legally re-established the covenant between God and man, broken by man but kept by God. On that one day of the suffering of that One there took place the comprehensive turning in the history of all creation—with all that this involves.

Because it is a matter of this person and His mission, the suffering, crucifixoin and death of this one man is a unique occurrence. His passion has a real dimension of depth which it alone can have in the whole series of human passions. In it—from God's standpoint as well as man's—we have to do not merely with something but with everything : not merely with one of the many hidden but gracious overrulings of God, but in the fulness of its hiddenness with an action in which it is a matter of His own being or not being, and therefore of His own honour or dishonour in relation to His creation. We are not dealing merely with any suffering, but with the suffering of God and this man in face of the destruction which threatens all creation and every individual, thus compromising God as the Creator. We are dealing with the painful confrontation of God and this man not merely with any evil, not merely with death, but with eternal death, with the power of that which is not. Therefore we are not dealing merely with any sin, or with many sins, which might wound God again and again and only especially perhaps at this point, and the consequences of which this man had only to suffer in part and freely willed to do so. We are dealing with sin itself and as such : the preoccupation, the orientation, the determination of man as he has left his place as a creature and broken his covenant with God ; the corruption which God has made His own, for which He willed to take responsibility in this one man. Here in the passion in which as Judge He lets Himself be judged God has fulfilled this responsibility. In the place of all men He has Himself wrestled with that which separates them from* Him. He has Himself borne the consequence of this separation to bear it away.

The New Testament has this in mind when in the Gospels it looks forward to the passion story of Jesus Christ and in the Epistles it looks forward from it to the future of the community and therefore to the future of the world and of every man. It is a matter of history. Everything depends upon the fact that this turning as it comes from God for us men is not simply imagined and presented as a true teaching of pious and thoughtful people, but that it happened in this way, in the space and time which are those of all men. But it is a matter of this history. That it took place once at this time and place as this history is what distinguishes the passion, crucifixion and death of this one Jew from all the other occurrences in time and

space with which the passion of Jesus Christ is otherwise
similar in every respect. Distinguished in this way, it is
the subject of Christian faith and proclamation.

[IV, 1, pp. 246–248]

[59] It is one thing for God to elect and predestinate
Himself to fellowship with man, and quite another for
God to predestinate man to fellowship with Himself.
Both are God's self-giving to man.   But if the latter
means unequivocally that a gift is made to man, the
former certainly does not mean that God gives or procures
Himself anything—for what could God give or procure
Himself in giving to man a share in His own being ?
What we have to consider under this aspect is simply
God's hazarding of His Godhead and power and status.
For man it means an infinite gain, an unheard of advance-
ment, that God should give Himself to him as his own
possession, that God should be his God.   But for God it
means inevitably a certain compromising of Himself that
He should determine to enter into this covenant.   Where
man stands only to gain, God stands only to lose.   And
because the eternal divine predestination is identical with
the election of Jesus Christ, its twofold content is that
God wills to lose in order that man may gain.   There is a
sure and certain salvation for man, and a sure and certain
risk for God.   [II, 2, p. 162]

[60] What is quite certain is that for God it means
severe self-commitment. God does not merely give Himself up to the risk and menace, but He exposes Himself to
the actual onslaught and grasp of evil.   For if God Himself became man, this man, what else can this mean but
that He declared Himself guilty of the contradiction
against Himself in which man was involved ; that He
submitted Himself to the law of creation by which such a
contradiction could be accompanied only by loss and
destruction ;   that He made Himself the object of the
wrath and judgment to which man had brought himself ;
that He took upon Himself the rejection which man had
deserved ;   that He tasted Himself the damnation, death
and hell which ought to have been the portion of fallen
man ?   What did God choose of glory or of joy or of
triumph when in Jesus Christ He elected man ?   What
could this election bring except something of which God

is free in Himself and for which He cannot truly have any
desire : darkness, and the impossibility of our existence
before Him as sinners, as those who have fallen victim to
His penalties ? If we would know what it was that God
elected for Himself when He elected fellowship with man,
then we can answer only that He elected our rejection.
He made it His own. He bore it and suffered it with all
its most bitter consequences. For the sake of this choice
and for the sake of man He hazarded Himself wholly and
utterly. He elected our suffering (what we as sinners
must suffer towards Him and before Him and from Him).
He elected it as His own suffering. This is the extent to
which His election is an election of grace, an election of
love, an election to give Himself, an election to empty and
abase Himself for the sake of the elect. Judas who betrays
Him He elects as an apostle. The sentence of Pilate He
elects as a revelation of His judgment on the world. He
elects the cross of Golgotha as His kingly throne. He
elects the tomb in the garden as the scene of His being as
the living God. That is how God loved the world. That
is how from all eternity His love was so selfless and genuine.
And, conversely, if we would know what rejection is as
determined in God's eternal counsel, the rejection of which
we cannot but speak even in our doctrine of predestination,
then we must look in the same direction. We must look
to what God elected for Himself in His Son when in that
Son He elected for Himself fellowship with man.

[II, 2, p. 164 f.]

[61] For how can we explain the rise of a tradition
whose content is so singular and contradictory—not the
acts and achievements and works of a historical figure, but
his shameful end, his destruction which so totally compromises everything that precedes it ? and this as an
event of such dimensions, of a relevance which is so positive in every respect ? How does it help us to refer to the
possibilities of myth, its invention, formation and elabora-
tion ? How could a myth originate at this point or
develop in these surroundings ? How could it come
about that only 30–70 years after the death of a historical
man, and in these different ways, all this could be narrated
and said with such remarkable concentration about His
death ? However that may be, there is no doubt that in

the 1st century there were people—and they were the first
members of the Christian community and Church—who
did know and tell and say of His death, His death on the
cross, that it had positive meaning as a decisive redemptive
turning-point for them and for all men, His life being the
way which led to this turning-point, and therefore to His
death on the cross as the confirmation of His existence,
His relationship to God, and all that He said and did.
And if they were asked how they knew this, and could
tell and say it, their answer (and they usually volunteered
the information of themselves) was simply that He had
encountered them as the One who had risen again from
the dead, thus revealing the secret of His death, and
therefore of His life, as the work of the saving and enlighten-
ing power of God, or, decisively and comprehensively,
revealing Himself as the incomparable royal man. We
cannot develop the theme in this context. But at some
point and in some way the Christian Church did in fact
begin to have this massive certainty. And we must beware
of facile explanations of this beginning.   [IV, 2, p. 257 f.]

[62] We must pause for a moment to consider a statement which plays no little part in the New Testament,
that the coming into the world of the Son of God includes
within itself the appearance and work of the Judge of the
world and of every man. If He were not the Judge, He
would not be the Saviour. He is the Saviour of the world
in so far as in a very definite (and most astonishing) way
He is also its Judge. . . .

All sin has its being and origin in the fact that man
wants to be his own judge. And in wanting to be that,
and thinking and acting accordingly, he and his whole
world is in conflict with God. It is an unreconciled world,
and therefore a suffering world, a world given up to
destruction.

It is for this reason—the fault and evil are evidently
great and deep enough to make it necessary—it is for this
reason that God Himself encounters man in the flesh and
therefore face to face in the person of His Son, in order
that He may pass on the one who feels and accepts himself as his own judge the real judgment which he has
merited. This judgment sets him in the wrong as the one
who maintains his own right against God instead of bowing

to God's right. We will have to explain this when we come to speak of sin as such. For the moment it is enough to maintain that because it is a matter of the appearance and work of the true Judge amongst those who think they can and should judge and therefore exalt themselves, therefore the abasement of the Son to our status, the obedience which He rendered in humility as our Brother, is the divine accusation against every man and the divine condemnation of every man. The whole world finds its supreme unity and determination against God in looking for justification from itself and not from God. And as a world hostile to God it is distinguished by the fact that in this way it repeats the very sin of which it acquits itself. In this way that which is flesh is flesh. And for this reason the incarnation of the Word means the judgment, the judgment of rejection and condemnation, which is passed on all flesh. Not all men commit all sins, but all men commit this sin which is the essence and root of all other sins. There is not one who can boast that he does not commit it. And this is what is revealed and rejected and condemned as an act of wrong-doing by the coming of the Son of God. This is what makes His coming a coming to judgment, and His office as Saviour His office as our Judge.

But those who are judged and rejected and condemned by God as wrong-doers are lost and condemned to perish, indeed, they are already perishing. They stand on the left hand of God, under the divine No, in the sphere of that which God does not will but rejects, and therefore in the sphere of that which is not, in the darkness in which there is no light, in the affliction in which there is no help, in the need from which there is no redemption. The power of God still rules over them, but as the power which holds and imprisons them, the power of His condemnation. The loves of God burns where they are, but as the fire of His wrath which consumes and destroys them. God lives for them, but the life of God can only mean death for those who are His enemies. That is how the men exist who will be their own judges, who will acquit themselves, who in so doing commit all sins *in nuce*, and who are therefore judged and rejected and condemned by God as wrong-doers. And because all men are determinedly against God in this, this is how every man necessarily exists—in a lost state as one who is lost. God would not be God if there could be any altering the universality and logic and completeness of what is necessarily done here, if there could be any escaping this sequence of sin and destruction. It means eternal perdition to have God against us. But if we will what God does not will, we do have God against us, and therefore we hurry and run and stumble and fall into eternal perdition.

But again God would not be God if His reaction to wrong-doers could be compared to a mechanism which functions, as it were, independently of His free ruling and disposing. That is not how it is on His right hand, where He says Yes to the creature, where He frees his powers and blesses his love and gives him life which is life indeed. God is the Lord in all His rule, even in that of His wrath and the destruction and perdition which it brings. He Himself determines the course and direction and meaning of it : not some necessity immanent to its occurrence ; not a force to which man when he sins against God becomes subject absolutely, i.e., otherwise than in conformity to the sovereign will and disposing of God which obtains even in His rule on the left hand. How God will fulfil the sentence to which man has fallen inescapably victim is a matter for Him to decide. He can fulfil it—in all its strictness—in such a way that in fulfilling it there is attained that which man in his perversity tried and never could secure for himself—his pardon. Without relaxing or mitigating the sentence, let alone as a judge who is unjust by reason of his laxity, He can exercise grace even with His judgment and in execution of it. He can be so much in earnest against sinful man that He is for him. He can bring on him all that must come on him as a wrong-doer at the left hand of God and under His No, in order to set him at His right hand, in order finally to say Yes to him, in order to address and treat him as one who does right and not wrong. God is free to judge in this way. He is not obliged to do so. There is no inner compulsion forcing Him to exercise this strange judgment. Even less is there any right or claim on the part of man on the ground of which he can expect this strange judgment. Everything is against any such judgment being even conceivable : a serious judgment of God's enemies the result of which is grace, liberation, redemption proceeding out of captivity, love out of wrath, life out of death ; a judgment which in the event makes the enemies of God His friends ; a judgment in which this does not happen arbitrarily but in a fixed order, not in a wild divine inconsequence but with a clear purpose and according to a firm plan ; and therefore a judgment beside and after and beyond which there need be no further fear of judgment ; a judgment which concludes once and for all with the redemption and salvation of the man who had been rightly accused and condemned and had fallen a helpless victim to destruction. Everything is against the possibility of a judgment like that. But we cannot encroach on the freedom of God. We cannot, therefore, say that it could not please God in His grace, out of sheer faithfulness and mercy to us men, to be our Judge in this strange fashion.

But in the last resort there is only one thing which tells us that this is in fact possible—that in Jesus Christ His Son our Lord He has acted in this and no other way as our Judge and the Judge of all men. We now return to our question : Why did the Son of God become man, one of us, our Brother, our Fellow in the human situation ? The answer is : In order to judge the world. But in the light of what God has actually done we must add at once : In order to judge it in the exercise of His kingly freedom to show His grace in the execution of His judgment, to pronounce us free in passing sentence, to free us by imprisoning us, to ground our life on our death, to redeem and save us by our destruction. That is how God has actually judged in Jesus Christ. And that is why He humbled Himself. That is why He went into the far country as the obedient Son of the Father. That is why He did not abandon us, but came amongst us as our Brother. That is why the Father sent Him. That was the eternal will of God and its fulfilment in time—the execution of this strange judgment. If this strange judgment had not taken place, there would be only a lost world and lost men. Since it has taken place, we can only recognise and believe and proclaim to the whole world and all men : Not lost. And since it did take place, what does it matter what may be said against the possibility of it ?

But what did take place ? At this point we can and must make the decisive statement : What took place is that the Son of God fulfilled the righteous judgment on us men by Himself taking our place as man and in our place undergoing the judgment under which we had passed. That is why He came and was amongst us. In this way, in this " for us," He was our Judge against us. That is what happened when the divine accusation was, as it were, embodied in His presence in the flesh. That is what happened when the divine condemnation had, as it were, visibly to fall on this our Fellow-man. And that is what happened when by reason of our accusation and condemnation it had to come to the point of our perishing, our destruction, our fall into nothingness, our death. Everything happened to us exactly as it had to happen, but because God willed to execute His judgment on us in His Son it all happened in His person, as His accusation and condemnation and destruction. He judged, and it was the Judge who was judged, who let Himself be judged. Because He was a man like us, He was able to be judged like us. Because He was the Son of God and Himself God, He had the competence and power to allow this to happen to Him. Because He was the divine Judge come amongst us, He had the authority in this way—by this giving up of Himself to judgment in our place—to exercise the divine justice of grace, to pronounce us righteous on the ground of what happened to Him, to free us therefore from the accusation and condemnation and punishment, to save us from the impending loss and destruction. And because in divine freedom He was on the way of obedience, He did not refuse to accept the will of the Father as His will in this self-giving. In His doing this for us, in His taking to Himself—to fulfil all righteousness—our accusation and condemnation and punishment, in His suffering in our place and for us, there came to pass our reconciliation with God. *Cur Deus homo ?* In order that God as man might do and accomplish and achieve and complete all this for us wrong-doers, in order that in this way there might be brought about by Him our reconciliation with Him and conversion to Him.   [IV, 1, pp. 216 f., 220–223]

[63] But how is man to see this, to take sin as seriously as this—his own sin and that of others, however plain ?

Are we not continually surprised by the insignificance of
that act in which the first man—and with him every other
man—became a sinner according to the story in Genesis ?
And do we not take a restricted view of the guilt and sin-
fulness of evil in all the measures that we believe we can
and should take against its origins and effects (our pedagogic and political and moral enterprises) ? How small
the harm appears when we think we can botch it up in
this way ! The truth is that Anselm's question : *quanti
ponderis sit peccatum ?* is given an answer either from the
cross of Christ or not at all. It is given an answer from
the cross of Christ. The serious and terrible nature of
human corruption, the depth of the abyss into which man
is about to fall as the author of it, can be measured by the
fact that the love of God could react and reply to this
event only by His giving, His giving up, of Jesus Christ
Himself to overcome and remove it and in that way to
redeem man, fulfilling the judgment upon it in such a
way that the Judge allowed Himself to be judged and
caused the man of sin to be put to death in His own person.
It is only when it is seen that this was the cost to God—
in the person of His Son—of our reconciliation with Him,
that the frivolously complacent assumption is destroyed
that our evil is always limited by our good (our good
nature and our good actions), and that it is excused and
mitigated by this compensation. Our evil is indeed limited
and compensated and more than counterbalanced, but
not by our good, only by the goodness of God. And
because this is the only possible limitation and compensation we cannot think too stringently or soberly about the
seriousness of the human situation.   [IV, 1, p. 411 f.]

[64] There, on the cross of Golgotha, hangs the man
who in His own name and person represented me, my
name and person, with God ; and who again in His own
name and person represented God to me in my name and
person. Everything, therefore, that God has to say in His
relationship to me is originally and properly said to Him ;
everything that I have to say to God in this relationship
is originally and properly said by Him. All that I have
to do, therefore, is to repeat what is already said in this
conversation between God and the Son. But what takes
place in this conversation is that in the person of Jesus

Christ I am addressed as a sinner, a lost son, and that again in the person of Jesus Christ I confess myself to be a sinner, a lost son. In this conversation the voice of denial is absolutely silenced. For in the death of Jesus Christ, this conversation between Father and Son is conducted with me and about me—with me and about me in His person as my Advocate before God. Even in the soliloquy and self-judgment which I cannot escape in face of the divine colloquy and judgment the voice of denial cannot be raised. I am not one who, as a hearer of this divine conversation, and a participator in this divine judgment, can either hear or make any kind of excuse. At the point where God deals with me, where He has sought and found me, at the cross of Golgotha, I am exposed and addressed as a sinner. Indeed, I have found and confessed myself to be this. I have nothing to add to what is said and confessed there, nor to subtract from it. The transgression in all transgressions, the sin in all sins, namely, that I should refuse the name of a sinner, is made quite impossible. It is literally nailed to the cross with Jesus Christ. It can only die. The only thing that I can do is recognise that my sin is really dead—the sin from which I cannot cleanse myself, the sin which I cannot even recognise and confess, the sin which I could only see awakening, and myself awaken, to constantly new forms of life if it were not already dead in the fact that God has pronounced and executed His sentence on His beloved Son in my place, and that the latter has accepted it in my place.   [II, 2, p. 750 f.]

[65] How, then, did He traverse this earth of ours? How was He and is He among us? As a man like ourselves, with all our frailty and limitation! In solidarity with us—indeed bearing our guilt and shame and misery in our place! Finally betrayed and rejected and condemned, dying a criminal's death! Yet all this pales before the way in which He was man and lived and acted and suffered as such. For in all this, not least but supremely in His death and passion, He lived the superior life of a new man completely different from us. What a Lord among a race of servants was this one perfect servant in His very being as a servant! What a cause He espoused for us all against us all—for us who are so occupied with

wretched causes ! What words He spoke—in human
language and with human limitations—but what words !
And what acts He performed—human acts and with
human limitations—but what acts ! This man came, and
in and with Him there came the kingdom. In and with
Him there took place the divine seizure of power on earth.
Nor was this arrested or reversed by His death, when He
trod the way of His humiliation to the bitter end. On the
contrary, it was completed, definitively completed, by His
death. What is it that we beheld ? Flesh of our flesh ?
And therefore the judgment of God fulfilled on all flesh in
Him ? And therefore His own and our misery ? No, we
beheld His glory—" the glory as of the only begotten of the
Father, full of grace and truth " (Jn. 1^{14}). What is it
that we heard ? That no man has seen God at any time ?
That we are so far from God, so godless and god-forsaken ?
No, for although we did hear this, we heard also the
declaration of God brought us by the One who is in the
bosom of the Father, and " of his fulness have all we
received, and grace for grace " (Jn. 1^{16}). This is paradoxical, not merely because it is said of the man Jesus, of
the eternal Word which became flesh, of the humiliated
Son of God as the Son of Man, of the One who entered
into the great concealment of His Godhead, but also
because this man was so superior and exalted, so genuine
and glorious a man. The riddle of the existence of Jesus
Christ has also this quite other side. There is in it not
only night but also day, not only confusing darkness but
also—no less and perhaps even more strangely—blinding
light ; the sharp light of contrast, but genuine light. Thus
we have not only to ask where and how we are to see and
have access to the reconciliation of the world with God as
it has taken place in Him, its and our salvation, the kingdom of God drawn near and its peace. With the answer
to this question we have also to ask how that which is
really present and visible can be seen by human eyes ;
how we can stand before this man ; where and how there
is a place in our heart and reason for the glory of man as
it is present in Him ; whether and how we are endowed
and adapted to receive grace of His fulness, or even to
realise the presence of the fulness of divine, and therefore
of human, glory. Is it really the case that the riddle of the

existence of Jesus Christ has only the aspect on which it appears to signify that on account of the lowliness in which God meets us in it we can make too little, or nothing at all, of this God? Is it not perhaps the case that it has, especially, this other aspect on which it signifies that we are quite impotent in face of it because in this man too much, indeed everything, is made of us, because there has taken place in Him an exaltation, a new beginning of our human being, which is quite beyond us, because there encounters us in Him a life that we cannot even conceive, let alone think or live, either as the life of this man or as the life which we are also given in Him?

It is again the case that the Christian community and the individual Christian, coming from the resurrection of Jesus Christ, find themselves on the far side of this question, actually saying Yes to this royal man, to the glory of the Son of God revealed in His human majesty, to His human life and therefore to the exaltation of our life as it has taken place in Him. If we assume that we are Christians, and that we come from Easter, we do not close our eyes to this light, or gape and stare at it as at an alien marvel. There is a place in our heart and reason for the reconciliation of the world with God as it has taken place in this true Son of God and Son of Man, for the covenant as it has been fulfilled even on man's side for the kingdom, the peace, the salvation of God, concluded in the existence of this man. We hear the Word incarnate, this man, and we obey Him. We can and must be His witnesses. We believe in the Lord Jesus Christ, the Crucified, but the One who conquers as the Crucified, and the One who is raised again and manifested as the Conqueror. We confess His human name as the name which is above every name. Whether we fully understand this and give ourselves to it, or draw back half-way, the fact itself is indisputable. The Christian community is the Easter community. Our preaching is Easter preaching, our hymns are Easter hymns, our faith is an Easter faith. We not only have a *theologia crucis*, but a *theologia resurrectionis* and therefore a *theologia gloriae*, i.e., a theology of the glory of the new man actualised and introduced in the crucified Jesus Christ who triumphs as the Crucified; a theology of the promise of our eternal life which has its

basis and origin in the death of this man. It would be a
false seriousness to try to disguise the fact that the Christian
answer to the one puzzle of the existence of Jesus Christ
has also this other aspect. To affirm it is not to deny or
forget or conceal the first side. It is only in the light of
the first that it can have this second aspect. It is great
and wonderful and necessary enough that in face of the
deep humiliation and concealment of the Son of God there
should be a violently resisting and attacking Christian
Notwithstanding and Nevertheless ; that in face of the
cross there should be an acceptance and repetition, piercing
the threatened despair, of the Yes that is spoken in and
under this powerful No ; that there should be therefore a
Good Friday faith, a *theologia crucis*. At all periods in its
history the Christian community has ventured fearfully
but boldly to proclaim this Notwithstanding and Nevertheless. And it will never cease fearfully but boldly to
proclaim it. The Holy Spirit encourages and instructs and
impels it to make this defiant penetration, and will never
cease to kindle and therefore to characterise Christian
faith and confession on this first side. But is it not more
great and wonderful and necessary that the one riddle of
the existence of Jesus Christ is disclosed to the same
Christian community—at all periods in its history—by a
very different aspect ? that the same faith in Him is set
in its heart, and the same confession on its lips, in a very
different form, in the form in which the Nevertheless has
become a Hence and the Notwithstanding a Therefore ?
This is in fact the case. The acceptance and repetition of
that Yes are more than a desperate resistance and attack.
They are more than the piercing of a threatened despair.
They are this, but they are also more. They are a simple
acceptance free from all the strain and stress of conflict.
It is not merely that the Yes is spoken in and under the
powerful No of the cross, and has to be received and
repeated in defiance of it. The fact is that in and under
the No of the cross a powerful Yes is also spoken : " Christ
is risen," and that this powerful Yes may also be received
and repeated. This being the case, faith and confession
are characterised more by joy and thankfulness than by
fearfulness and boldness. The liberation has given rise
to liberty. The riddle of the existence of Jesus Christ,

which is the point of reference for the Christian answer
and Christian faith and confession, is thus the fact that in
the humiliation of the Son of God there is actualised and
revealed the exaltation of the Son of Man, and our own
exaltation in Him as our Brother and Head.

[IV, 2, pp. 353–355]

III. NOTHINGNESS

The question of the origin and purpose of evil has always been a basic question of human thought. In Christian thinking certain tenets are sure even though they are hard to bring into logical connexion : (1) that God, the Author of all that is, is not the Author of evil, and yet the latter is a powerful reality and not a mere appearance ; (2) that evil is really evil, i.e., that it is that which is not willed by God, and cannot therefore be somehow regarded as purposeful, and yet God is a match for it, mastering it and turning it to good ; and (3) that the creaturely nature of man makes it possible for him to choose evil and sin, and yet this is not the will or plan of God, so that man alone is responsible and not God. Barth takes up the questions raised by these basic propositions. In his attempt the following points are to be noted : (1) the title " nothingness," which he gives to evil, does not mean that it does not exist but that it is rejected and overcome, so that man can only turn away from it and cannot respect it ; (2) he differentiates evil strictly from the shadow-side of creation—night, sorrow, finitude and need—which are meaningful and belong to the good creation of God, in no way detracting from it ; (3) he thinks that justice is done to the resurrection of Christ, the triumph of grace, only when the triumph of God is believed and evil is not therefore taken with final seriousness.

[66] It is a mark of the divine nature as distinct from that of the creature that in it a conflict with Himself is not merely ruled out, but is inherently impossible. If this were not so, if there did not exist perfect, original and ultimate peace between the Father and the Son by the Holy Spirit, God would not be God. Any God in conflict with Himself is bound to be a false God. On the other hand, it is a mark of created being as distinct from divine that in it conflict with God and therefore mortal conflict with itself is not ruled out, but is a definite possibility even if it is only the impossible possibility, the possibility of self-annulment and therefore its own destruction. Without this possibility of defection or of evil, creation would not be distinct from God and therefore not really His creation. The fact that the creature can fall away from God and perish does not imply any imperfection on the part of creation or the Creator. What it does mean positively is that it is something created and is therefore

134

dependent on preserving grace, just as it owes its very existence simply to the grace of its Creator. A creature freed from the possibility of falling away would not really be living as a creature. It could only be a second God—and as no second God exists, it could only be God Himself. Sin is when the creature avails itself of this impossible possibility in opposition to God and to the meaning of its own existence. But the fault is that of the creature and not of God. In no sense does it follow necessarily from what God is in Himself. Nor does it result from the nature of creation. It follows inevitably only from the incomprehensible fact that the creature rejects the preserving grace of God. What belongs to the nature of the creature is that it is not physically hindered from doing this. If it was hindered in this way, it could not exist at all as a creature. In that case, grace would not be grace and the creature would inevitably be God Himself. The fact of evil in the world does not cast any shadow on God, as if evil, i.e., opposition to Him, had any place either in Himself or in His being and activity as the Creator.

[II, 1, p. 503 f.]

[67] We cannot complain because God put a creaturely being on this frontier, a being unlike Himself in that it was subject to temptation. We cannot blame God for confronting man with evil, an evil which in His own case was excluded by the divine nature, but which in man's case could be excluded only by the divine Word and commandment. We cannot hold it against God that He did not prevent but permitted the fall of man, i.e., his succumbing to the temptation of the devil and his incurring of actual guilt. In God's eternal decree these things did not involve any injustice to the creature, for by this same decree God decided that the risk which He allowed to threaten the creature and the plight into which He allowed it to plunge itself should be His own risk and His own plight. God created man. In that sense He exposed him to the risk. Yet from all eternity God did not let him fall, but He upheld him even when Satan's temptation and his own culpability resulted in a fall into sin. Thus even when we think of man in this negative determination, we still think of him as the one whom God loved from all eternity in His Son, as the one to whom He gave Himself

from all eternity in His Son, gave Himself that He might
represent him, gave Himself that He might bear and
suffer on His behalf what man himself had to suffer. We
must insist upon man's responsibility for his failure to do
on that frontier what he ought to have done as a creature
of God and hearer of the Word of God. But much more,
we must insist upon the responsibility which God Himself
shouldered when He created man and permitted the fall
of man. Man cannot evade his own responsibility by
complaining that God required too much of him, for what
God required of Himself on man's behalf is infinitely greater
than what He required of man. In the last analysis what
God required of man consists only in the demand that he
should live as the one on whose behalf God required the
uttermost of Himself. " Thou wilt say then unto me,
Why doth he yet find fault ? For who hath resisted his
will ? Nay but, O man, who art thou that repliest against
God ? " (Rom. 9¹²ᶠ·). And the answer is : The man to
whom God Himself turned from all eternity in His Son,
even in the subordination to His will which is so strange
to you ; the man at whose strange need and danger God
estranged Himself from all eternity, making it His own ;
the man who has no cause to reproach God, but if he will
reproach anyone can only reproach himself ; the man who
is justly reproached by God if he attempts to reply against
Him, if he does not live as the one on whose behalf God
has taken to Himself every reproach, if he does not live
in a state of thankfulness towards God.

[II, 2, p. 165 f.]

[68] What is real nothingness ?

1. In this question objection may well be taken to the
word " is." Only God and His creature really and properly
are. But nothingness is neither God nor His creature.
Thus it can have nothing in common with God and His
creature. But it would be foolhardy to rush to the conclusion that it is therefore nothing, i.e., that it does not
exist. God takes it into account. He is concerned with it.
He strives against it, resists and overcomes it. If God's
reality and revelation are known in His presence and
action in Jesus Christ, He is also known as the God who
is confronted by nothingness, for whom it constitutes a
problem, who takes it seriously, who does not deal with it

136

incidentally but in the fulness of the glory of His deity, who is not engaged indirectly or mediately but with His whole being, involving Himself to the utmost. If we accept this, we cannot argue that because it has nothing in common with God and His creature nothingness is nothing, i.e., it does not exist. That which confronts God in this way, and is seriously treated by Him, is surely not nothing or non-existent. In the light of God's relationship to it we must accept the fact that in a third way of its own nothingness " is." All conceptions or doctrines which would deny or diminish or minimise this " is " are untenable from the Christian standpoint. Nothingness is not nothing. Quite apart from the inadmissibility of its content, this proposition would be self-contradictory. But it " is " nothingness. Its nature and being are those which can be assigned to it within this definition. But because it stands before God as such they must be assigned to it. They cannot be controverted without misapprehending God Himself.

2. Again, nothingness is not simply to be equated with what is *not*, i.e., not God and not the creature. God is God and not the creature, but this does not mean that there is nothingness in God. On the contrary, this " not " belongs to His perfection. Again, the creature is creature and not God, yet this does not mean that as such it is null or nothingness. If in the relationship between God and creature a " not " is involved, the " not " belongs to the perfection of the relationship, and even the second " not " which characterises the creature belongs to its perfection. Hence it would be blasphemy against God and His work if nothingness were to be sought in this " not," in the non-divinity of the creature. The diversities and frontiers of the creaturely world contain many " nots." No single creature is all-inclusive. None is or resembles another. To each belongs its own place and time, and in these its own manner, nature and existence. What we have called the " shadow side " of creation is constituted by the " not " which in this twofold respect, as its distinction from God and its individual distinctiveness, pertains to creaturely nature. On this shadow side the creature is contiguous to nothingness, for this " not " is at once the expression and frontier of the positive will, election and

activity of God. When the creature crosses the frontier from the one side, and it is invaded from the other, nothingness achieves actuality in the creaturely world. But in itself and as such this frontier is not nothingness, nor has the shadow side of creation any connexion with it. Therefore all conceptions and doctrines which view nothingness as an essential and necessary determination of being and existence and therefore of the creature, or as an essential determination of the original and creative being of God Himself, are untenable from the Christian standpoint. They are untenable on two grounds, first, because they misrepresent the creature and even the Creator Himself, and second, because they confound the legitimate " not " with nothingness, and are thus guilty of a drastic minimisation of the latter.

3. Since real nothingness is real in this third fashion peculiar to itself, not resembling either God or the creature but taken seriously by God Himself, and since it is not identical either with the distinction and frontier between God and creation or with those within the creaturely world, its revelation and knowledge cannot be a matter of the insight which is accessible to the creature itself and is therefore set under its own choice and control. Standing before God in its own characteristic way which is very different from that of the creature, the object of His concern and action, His problem and adversary and the negative goal of His victory, nothingness does not possess a nature which can be assessed nor an existence which can be discovered by the creature. There is no accessible relationship between the creature and nothingness. Hence nothingness cannot be an object of the creature's natural knowledge. It is certainly an objective reality for the creature. The latter exists objectively in encounter with it. But it is disclosed to the creature only as God is revealed to the latter in His critical relationship. The creature knows it only as it knows God in His being and attitude against it. It is an element in the history of the relationship between God and the creature in which God precedes the creature in His acts, thus revealing His will to the creature and informing it about Himself. As this occurs and the creature attains to the truth—the truth about God's purpose and attitude and therefore about

itself—through the Word of God, the encounter of the creature with true nothingness is also realised and recognised. Of itself, the creature cannot recognise this encounter and what it encounters. It experiences and endures it. But it also misinterprets it, as has always happened. Calumniating God and His work, it misrepresents it as a necessity of being or nature, as a given factor, as a peculiarity of existence which is perhaps deplorable, perhaps also justifiable, perhaps to be explained in terms of perfection or simply to be dismissed as non-existent, as something which can be regarded as supremely positive in relation to God, or even as a determination of God Himself. All these conceptions and doctrines, whatever their content, are untenable from a Christian standpoint if only because they are contingent upon an arbitrary and impotent appraisal of what can only make itself known in the judgment of God, and is thus knowable only as God pronounces His sentence, while its malignity and corruption find supreme expression in the assumption of the creature that of itself and at its own discretion it is able to discover its nature and existence.

4. The ontic context in which nothingness is real is that of God's activity as grounded in His election, of His activity as the Creator, as the Lord of His creatures, as the King of the covenant between Himself and man which is the goal and purpose of His creation. Grounded always in election, the activity of God is invariably one of jealousy, wrath and judgment. God is also holy, and this means that His being and activity take place in a definite opposition, in a real negation, both defensive and aggressive. Nothingness is that from which God separates Himself and in face of which He asserts Himself and exerts His positive will. If the biblical conception of the God whose activity is grounded in election and is therefore holy fades or disappears, there will also fade and disappear the knowledge of nothingness, for it will necessarily become pointless. Nothingness has no existence and cannot be known except as the object of God's activity as always a holy activity. The biblical conception, as we now recall it, is as follows. God elects, and therefore rejects what He does not elect. God wills, and therefore opposes what He does not will. He says Yes, and therefore says No to that to

which He has not said Yes. He works according to His purpose, and in so doing rejects and dismisses all that gainsays it. Both of these activities, grounded in His election and decision, are necessary elements in His sovereign action. He is Lord both on the right hand and on the left. It is only on this basis that nothingness " is," but on this basis it really " is." As God is Lord on the left hand as well, He is the basis and Lord of nothingness too. Consequently it is not adventitious. It is not a second God, nor self-created. It has no power save that which it is allowed by God. It, too, belongs to God. It " is " problematically because it is only on the left hand of God, under His No, the object of His jealousy, wrath and judgment. It " is," not as God and His creation are, but only in its own improper way, as inherent contradiction, as impossible possibility. Yet because it is on the left hand of God, it really " is " in this paradoxical manner. Even on His left hand the activity of God is not in vain. He does not act for nothing. His rejection, opposition, negation and dismissal are powerful and effective like all His works because they, too, are grounded in Himself, in the freedom and wisdom of His election. That which God renounces and abandons in virtue of His decision is not merely nothing. It is nothingness, and has as such its own being, albeit malignant and perverse. A real dimension is disclosed, and existence and form are given to a reality *sui generis*, in the fact that God is wholly and utterly not the Creator in this respect. Nothingness is that which God does not will. It lives only by the fact that it is that which God does not will. But it does live by this fact. For not only what God wills, but what He does not will, is potent, and must have a real correspondence. What really corresponds to that which God does not will is nothingness. [III, 3, pp. 349–352]

[69] The character of nothingness derives from its ontic peculiarity. It is evil. What God positively wills and performs in the *opus proprium* of His election, of His creation, of His preservation and overruling rule of the creature revealed in the history of His covenant with man, is His grace—the free goodness of His condescension in which He wills, identifying Himself with the creature, to accept solidarity and to be present with it, to be Him-

140

self its Guarantor, Helper and King, and therefore to do the best possible for it. What God does not will and therefore negates and rejects, what can thus be only the object of His *opus alienum*, of His jealousy, wrath and judgment, is a being that refuses and resists and therefore lacks His grace. This being which is alien and adverse to grace and therefore without it, is that of nothingness. This negation of His grace is chaos, the world which He did not choose or will, which He could not and did not create, but which, as He created the actual world, He passed over and set aside, marking and excluding it as the eternal past, the eternal yesterday. And this is evil in the Christian sense, namely, what is alien and adverse to grace, and therefore without it. In this sense nothingness is really privation, the attempt to defraud God of His honour and right and at the same time to rob the creature of its salvation and right. For it is God's honour and right to be gracious, and this is what nothingness contests. It is also the salvation and right of the creature to receive and live by the grace of God, and this is what it disturbs and obstructs. Where this privation occurs, nothingness is present ; and where nothingness is present this privation occurs, i.e., evil, that which is utterly inimical first to God and then to His creature. The grace of God is the basis and norm of all being, the source and criterion of all good. Measured by this standard, as the negation of God's grace, nothingness is intrinsically evil. It is both perverting and perverted. In this capacity it does not confront either God or the creature neutrally. It is not merely a third factor. It opposes both as an enemy, offending God and threatening His creature. From above as well as from below, it is the impossible and intolerable. By reason of this character, whether in the form of sin, evil or death, it is inexplicable as a natural process or condition. It is altogether inexplicable. The explicable is subject to a norm and occurs within a standard. But nothingness is absolutely without norm or standard. The explicable conforms to a law, nothingness to none. It is simply aberration, transgression, evil. For this reason it is inexplicable, and can be affirmed only as that which is inherently inimical. For this reason it can be apprehended in its aspect of sin only as guilt, and in its aspect of evil and death only as retribution and misery, but never as a natural process or condition, never as a subject of systematic formulation, even though the system be dialectical. Being hostile before and against God, and also before and against His creature, it is outside the sphere of systematisation. It cannot even be viewed dialectically, let alone resolved. Its defeat can be envisaged only as the purpose and end of the history of God's dealings with His creature, and in no other way. As it is real only by reason of the *opus Dei alienum*, the divine negation and rejection, so it can be seen and understood only in the light of the *opus Dei proprium*, only in relation to the sovereign counter-offensive of God's free grace. It " is " only as the disorder at which this counter-offensive is aimed, only as the non-essence which it judges, only as the enemy of God and His creation. We thus affirm that it is necessary to dismiss as non-Christian all those conceptions in which its character as evil is openly or secretly, directly or indirectly, conjured away, and its reality is in some way regarded or grouped with that of God and His creature. Where God and His creature are known, and His free grace as the basic order of their relationship, nothingness can only be understood as opposition and resistance to this basic order and cannot therefore be regarded or grouped with God and His creature.

[III, 3, p. 353 f.]

[70] Thus it follows that the controversy with nothingness, its conquest, removal and abolition, is primarily and properly the cause of God Himself. At first sight we might regard the converse as true. Nothingness is the danger, assault and menace under which the creature as such must exist. Therefore the creature as such is surely the hero who must suffer and fight and finally conquer this adversary, and the conflict with it is the problem of his destiny and decision, his tragedy and courage, his impotence and comparative successes. But there can be no greater delusion nor catastrophe than to take this view. For it would not be real nothingness, but only an ultimately innocuous counterfeit, if the attack were primarily and properly directed against the creature, and its repulse could and should be primarily and properly the creature's concern. And while the creature is preoccupied with the assault and repulse of these counterfeits, it is already

subject to the attack of real nothingness and its defence against it is already futile. In face of real nothingness the creature is already defeated and lost. For, as Gen. 3 shows, it regards the conflict with it as its own cause, and tries to champion it as such. It tries to be itself the hero who suffers and fights and conquers, and therefore like God. And because this decision is a decision against the grace of God, it is a choice of evil. For good—the one and only good of the creature—is the free grace of God, the action of His mercy, in which He who has no need to do so has made the controversy with nothingness His own, exposing Himself to its attack and undertaking to repel it. He knows nothingness. He knows that which He did not elect or will as the Creator. He knows chaos and its terror. He knows its advantage over His creature. He knows how inevitably it imperils His creature. Yet He is Lord over that which imperils His creature. Against Him, nothingness has no power of its own. And He has sworn fidelity to His threatened creature. In creating it He has covenanted and identified Himself with it. He Himself has assumed the burden and trouble of confrontation with nothingness. He would rather be unblest with His creature than be the blessed God of an unblest creature. He would rather let Himself be injured and humiliated in making the assault and repulse of nothingness His own concern than leave His creature alone in this affliction. He deploys all His majesty in the work of His deepest condescension. He intervenes in the struggle between nothingness and the creature as if He were not God but Himself a weak and threatened and vulnerable creature. " As if "—but is that all ? No, for in the decisive action in the history of His covenant with the creature, in Jesus Christ, He actually becomes a creature, and thus makes the cause of the creature His own in the most concrete reality and not just in appearance, really taking its place. This is how God Himself comes on the scene.

But it is really God who does so in His free grace. And therefore it is He as the first and true and indeed the only man, as the Helper who really takes the creature's place, lifting from it all its need and labour and problem and placing them upon Himself, as the Warrior who assumes the full responsibility of a substitute and suffers and does everything on its behalf. In the light of this merciful action of God, the arrogant delusion of the creature that it is called and qualified to help and save and maintain itself in its infinite peril is shown to be evil as well as foolish and unnecessary. So, too, is the arrogant illusion that it is the principal party affected, that its own strength or weakness, despair or elation, folly or wisdom, modicum of " existential " insight and freedom, is the problem in solution of which there takes place the decisive encounter with nothingness, the repelling of its assault, and perhaps its defeat. In the light of the merciful action of God, only God Himself, and trust in Him, and perseverance in His covenant, can be called good, even for the creature too. Hence the creature has only one good to choose, namely, that it has God for it, and that it is thus opposed by nothingness as God Himself is opposed, the God who can so easily master it.

In this way, in this trust and perseverance, in this choice of God's help as its only good, the creature can and will have a real part in the conflict with nothingness. It is certainly no mere spectator. But only in this way does it cease to be such. Only in this way is it rescued from illusory struggles and strivings with what are only counterfeits of nothingness, and from inaction in the event in which the onslaught of nothingness is real but its repulse is effective and its conquest in sight. In this way alone is the situation of the creature, its fall and rehabilitation, its suffering, action and inaction, full of meaning and promise. As the action of God is primary, the creature can and will also play its part. For it is the salvation of the creature which God makes a matter of His own honour. It is for the right of the creature that He establishes and defends His own right. The *opus alienum* of divine jealousy, wrath and judgment is no less for the creature than the *opus proprium* of divine grace. For it is the sin and guilt, the suffering and misery of the creature that God makes His own problem. The creature is not its own. It is the creature and possession of God. It is thus the object of His concern. And therefore conflict with nothingness is its own problem as it is the cause of God. The full intervention of God is needed, and this action of His mercy is the only compelling force, to make the creature willing and able to act on its own behalf in the conflict with nothingness. As God takes action on its behalf, the creature itself is summoned and empowered. It has no arrogant illusion as to its own authority or competence. It really trusts in God, perseveres in His covenant and chooses His help as the only effective good. But if it does this it can and will take action in the conflict with nothingness. It is not under the wings of divine mercy but in the vacuum of creaturely self-sufficiency that the laziness thrives which induces man to yield and succumb to nothingness. And it is not in the vacuum of creaturely self-sufficiency but under the wings of divine mercy that the fortitude thrives in which man is summoned and equipped to range himself with God, so that in his own place he opposes nothingness and thus has a part in the work and warfare of God.

[III, 3, pp. 357–359]

[71] What is nothingness ? In the knowledge and confession of the Christian faith, i.e., looking retrospectively to the resurrection of Jesus Christ and prospectively to His coming again, there is only one possible answer. Nothingness is the past, the ancient menace, danger and destruction, the ancient non-being which obscured and defaced the divine creation of God but which is consigned to the past in Jesus Christ, in whose death it has received its deserts, being destroyed with this consummation of the positive will of God which is as such the end of His non-willing. Because Jesus is Victor, nothingness is routed and extirpated. It is that which in this One who was both very God and very man has been absolutely set behind, not only by God, but in unity with Him by man and therefore the creature. It is that from whose influence, dominion and power the relationship between Creator and creature was absolutely set free in Jesus Christ, so that it is no longer involved in their relationship as a third factor. This is what has happened to nothingness once and for all in Jesus Christ. This is its status and appearance now that God has made His own and carried through the conflict with it in His Son. It is no longer to be feared. It can no longer " nihilate." But obviously we may make these undoubtedly audacious statements only on the ground of one single presupposition. The aspect of creaturely activity both as a whole and in detail, our consciousness both of

the world and of self, certainly do not bear them out. But
what do we really know of it as taught by this consciousness ? How can this teach us the truth that it is really
past and done with ? The only valid presupposition is a
backward look to the resurrection of Jesus Christ and a
forward look to His coming in glory, i.e., the look of
Christian faith as rooted in and constantly nourished by
the Word of God. The knowledge and confession of
Christian faith, however, inevitably entails the affirmation
that by the divine intervention nothingness has lost the
perpetuity which it could and must and indeed did have
apart from this intervention. It can no longer be validly
regarded as possessing any claim or right or power in
relation to the creature, as though it were still before and
above us, as though the world created by God were still
subject to and dominated by it, as though Christians must
hold it in awe, as though it were particularly Christian to
hold it in the utmost awe and to summon the world to
share in this awe. It is no longer legitimate to think of it
as if real deliverance and release from it were still an event
of the future. It is obvious that in point of fact we do
constantly think of it in this way, with anxious, legalistic,
tragic, hesitant, doleful and basically pessimistic thoughts,
and this inevitably where we are neither able nor prepared
to think from the standpoint of Christian faith. But it is
surely evident that when we think in this way it is not from
a Christian standpoint, but in spite of it, in breach of the
command imposed with our Christian faith. If our thought
is conditioned by the obedience of Christian faith, we have
only one freedom, namely, to regard nothingness as finally
destroyed and to make a new beginning in remembrance
of the One who has destroyed it. Only if our thought is
thus conditioned by the obedience of Christian faith is it
possible to proclaim the Gospel to the world as it really is,
as the message of freedom for the One who has already
come and acted as the Liberator, and therefore of the
freedom which precludes the anxiety, legalism and pessi-
mism so prevalent in the world. We need hardly describe
how throughout the centuries the Christian Church has
failed to shape its thought in the obedience of Christian
faith, to proclaim it to the world in this obedience, to live
in this freedom and to summon the world to it. For this

reason and contrary to its true nature, so-called Christianity has become a sorry affair both within and without. It is shameful enough to have to admit that many of the interpretations of nothingness which we are forced to reject as non-Christian derive their power and cogency from the fact that for all their weakness and erroneousness they attest a Christian insight to the extent that they do at least offer a cheerful view and describe and treat nothingness as having no perpetuity. It ought to be the main characteristic of the Christian view that it can demonstrate this more surely because on surer ground, more boldly because in the exercise and proclamation of the freedom granted to do so, and more logically because not in a venture but in simple obedience. We must not imagine that we serve the seriousness of Christian knowledge, life and proclamation by retreating at this point and refusing to realise and admit that the apparently audacious is the norm, the only true possibility. The true seriousness of the matter, and we may emphasise this point in retrospect of the whole discussion, does not finally depend upon pessimistic but upon optimistic thought and speech. From a Christian standpoint " to be serious " can only mean to take seriously the fact that Jesus is Victor. If Jesus is Victor, the last word must always be secretly the first, namely, that nothingness has no perpetuity.

[III, 3, p. 363 f.]

IV. CREATION AS BENEFIT

Barth's exposition of the first article of the creed is characterised by the fact that he does not regard the creatureliness of the world and the providence of God as something which can be known from other indications and demonstrated as attempted by the older proofs of God, but as something which can be known only in faith, i.e., in acknowledgment of the Word of revelation. It is also characterised by the closely related fact that he does not see only a subsequent but an original relationship between creation and salvation. God does not first posit in being and then bring salvation to certain creatures under specific conditions. He creates out of grace. This is what is meant by the two main propositions that creation is the external basis of the covenant and the covenant the internal basis of creation. In relation to God this means that His creation is not a causation but the overflowing of His love, His being for the creature. And in relation to us it means the unheard-of fact that our very being is grace, for which all of us, whoever we are, can only be absolutely thankful and with which we can only come to terms.

[72] God is unknown to us as our Father or as the Creator to the extent that He is not known through Jesus. . . . If this exclusive statement is accepted and taken seriously . . . there can be no possibility of regarding the first article of the creed as an article of natural theology. The message of Jesus concerning God the Father cannot be taken to mean that Jesus uttered the well-known truth that the world must have and really has a Creator, that He ventured to give to this Creator the familiar human name of *' Father,"* that He took what all serious philosophy has called the supreme good, the *esse a se*, the *ens perfectissimum*, the *universum*, the ground or abyss of meaning, the unconditional, the limit, the critical negation or the origin, and gave to it this name which was already current in the language of religion, thus baptising it and interpreting it in a Christian sense. Concerning such a view we can only say that, whether or not it is given the name of Father, this entity, the supposed philosophical equivalent of the Creator God, has nothing whatever to do with the message of Jesus concerning God the Father. It still has nothing whatever to do with it even

if it is related and perhaps identified with the principle of dying to become, with the superior origin and goal of the dialectic of losing one's life to gain it. An idea projected with the claim to be the idea of God is as such an idol in the light of the exclusiveness of the biblical witnesses, not because it is an idea but because of its claim. This applies even to the genuinely pure and for that reason misleading idea of God advanced by a Plato. If our exclusive statement is true, Jesus did not proclaim again the well-known Creator of the world and reinterpret Him by investing Him with the not unknown name of Father. On the contrary, He revealed the unknown Father, His Father, and in so doing, but only in so doing, He said who and what the Creator is, and that the Creator as such is our Father. [I, 1, p. 448 f.]

[73] The doctrine of the creation no less than the whole remaining content of Christian confession is an article of faith, i.e., the rendering of a knowledge which no man has procured for himself or ever will ; which is neither native to him nor accessible by way of observation and logical thinking ; for which he has no organ and no ability ; which he can in fact achieve only in faith ; but which is actually consummated in faith, i.e., in the reception of and response to the divine witness, so that he is made to be strong in his weakness, to see in his blindness and to hear in his deafness by the One who, according to the Easter story, goes through closed doors. It is a faith and doctrine of this kind which is expressed when in and with the whole of Christendom we confess that God is the Creator of heaven and earth. [III, 1, p. 3 f.]

[74] Creation is the freely willed and executed positing of a reality distinct from God. The question thus arises : What was and is the will of God in doing this ? We may reply that He does not will to be alone in His glory ; that He desires something else beside Him. But this answer cannot mean that God either willed and did it for no purpose, or that He did so to satisfy a need. Nor does it mean that He did not will to be and remain alone because He could not do so. And the idea of something beside Him which would be what it is independently of Him is quite inconsistent with His freedom. In constituting this reality He cannot have set a limit to His glory, will and

149

power. As the divine Creator He cannot have created a remote and alien sphere abandoned to itself or to its own teleology. If, then, this positing is not an accident, if it corresponds to no divine necessity and does not in any sense signify a limitation of His own glory, there remains only the recollection that God is the One who is free in His love. In this case we can understand the positing of this reality—which otherwise is incomprehensible—only as the work of His love. He wills and posits the creature neither out of caprice nor necessity, but because He has loved it from eternity, because He wills to demonstrate His love for it, and because He wills, not to limit His glory by its existence and being, but to reveal and manifest it in His own co-existence with it. As the Creator He wills really to exist for His creature. That is why He gives it its own existence and being. That is also why there cannot follow from the creature's own existence and being an immanent determination of its goal or purpose, or a claim to any right, meaning or dignity of its existence and nature accruing to it except as a gift. That is why even the very existence and nature of the creature are the work of the grace of God. It would be a strange love that was satisfied with the mere existence and nature of the other, then withdrawing, leaving it to its own devices. Love wills to love. Love wills something with and for that which it loves. Because God loves the creature, its creation and continuance and preservation point beyond themselves to an exercise and fulfilment of His love which do not take place merely with the fact that the creature is posited as such and receives its existence and being alongside and outside the being and existence of God, but to which creation in all its glory looks and moves, and of which creation is the presupposition.   [III, 1, p. 95 f.]

[75] Creation is one long preparation, and therefore the being and existence of the creature one long readiness, for what God will intend and do with it in the history of the covenant. Its nature is simply its equipment for grace. Its creatureliness is pure promise, expectation and prophecy of that which in His grace, in the execution of the will of His eternal love, and finally and supremely in the consummation of the giving of His Son, God plans for man and will not delay to accomplish for his benefit. In this

way creation is the road to the covenant, its external power and external basis, because for its fulfilment the latter depends wholly on the fact that the creature is in no position to act alone as the partner of God, that it is thrown back wholly and utterly on the care and intercession of God Himself, but that it does actually enjoy this divine care and intercession. . . . The covenant is the internal basis of creation. . . . This consists in the fact that the wisdom and omnipotence of God the Creator was not just any wisdom and omnipotence but that of His free love. . . . The fact that the covenant is the goal of creation is not something which is added later to the reality of the creature. . . . It already characterises creation itself and as such, and therefore the being and existence of the creature. The covenant whose history had still to commence was the covenant which, as the goal appointed for creation and the creature, made creation necessary and possible, and determined and limited the creature. If creation was the external basis of the covenant, the latter was the internal basis of the former. If creation was the formal presupposition of the covenant, the latter was the material presupposition of the former. If creation takes precedence historically, the covenant does so in substance. [III, 1, p. 231 f.]

[76] The ordaining of salvation for man and of man for salvation is the original and basic will of God, the ground and purpose of His will as Creator. It is not that He first wills and works the being of the world and man, and then ordains it to salvation. But God creates, preserves and overrules man for this prior end and with this prior purpose, that there may be a being distinct from Himself ordained for salvation, for perfect being, for participation in His own being, because as the One who loves in freedom He has determined to exercise redemptive grace—and that there may be an object of this His redemptive grace, a partner to receive it. . . . The " God with us " has nothing to do with chance. As a redemptive happening it means the revelation and confirmation of the most primitive relationship between God and man, that which was freely determined in eternity by God Himself before there was any created being. In the very fact that man is, and that he is man, he is as such chosen by God for salvation . . .

not because God owes it to him; not in virtue of any quality or capacity of his own being; completely without claim.   [IV, 1, p. 9 f.]

[77] Divine creation is divine benefit. What takes shape in it is the goodness of God. This is the character without which it would not be a work of God. . . .

This statement is not made in the void, nor need it to used with such reserve as is sometimes the case, but it is of essential importance if it is referred to the character proper to creation in virtue of its connexion with the covenant. The process whose fundamental purpose, as we have learnt from the biblical testimony to creation, is the history of salvation which culminates in Jesus Christ, cannot itself be hostile or indifferent, but can only be a benefit and can only be understood as such. . . .

Creation is blessing because it has unchangeably the character of an action in which the divine joy, honour and affirmation are turned towards another. What God has created is as such well done. . . .

This affirmation is not an irresponsible venture. It is not only permitted; it is commanded. We cannot understand the divine creation otherwise than as benefit. We are not free to think and speak in this matter otherwise or even uncertainly and equivocally. The Christian apprehension of creation requires and involves the principle that creation is benefit. It shows us God's good-pleasure as the root, the foundation and the end of divine creation. It suggests the peace with which God separated and protected what He truly willed from what He did not will, and therefore from the unreal. It implies that God Himself, in and with the beginning of all things, decided for His creation and made Himself the responsible Guarantor of it. Creation, as it is known by the Christian, is benefit. . . . We may add in explanation that this statement is demanded and supported by the Christian knowledge of the Lord who alone can be the Creator at the beginning of all things. Who is this Lord? He is the God of Israel who in Jesus Christ has loved man, and sought and found him in his lostness and drawn him to Himself, averting from him the suffering of His righteous judgment, and in grace giving him life with the promise of eternal life. If the God who has expressed and revealed His nature in this way is the Creator, He has already expressed and revealed the same nature as the Creator, not saying No, or Yes and No, but an unqualified Yes to what He has really willed and created. What this God has created is good as such. Only if we lose sight of this God and His nature can we say otherwise. [III, 1, pp. 330–332]

[78] We have referred to the subordination of all creaturely occurrence to the one goal posited by God, which is itself God, and also to the mutual co-ordination of its individual moments and actions as thereby conditioned. Now it is clear that both these concepts involve a thoroughgoing relativisation of all creaturely occurrence. If God gives it His own end and ends, then this means that the occurrence has a significance outside itself. It is not moving in circles, but moving towards a destiny which is posited and given from without, whose fulfilment it can only await as it makes this movement. In the most literal sense creaturely occurrence is only preparatory, i.e., it is engaged in a process. The creature itself cannot decide either why it moves or whither it moves. This decision belongs to God who rules the creature. It is His action which determines the world-process in its true and definitive form. This is in a sense the vertical relativisation of creaturely occurrence. God co-ordinates the various events and the various activities and effects of individual creaturely subjects. He allots to each one its own place and time and function in relation to all the rest. And this means that we can speak of the significance of any one thing only in the light of its connexion with all other things. The individual thing is as it were a word or sentence within a context. It is indispensable to this context. But only within this context does it say what is really intended. Only within this context can it be read and understood rightly. And this is in a sense the horizontal relativisation of creaturely occurrence.

But we must be more precise. The twofold relativisation of creaturely occurrence has reference to its relationship to the rule of God. It is God who arranges for each creature its end and ends. Thus He subordinates all creatures to Himself. And under Himself He co-ordinates all the ends, and therefore all the activities and effects of all creatures into a totality. To this extent all creaturely occurrence and all creatures are relegated to a position of lowliness and dependence and relativity. This means that in themselves they are nothing, and that of themselves they can neither mean anything nor do anything. God is the " yonderside " of all creaturely being and activity from which alone the light and life and power of creaturely occurrence can derive. In relation to God the creature is lowly and dependent and relative. But this position of lowliness and dependence and relativity in relation to God does not involve a degradation or depreciation or humiliation of the creature. To be lowly before God is its exaltation. If it is nothing without Him it is everything by Him : everything, that is, that He its Creator and Lord has determined and ascribed and allotted to it ; everything that He will continue to be for it, and to execute with and by it. And since this is the optimum of light and life and power, making possible its own value and dignity, it is really everything. If we are to understand the divine world-governance rightly, there is one idea that we can never resist too strongly, one notion that we can never reject too sharply. The fact that God causes His will and His will alone to be done in all things, does not mean that the ruling God is an oppressor who grudges it to the creature even to exist at all, let alone to have its own value and dignity over against him. It is the glory of the creature to be lowly in relation to God. For when it is relative to Him, it participates with all its activities and effects in His absoluteness. To be able to serve Him alone with all its activities and in all its joint-effects, to be in His hands and under His control only as a means, an instrument, the clay of the potter—this is its direct and original glory. It is exalted in this necessity ; it is rich in this poverty ; it can go forward on the basis of this humiliation. To exist in any other way but in this relativity towards God would mean misery and shame and ruin and death for the creature. Its full and perfect salvation consists in this subordination to Him, and in this subordination in the co-ordination with its fellow-creatures which is ordained by Him. [III, 3, 170 f.]

[79] The theological concept of Creator and creating, of creation and creature, must be kept in view. God the Creator must not be equated with a mere manufacturer,

or His work with a manufactured article. The man who makes something, however noble, talented or powerful he may be, can easily leave what he makes to itself, and the more easily the more perfect it is. But the Creator cannot do this in relation to His creature. Between Creator and creature in the sense of biblical theology there is a connexion which makes it impossible for the Creator to leave His work to itself, and makes immediately necessary the reality and knowledge of a second action of the Creator following the first, i.e., His action in the sense of the concept of providence. In no sense is God a creature in Himself. He has in Himself absolutely nothing of the nature of a creature. He does not need a creature to be perfect in Himself. Alongside and apart from Him there can be nothing like Him with its origin, meaning and purpose in itself. Yet on these strict conditions of His own being this God posits Himself as Creator, and apart from and alongside Himself He posits the creature, a reality distinct from Himself. This God who confronts His creature with such transcendence obviously stands, in respect of its continuation and history, in a relationship which could only be contingent and possibly alien to a supreme being or demiurge. The majestic freedom in which the relationship of Creator and creature is grounded is the guarantee of its preservation. The eternity of God is the pledge that He will give it time so long as He wills.

[III, 3, p. 9 f.]

[80] Of all creatures the Christian is the one which not merely is a creature, but actually says Yes to being a creature. Innumerable creatures do not seem to be even asked to make this affirmation. Man is asked. But man as such is neither able nor willing to make it. From the very first man as such has continual illusions about himself. He wants always to be more than a creature. He does not want merely to be under the universal lordship of God. But the Christian makes the affirmation that is demanded of man. . . .

He sees what the others do not see. The world-process in which he participates in solidarity with all other creatures might just as easily be a vain thrusting and tumult without either master or purpose. This is how many see it. But the Christian sees in it a universal lordship.

155

The lordship might just as easily be that of natural law, or fate, or chance, or even the devil. This is how many see it. But the Christian sees in it the universal lordship of God, of the God who is the Father, who is the Father to him, his Father. He sees the constitutive and organising centre of the process. What makes him a Christian is that he sees Jesus Christ, the Son of God, in the humiliation but also in the exaltation of His humanity, and himself united with Him, belonging to Him, his life delivered by Him, but also placed at His disposal. And seeing Him, he sees the legislative, executive and judicial authority over and in all things. He sees it as the authority of God. He sees it as the authority of the Father. He sees himself subjected to this authority as the one who is united with and belongs to the Son. Only the Christian sees this centre of the world-process. Only the Christian sees at this centre, as the One who has all power in heaven and on earth, the Son of God, and through Him God the Father, and on the circumference himself as a child of the Father for the sake of the Son. The whole Christian community is simply a gathering together by the Word which tells us this and explains and reveals it to us ; a gathering together of those whose eyes are opened to the fact of it. Only the Christian is a member of this community, i.e., one who is gathered together with others by this Word, one whose eyes are opened to this fact. There are some creatures which do not need to have eyes for it because even without seeing it they are carried along by the power of this order and are secure in its peace. There are other creatures which have eyes for it but they will not and cannot open them. But the Christian has open eyes. That is why he has the reality freely and joyfully to confess his creatureliness and his consequent subjection to the universal rule of God without reserve and without claim. What he sees at that centre and on that circumference is not something which frightens him, something which he has to reject. God the Father as the ruling Creator is obviously not an oppressor, and Christ as a subject creature is obviously not oppressed. There is nothing here which need frighten him. There is nothing here which need cause him to flee or rebel. To be wholly and unreservedly under the universal lordship of God, to be wholly and unreservedly a creaturely subject, is not in any sense a constraint, a misfortune, an outrage or a humiliation for the man who as a Christian can see actualised in Jesus Christ both the lordship of God and also the subordination of the creature. For him all attempts to evade this fact are purposeless, and the illusion by which it is obscured or avoided is superfluous. If the relation between the Creator and the creature is the relation which he can see in Jesus Christ, then existence in this relation is the existence which is to be truly desired, an existence in the highest possible freedom and felicity. To have to confess this is not an obscure law, but a friendly permission and invitation. It is not unwillingly but spontaneously, not grudgingly but gladly, that the Christian will affirm and lay hold of this relation and his own existence in it. Hence the reality does not cost him anything. He does not have to force it. He does not have to struggle to attain it. It comes to him in the same way as what he sees comes to him. And this means that he does not screw himself up to a height when he is a real creature. It also means that there does not arise any claim or merit on his part just because he confesses so unreservedly what other creatures and other men cannot and will not confess. The fact that he does so is not a kind of triumph for his individual honesty. Other people are just as honest, perhaps more so. He is simply made real by what he sees. And as such he is simply availing himself of a permission and invitation. He is going through an open door, but one which he himself has not opened, into a banqueting hall. And there he willingly takes his place under the table, in the company of publicans, in the company of beasts and plants and stones, accepting solidarity with them, being present simply as they are, as a creature of God. It is the fact that he sees, and that which he is able to see as the centre and the circumference, the Creator and the creature, which constitute the permission and invitation and open door to his peculiar reality. . . .

In practice, of course, he is faced every day afresh with the riddles of the world-process, with the precipices and plains, the blinding lights and obscurities, of the general creaturely occurrence to which his own life's history also belongs. Of course he can only keep on asking : Whence ? and Whither ? and Why ? and Wherefore ? Of course he has no master-key to all the mysteries of the great process of existence as they crowd in upon him every moment in a new form, to all the mysteries of his own existence as a constituent existence in the historical process of all created reality. On the contrary, he will be the one man who knows that there is no value in any of the master-keys which man has thought to discover and possess. He is the one man who will always be the most surprised, the most affected, the most apprehensive and the most joyful in the face of events. He will not be like an ant which has forseen everything in advance, but like a child in a forest, or on Christmas Eve; one who is always rightly astonished by events, by the encounters and experiences which overtake him, and the cares and duties laid upon him. He is the one who is constantly forced to begin afresh, wrestling with the possibilities which open out to him and the impossibilities which oppose him. If we may put it in this way, life in the world, with all its joys and sorrows and contemplation and activity, will always be for him a really interesting matter, or, to use a bolder expression, it will be an adventure, for which he for his part has ultimately and basically no qualifications of his own.

And all this is not because he does not know what it is all about, but just because he does know. All this is because he has an " understanding " with the source from which everything derives, from which directly or indirectly everything happens to him; the " understanding " of the creature with its Creator, which is, for him, that of the child with its father. One thing at least he does not need to puzzle about. About this one thing he has no need to enquire, to be always on the look-out for new answers, new solutions. For he has learned once and for all who is this source, and what basically he can expect from it, and what will always actually come from it. But how the decision is reached, and in what form everything will come as it proceeds from this source, he is as tense and curious as a child, always open and surprised in face of what comes. Yet whatever comes, and in whatever form it comes, he will see that it comes from this one source. However strange it may seem, however irksome in the form in which it comes, he will approve it as coming from this source. He will always be, not perhaps able, but at least willing and ready to perceive the positive—and in the light of its source the most definitely positive—meaning and content of what comes. He will always be willing and ready—again a daring expression—to co-operate with it instead of adopting an attitude of super-cilious and dissatisfied criticism and opposition, or, if it were possible, retiring sulkily into a corner as a sceptical spectator. He will always allow everything to concern him directly, and, with all the dialectic of his experiences and attitudes, he will ultimately and basically allow everything to concern him positively. Ultimately and basically he will always be thankful, and in the light of this thankfulness he will look forward to what has still to come. He will always know both what was intended and what is intended. He will always be the child having dealings with its father. This is the knowledge of the Christian in matters of the divine lordship. There is nothing arrogant about it. It remains within the bounds of the reality in which the Christian can know himself—know himself as a creature under the lordship of God like all other creatures.   [III, 3, pp. 240–243]

[81] I must again revert to Wolfgang Amadeus Mozart. Why is it that this man is so incomparable ? Why is it that for the receptive, he has produced in almost every bar he conceived and composed a type of music for which " beautiful " is not a fitting epithet : music which for the true Christian is not mere entertainment, enjoyment or edification but food and drink ; music full of comfort and counsel for his needs ; music which is never a slave to its technique nor sentimental but always " moving," free and liberating because wise, strong and sovereign ? Why is it possible to hold that Mozart has a place in theology, especially in the doctrine of creation and also in eschato-logy, although he was not a father of the Church, does not seem to have been a particularly active Christian, and was a Roman Catholic, apparently leading what might appear to us a rather frivolous existence when not occupied in his work ? It is possible to give him this position because he knew something about creation in its total goodness that neither the real fathers of the Church nor our Reformers, neither the orthodox nor Liberals, neither

the exponents of natural theology nor those heavily armed with the " Word of God," and certainly not the Existentialists, nor indeed any other great musicians before and after him, either know or can express and maintain as he did. In this respect he was pure in heart, far transcending both optimists and pessimists. 1756–1791 ! This was the time when God was under attack for the Lisbon earthquake, and theologians and other well-meaning folk were hard put to it to defend Him. In face of the problem of theodicy, Mozart had the peace of God which far transcends all the critical or speculative reason that praises and reproves. This problem lay behind him. Why then concern himself with it ? He had heard, and causes those who have ears to hear, even to-day, what we shall not see until the end of time—the whole context of providence. As though in the light of this end, he heard the harmony of creation to which the shadow also belongs but in which the shadow is not darkness, deficiency is not defeat, sadness cannot become despair, trouble cannot degenerate into tragedy and infinite melancholy is not ultimately forced to claim indisputed sway. Thus the cheerfulness in this harmony is not without its limits. But the light shines all the more brightly because it breaks forth from the shadow. The sweetness is also bitter and cannot therefore cloy. Life does not fear death but knows it well. *Et lux perpetua lucet* (sic !) *eis*—even the dead of Lisbon. Mozart saw this light no more than we do, but he heard the whole world of creation enveloped by this light. Hence it was fundamentally in order that he should not hear a middle or neutral note, but the positive far more strongly than the negative. He heard the negative only in and with the positive. Yet in their inequality he heard them both together, as, for example, in the Symphony in G-minor of 1788. He never heard only the one in abstraction. He heard concretely, and therefore his compositions were and are total music. Hearing creation unresentfully and impartially, he did not produce merely his own music but that of creation, its twofold and yet harmonious praise of God. He neither needed nor desired to express or represent himself, his vitality, sorrow, piety, or any programme. He was remarkably free from the mania for self-expression. He simply offered himself as the agent by which little bits of horn, metal and catgut could serve as the voices of creation, sometimes leading, sometimes accompanying and sometimes in harmony. He made use of instruments ranging from the piano and violin, through the horn and the clarinet, down to the venerable bassoon, with the human voice somewhere among them, having no special claim to distinction yet distinguished for this very reason. He drew music from them all, expressing even human emotions in the service of this music, and not *vice versa*. He himself was only an ear for this music, and its mediator to other ears. He died when according to the worldly wise his life-work was only ripening to its true fulfilment. But who shall say that after the " Magic Flute," the Clarinet Concerto of October 1791 and the Requiem, it was not already fulfilled ? Was not the whole of his achievement ˙implicit in his works at the age of 16 or 18 ? Is it not heard in what has come down to us from the very young Mozart ? He died in misery like an " unknown soldier," and in company with Calvin, and Moses in the Bible, he has no known grave. But what does this matter ? What does a grave matter when a life is permitted simply and unpretentiously, and therefore serenely, authentically and impressively, to express the good creation of God, which also includes the limitation and end of man.

I make this interposition here, before turning to chaos, because in the music of Mozart—and I wonder whether the same can be said of any other works before or after— we have clear and convincing proof that it is a slander on creation to charge it with a share in chaos because it includes a Yes and a No, as though orientated to God on the one side and nothingness on the other. Mozart causes us to hear that even on the latter side, and therefore in its totality, creation praises its Master and is therefore perfect. Here on the threshhold of our problem—and it is no small achievement—Mozart has created order for those who have ears to hear, and he has done it better than any scientific deduction could. This is the point which I wish to make. [III, 3, pp. 297–299]

V. THE DETERMINATION OF MAN

If Jesus Christ is not just one light among others, but the " light of the world," Christian thinking which takes this seriously can find only in this source definitive information concerning man and his nature and goal. Barth thus projects in III, 2 an anthropology which certainly allows that other anthropological sciences and theories can establish and work out phenomena of the human but which derives its decisive definitions of real man from the human being of Jesus Christ. The central definitions of his nature are (1) his fellow-humanity, (2) his being as body and soul in inseparable unity and indissoluble differentiation, and (3) his temporality as a unique opportunity in the span bounded by his beginning and end.

[82] God's glory is the answer evoked by Him of the worship offered Him by His creatures. This is not of their own ability and inclination, their creaturely capacity and good-will, least of all the wisdom and desire of man who is flesh. It derives from the presence of the Creator which is granted to the creature. This is not an idle or unfruitful presence. It is not the presence of a cold confrontation. It is not a presence which leaves blind eyes blind or deaf ears deaf. It is a presence which opens them. It is a presence which also looses at once tongues that were bound. God's glory is the indwelling joy of His divine being which as such shines out from Him, which overflows in its richness, which in its super-abundance is not satisfied with itself but communicates itself. All God's works must be understood also and decisively from this point of view. All together and without exception they take part in the movement of God's self-glorification and the communication of His joy. They are the coming into being of light outside Him on the basis of the light inside Him, which is Himself. They are expressions of the infinite exultation in the depth of His divine being. It is from this point of view that all His creatures are to be viewed both first and last. God wills them and loves them because, far from having their existence of themselves and their meaning in themselves, they have their being and existence in the movement of the divine

self-glorification, in the transition to them of His immanent joyfulness. It is their destiny to offer a true if inadequate response in the temporal sphere to the jubilation with which the Godhead is filled from eternity to eternity. This is the destiny which man received and lost, only to receive it again, inconceivably and infinitely increased by the personal participation of God in man's being accomplished in Jesus Christ. The reaction of God even against sin, the meaning even of His holiness, even of His judgment, the meaning which is not extinguished but fulfilled even in damnation and hell, is that God is glorious, and that His glory does not allow itself to be diminished, to be disturbed in its gladness and the expression of that gladness, to be checked in the overflowing of its fulness. And this is what is expected from all creation because this is the source from which they come. It is in this light that they are to be seen and heard. This is their secret that will one day come out and be revealed. And it is to this that we are always required and will always find it worth our while to attend and look. It is for this revelation that we should always wait. The creature has no voice of its own. It does not point to its own picture. It echoes and reflects the glory of the Lord. It does this in its heights and its depths, its happiness and its misery. The angels do it (and unfortunately we have almost completely forgotten that we are surrounded by the angels as crown witnesses to the divine glory). But even the smallest creatures do it too. They do it along with us or without us. They do it also against us to shame us and instruct us. They do it because they cannot help doing it. They would not and could not exist unless first and last and properly they did this and only this. And when man accepts again his destiny in Jesus Christ in the promise and faith of the future revelation of his participation in God's glory as it is already given Him here and now, he is only like a late-comer slipping shamefacedly into creation's choir in heaven and earth, which has never ceased its praise, but merely suffered and sighed, as it still does, that in inconceivable folly and ingratitude its living centre man does not hear its voice, its response, its echoing of the divine glory, or rather hears it in a completely perverted way, and refuses to co-operate in the jubilation

163

which surrounds him. This is the sin of man which is judged and forgiven in Jesus Christ, which God Himself has made good and cast behind man's back. It is this which in Jesus Christ has once for all become his past. In the eternal glory before us it will not exist at all even as the past. In the eternity before us the groaning of creation will cease, and man too will live in his determination to be the reflection and echo of God and therefore the witness to the divine glory that reaches over to him, rejoicing with the God who Himself has eternal joy and Himself is eternal joy.   [II, 1, pp. 647–649]

[83] And inevitably this distinction of man sheds light at least on earth and heaven and the whole cosmos as well. Man is not the world ; not even a reflection of the world ; not even its epitome or compendium. He is less than this, we said, but we also say that he is more than this. He is the point in the cosmos where, in spite of its very different nature, its relationship to God is illuminated. That the purpose of God towards it is revealed here, cannot be without significance for an understanding of its different nature. Heaven and earth, man's beyond and present, were created by the counsel and the act of God who created man. To the same end ? We have no direct knowledge of heaven and earth to justify us in affirming as much. And yet we affirm it by the indirect knowledge which we owe to our knowledge of man as grounded in the Word of God. He who is the Creator of man is also the Creator of the cosmos, and His purpose towards the latter, although hidden as such, is none other than His revealed purpose for us. Hence in the disclosed relationship of God with man there is disclosed also His relationship with the universe. It is not without significance that in Old and New Testament alike heaven and earth and their elements and inhabitants are always described not only as witnesses but as co-workers in the work of God and that of human praise. This does not rest on a world-view, but on a view of man which sees in him the point in the cosmos where the thoughts of its Creator are disclosed, illuminating man in his totality and also shedding light on the deepest and ultimate force which moves the cosmos—the cosmos which has for us no intrinsic light and cannot reveal the divine plan which governs it.

164

It is man in covenant with God who reveals this plan. He does so representatively for the whole cosmos. He is not actually alone. He is in the cosmos. He alone sheds light on the cosmos. As he is light, the cosmos is also light. As God's covenant with him is disclosed, the cosmos is shown to be embraced by the same covenant.

[III, 2, p. 18 f.]

[84] The grace of God in Jesus Christ is the noetic basis as and because it is also the ontic basis of man's creaturely being. But here it is both in almost indissoluble unity, and to avoid repetition we may consider it at once in this double quality.

What we really know of man, we know by means of this grace. For how things really stand with man, who and what he is, is grounded in it. What we claim to know about man apart from it, we only claim to know. On a closer examination, it consists only of the working hypotheses of man's self-understanding : perhaps in relation to his being as a natural being beside others and in the context of the being of nature as discernible to us ; perhaps in relation to his being as an ethical rational being with his ability to distinguish himself from nature and to become to a certain extent its master ; perhaps in relation to his being in the act of his existence with the capacity therein demonstrated to limit himself and to that extent to transcend himself in his totality ; or perhaps in relation to his being in the community of the history of his race with his ability to experience history and at the same time to make it. These are all permissible and necessary hypotheses with regard to definite aspects of human being, but they do not solve the question of the common denominator, i.e., of man himself. This question is solved, however, if we set out from the fact that man is the being to whom God is gracious in Jesus Christ. From this there result definitions which certainly do not extinguish as such or even obscure these phenomena of human existence, which do not contradict or render superfluous these working hypotheses of human self-consciousness, which give them a firm basis as hypotheses, but which, as opposed to them, refer to the real man, to man himself. In the fact, revealed to us in God's Word, that God is gracious to man in Jesus Christ, we do not see any of these views of man, either confirmed or questioned, nor do we see any new view of man, but we see man himself, what and how he really is.

This fact includes not only the " Behold your God," but also the *Ecce homo !* It is not only the mirror of the fatherly heart of God, but also of the particularity of man. In what way, and to what extent ? Simply to the extent that in distinction from all mere religion—even that of grace—it is the fact in which the true God is present and revealed in the true man. When we see the glory of God residing in Jesus Christ, then in and with the most high God Himself, we also see man : humbled, accused and judged as a guilty and lost creature, and only as such, only in the fire of judgment, upheld and saved ; but also exalted and glorified as the creature elected and affirmed by God from all eternity. This is real man, man himself in the mirror of God's grace addressed to him in Jesus Christ.   [III, 4, p. 41 f.]

[85] This grace of God decides and has already decided concerning our human existence. What does it mean to be a man now that this decision has been reached by the grace of God ? It obviously means to be one who stands and walks and lives and dies within the fact that God is gracious to him, that He has made him His own. It obviously means to be one for whom God has intervened in this way, with whom He has dealt in this way. It obviously means to be one for whose human existence Jesus Christ Himself stands before God according to the will, in the name, and by the commission of God, in all the wisdom and the fulness of the might of God—so stands before God that he is completely covered by Him, completely destroyed both in his weakness and in his self-will, completely offered as a living sacrifice, but in this way made completely holy and completely glorious.

[II, 2, p. 558 f.]

[86] The ontological determination of humanity is grounded in the fact that one man among all others is the man Jesus. So long as we select any other starting-point for our study, we shall reach only the phenomena of the human. We are condemned to abstractions so long as our attention is riveted as it were on other men, or rather on man in general, as if we could learn about real man from a study of man in general, and in abstraction from the

fact that one man among all others is the man Jesus. In this case we miss the one Archimedean point given us beyond humanity, and therefore the one possibility of discovering the ontological determination of man. Theological anthropology has no choice in this matter. It is not yet or no longer theological anthropology if it tries to pose and answer the question of the true being of man from any other angle.

We remember who and what the man Jesus is. As we have seen, He is the one creaturely being in whose existence we have to do immediately and directly with the being of God also. Again, He is the creaturely being in whose existence God's act of deliverance has taken place for all other men. He is the creaturely being in whom God as the Saviour of all men also reveals and affirms His own glory as the Creator. He is the creaturely being who as such embodies the sovereignty of God, or conversely the sovereignty of God which as such actualises this creaturely being. He is the creaturely being whose existence consists in His fulfilment of the will of God. And finally He is the creaturely being who as such not only exists from God and in God but absolutely for God instead of for Himself.

From this knowledge of the man Jesus we have derived the criteria which indicate the limits within which the attempt to attain knowledge of human existence must always move. We have thus been warned against confusing the reality of man with mere phenomena of man. We have been unable to accept those determinations of man in which his relationship to God, his participation in the history inaugurated between him and God, and the glory, lordship, purpose and service of God, are not brought out as the meaning of human life. We have also had to be critical even where the concept of God seemed to play a certainly not unimportant role, but where it remained empty to the extent that there did not emerge anything of His saving action and the related actuality of the being of man. We have now to show the fact and extent that the ontological determination of man results from the fact that one man among all others is this creaturely being, the man Jesus.

Our first point is that the message of the Bible about

this one man has amongst other things this ontological significance. Speaking of this one man, it says of all other men—those who were before Him and those who were after Him, those who knew Him and those who did not know Him or did so only indirectly, those who accepted Him and those who rejected Him—at least that they were and are creaturely beings whom this man is like for all His unlikeness, and in whose sphere and fellowship and history this one man also existed in likeness with them. This means that a decision has been made concerning the being and nature of every man by the mere fact that with him and among all other men He too has been a man. No matter who or what or where he may be, he cannot alter the fact that this One is also man. And because this One is also man, every man in his place and time is changed, i.e., he is something other than what he would have been if this One had not been man too. It belongs to his human essence that Jesus too is man, and that in Him he has a human Neighbour, Companion and Brother. Hence he has no choice in the matter. The question whether and to what extent he knows this Neighbour, and what attitude he adopts to Him, is no doubt important but it is secondary to that which has already been decided, namely, whether he can be a man at all without this Neighbour. Once for all this question has been decided in the negative for every man. We cannot break free from this Neighbour. He is definitely our Neighbour. And we as men are those among whom Jesus is also a man, like us for all His unlikeness.

Theological anthropology must not be so timid that it does not firmly insist on this simplest factor in the situation. Nor must it be so distracted that it suggests every possible and impossible foundation for its thesis except the first and simplest of all, namely, that every man as such is the fellow-man of Jesus. The biblical message to which we must keep is neither timid nor distracted in this respect. It dares to be the message of this one man, and with all that it tells us concerning Him, and obviously in the light of it, it makes the massively self-evident ontological pre-supposition that the existence of this one man concerns every other man as such, and that the fact that He too is a man is the ground on which every other man is to be

addressed and to which every other man is to be kept.
It is worth noting that the biblical message never addresses
man on any other basis. It does not appeal to his rationality or responsibility or human dignity or intrinsic
humanity. No other decisive presupposition is made except
that every one who bears the name of man is to be addressed
as such in the name of Jesus, and therefore that he stands
in an indisputable continuity with Him which is quite
adequate as a point of contact. The biblical message
reckons with a humanity which as such stands in this
continuity, and therefore with man as a being whom we
immediately expect to respond to the call to order, to his
own order, addressed in the name of Jesus. It reckons
only with a creatureliness of man constituted by the fact
that one man among all others is this man. This is the
ontological undertone which we must not miss if we are to
understand why as a message about what this One is and
does, and as a message about faith in Him, it is so confident and unreserved, and yet not "enthusiastic" but
sober. It speaks in fact about the One who not merely
a posteriori but *a priori*, from the very outset, is the Neighbour, Companion and Brother of every man.

[III, 2, pp. 132–134]

[87] As the One who has done that, in whom God Himself has done that, who lives as the doer of that deed, He
is our man, we are in Him, our present is His, the history
of man is His history, He is the concrete event of the existence and reality of justified man in whom every man can
recognise himself and every other man—recognise himself
as truly justified. There is not one for whose sin and
death He did not die, whose sin and death He did not
remove and obliterate on the cross, for whom He did not
positively do the right, whose right He has not established.
There is not one to whom this was not addressed as his
justification in His resurrection from the dead. There is
not one whose man He is not, who is not justified in Him.
There is not one who is justified in any other way than in
Him—because it is in Him and only in Him that an end,
a bonfire, is made of man's sin and death, because it is in
Him and only in Him that man's sin and death are the
old thing which has passed away, because it is in Him and
only in Him that the right has been done which is

demanded of man, that the right has been established to which man can move forward. Again, there is not one who is not adequately and perfectly and finally justified in Him. There is not one whose sin is not forgiven sin in Him, whose death is not a death which has been put to death in Him. There is not one whose right has not been established and confirmed validly and once and for all in Him. There is not one, therefore, who has first to win and appropriate this right for himself. There is not one who has first to go or still to go in his own virtue and strength this way from there to here, from yesterday to to-morrow, from darkness to light, who has first to accomplish or still to accomplish his own justification, repeating it when it has already taken place in Him. There is not one whose past and future and therefore whose present He does not undertake and guarantee, having long since accepted full responsibility and liability for it, bearing it every hour and into eternity. There is not one whose peace with God has not been made and does not continue in Him. There is not one of whom it is demanded that he should make and maintain this peace for himself, or who is permitted to act as though he himself were the author of it, having to make it himself and to maintain it in his own strength. There is not one for whom He has not done everything in His death and received everything in His resurrection from the dead.   [IV, 1, p. 630]

[88] If it is not indifferent, incidental or subordinate but ontologically decisive, that one man among all others is the man Jesus ; if to be a man is to dwell with this man who is our true and absolute Counterpart ; if to be a man is to be concretely confronted with this man who is like us for all that He is so unlike in the full majesty of God, then the fact that we are with God is not merely one of many determinations of our being, derivative and mutable, but the basic determination, original and immutable.

Godlessness is not, therefore, a possibility, but an ontological impossibility for man. Man is not without, but with God. This is not to say, of course, that godless men do not exist. Sin is undoubtedly committed and exists. Yet sin itself is not a possibility but an ontological impossibility for man. We are actually with Jesus, i.e., with God. This means that our being does not include but excludes sin. To be in sin, in godlessness, is a mode of being contrary to our humanity. For the man who is with Jesus—and this is man's ontological determination—is with God. If he denies God, he denies himself. He is then something which he cannot be in the Counterpart in which he is. He chooses his own impossibility. And every offence in which godlessness can express itself, e.g., unbelief and idolatry, doubt and indifference to God, is as such, both in its theoretical and practical forms, an offence with which man burdens, obscures and corrupts himself. It is an attack on the continuance of his own creatureliness: not a superficial, temporary or endurable attack, but a radical, central and fatal attack on its very foundation, and therefore its continuance. His very being as man is endangered by every surrender to sin. And conversely, every vindication and restoration of his relation to God is a vindication and restoration of his being as man. For he himself as a man is with Jesus and therefore with God. He himself stands from the very first and inescapably in the order which this fact implies. He himself is thus upheld if he keeps to this order, and he plunges into the void if he falls away from it.   [III, 2, p. 135 f.]

[89] I could not believe in the Church if in it and by it I did not find hope even for man as such.

We could call this awareness of the destiny of man the Christian conception of humanity. It is distinguished from the Stoic in three ways. First, it is not based on the perception and assessment of a so-called " nature " of man. Second, in ascribing to man as such a *character indelebilis* it does not mean statically a quality of his own. Third, it does not ascribe to him only—which is not enough—a so-called disposition or capacity which may perhaps be developed by instruction and education. It means actually and concretely his destiny, a historical differentiation of man and humanity, which consists in a mission and authorisation, and is fulfilled in an actual confrontation with the Church of Jesus Christ. It was in the light of this historical differentiation that in a particularly impressive way Paul (and, of course, all the mission of the primitive Church) considered the Gentiles. . . . The Church would not take itself seriously if confronting the world it did not regard it as a world already changed by this fact, if it did not find hope for man, not as such and before it has claimed him, but simply because it exists and will claim him. How can it ever cease to see him in advance in the light of " thou wilt," by which it lives itself ? How can it rest towards him in a barren " thou shalt " and therefore " thou art not " ? The Christian conception of humanity is, therefore, a very different one from the Stoic. But it is to be distinguished from it not by a lesser, but by a disproportionately much greater intensity and definition. What kind of power can and will that conception have which deals only with the " nature " of man and the still to be realised possibilities of education which must be weighed against it ? Again and again it will be corroded by a very justifiable scepticism, not only in respect of human nature, but also in respect of all human education. It is only in the Church or from the Church that there has ever been a free, strong, truly open and confident expectation in regard to the natural man, a quiet and joyful hope that he will be my neighbour, a conception of humanity which is based on ultimate certainty. [I, 2, p. 423]

VI. AGAPE AND EROS

In the self-giving of Jesus Christ fulfilled in His crucifixion, God Himself intervenes for man who cannot help himself, as God the Son obedient to the will of God the Father, as the Judge bearing the judgment for the judged. To this action of God there corresponds on man's side the obedience of faith which accepts what is done (IV, 1). In the assumption of human nature by the incarnation of Jesus Christ God raises fallen man up again and exalts him to be a partner of His covenant and to new life in righteousness. To this action of God there corresponds on man's side the obedience of love in which man, freed for right action, imitates in relation to God and neighbour that which God has done towards him and for him. This is described in the second part of the volume on reconciliation (IV, 2) from which we take the great comparison of agape and eros.

[90] Christian love turns to the other purely for the sake of the other. It does not desire it for itself. It loves it simply because it is there as this other, with all its value or lack of value. It loves it freely. But it is more than this turning. In Christian love the loving subject gives to the other, the object of love, that which it has, which is its own, which belongs to it. It does so irrespective of the right or claim that it may have to it, or the further use that it might make of it. It does so in confirmation of the freedom in respect of itself which it has in its critical beginning. It does so with a radically unlimited liberality. Nor is this liberality confined to that which the loving subject " has." For in Christian love the loving subject reaches back, as it were, behind itself to that which at the first it denies and from which it turns away, namely, itself : to give itself (for everything would lack if this final thing were lacking) ; to give itself away ; to give up itself to the one to whom it turns for the sake of this object. To do this the loving man has given up control of himself to place himself under the control of the other, the object of his love. He is free to do this. It is in this freedom that the one who loves as a Christian loves. Where this movement is fulfilled in all its aspects, and reaches its goal in this self-giving of the loving subject,

173

there is Christian love. And this movement, together with faith (and hope, etc.) and inseparably and simultaneously fulfilled with them, is the life-act of the Christian both in detail and finally as a whole. Its fulfilment is the particular problem of Christian love.

As is apparent from this preliminary analysis, it is very different from any other movement which may have the name of " love " and in its own way is love, but which from first to last takes a very different form and direction. To sharpen the picture of the movement with which we are now concerned, we will attempt a brief analysis of this other kind of love. It does not have its origin in self-denial, but in a distinctively uncritical intensification and strengthening of natural self-assertion. It is in this that the loving subject finds itself summoned and stirred to turn to another. It is hungry, and demands the food that the other seems to hold out. This is the reason for its interest in the other. It needs it because of its intrinsic value and in pursuance of an end. As this other promises something—itself in one of its properties—there is the desire to possess and control and enjoy it. Man wants it for himself : for the upholding, magnifying, deepening, broadening, illuminating or enriching of his own existence ; or perhaps simply in a need to express himself ; or perhaps even more simply in the desire to find satisfaction in all his unrest. And so it takes place that, however much he may seem to give what is his, lavishing and dissipating it on the object of his love, he does not really give it up, but uses it as a means to win or keep or enjoy this object of his love (as the peacock displays its tail before its mate, or the woman exerts, as her own, all her inner and outer, natural and artificial advantages that the man may be hers also). And so it also takes place that the one who loves, however much he may apparently forget himself or however much he may transcend himself (in very high and noble and spiritual transports) in the direction of the object of his love, merely asserts himself the more strongly in face of it as he wins and keeps and enjoys it, since all the time it is himself that he has in view, and his own affirmation and development that he seeks. For all the self-emptying on the part of the one who loves, union with the beloved as the supreme goal of this love consists

174

in the fact that this object of love is taken to himself, if
not expressly swallowed up and consumed, so that in the
event he alone remains, like the wolf when it has devoured,
as it hopes, both Red Riding Hood and her grandmother.
The movement of this love takes the form of a circle. It
seeks the infinite in a transcendence of everything finite,
but from the very first it is disposed in such a way that
(even by way of the infinite) it must always return to its
beginning. Its objects do not need to be sensual. It may
be directed to the good, the true and the beautiful. Even
in its sexual form, it may have reference (perhaps wholly
and utterly) to the soul and not merely the body. Beyond
all other goods and values, it may even reach out to the
Godhead in its purest form and thus be a most wonderful
love of God. But in all its forms it will always be a grasping,
taking, possessive love—self-love—and in some way and
at some point it will always betray itself as such.

But as such it is the direct opposite of Christian love—
the love which seeks and attains its end as the self-giving
of the one who loves to the object of his love. It is no
light thing, of course, to dare to criticise and disqualify it
from the standpoint of Christian love. For one thing,
although Christian love is both permitted and commanded
in the case of Christians, in a crude or subtle form (and
perhaps both) they all love in this way too, according to
the standards of this very different love. Thus they are
all the first to be convicted by whatever may be said for
the one love and against the other. And they have so
much to do to wipe clean their own slate that it will be a
long time before they can be too loud in their exaltation
of Christian love and condemnation of the theoretical and
practical forms of the other (whether Greek or otherwise).
But above all reserve is enjoined by the fact that this
other love can claim some of the greatest figures in the
history of the human spirit, whom it would be a highly
questionable enterprise to reject and repudiate in a curt
and dogmatic Christianity, especially on the part of those
who do not really know them and cannot therefore estimate
them at their true worth. It has also to be taken into
account that all of us (even we Christians) exist in a world
which in its best and finest as well as its most basic phenomena is for the most part built upon this other rather than

Christian love, and that we live by the works and fruits and achievements of this love, so that when the Christian calls it in question in the light of Christian love he always takes on a highly ambiguous appearance. What is clearly brought out by this distinction between Christian and every other love as it may be seen—we stress this point— even in the life of the Christian himself, is the wholly alien character of Christianity in relation to the world around.

Yet these considerations must not prevent a sober affirmation of this distinction. Christian love cannot in fact be equated with any other, or with any of the forms (even the highest and purest) of this other, just as this other love has obviously no desire to be confused with Christian. Nor can Christian love be fused with this other to form a higher synthesis. We cannot say of any other love that it is a kind of preparatory stage for Christian love. Nor can we commend Christian love by representing and portraying it as the purified form, the supreme climax, of this other love. There is an element common to both types of love—we shall have to speak of this later. But remarkably enough it is precisely in view of this common element that there must and will always be decision and decisions between them : not only in the history of the Christian community in its relations with the world ; but also in the history of the Christian community itself, which is also of the world, and consists of men who both as a whole and as individuals can be moved by both types, but cannot possibly be moved by both at the same time or in the same way ; and finally and above all in the individual histories of these men themselves.

Even a superficial glance at the two phenomena and concepts, or rather at the realities of the two types of love, necessarily discloses that we have to do here with two movements in opposite directions, so that there can be no harmony but only conflict between them. The first type cannot pass over and be transformed into the second, nor the second into the first. Man loves either in one way or the other, and he has to choose whether it is to be in the one way or the other. If in fact he loves in both ways at the same time, as is often the case even with the Christian, this can only be with the disruption, the " falling out," which we had occasion to discuss in relation to " conversion." Where Christian love enters, there always begins at once the unceasing controversy between itself and every other love. The Christian life is existence in the history of the distinction between these opposing types of love. It has not yet begun, or has been extinguished again, where there is the desire or ability to be superior, or neutral, or tolerant in relation to the two ; where Christian love (perishing as such) can be brought to terms with this other love. Not the moment of this other love as such, but the moment of tolerance, of the agreement of Christian love with this other, of truce in the controversy, constitutes a hiatus, a cessation, a vacuum in the Christian life—a definitely non-Christian moment. There can be only conflict and not compromise between Christian love and this other. And there can be only conflict and not compromise between this other love and Christian.

The biblical basis for this distinction and opposition will emerge, like the material, only as we take up the various themes of the section. Our present task is simply to show that there is always this distinction and opposition.

Nevertheless, we are given a prior indication of the biblical basis when we remember the linguistic usage of the Bible. It is immediately apparent that the New Testament consistently avoids the use of the verb ἐρᾶν and the substantive ἔρως—the terms which in classical Greek plainly describe this other grasping, taking, possessing and enjoying love. Even in the apostolic fathers we find only a single occurrence of ἔρως (Ignatius, ad Rom. 7, 2), and here it is used only to denote the love which the author declares that he has left behind him as crucified. In the New Testament, however, it is not used at all, even in a depreciatory sense. The reader who meets the concept of love in these pages is obviously not even to be reminded of this other love. Apart from an occasional use of φιλεῖν with its emphasis on feeling, the normal term for love in the New Testament is ἀγαπᾶν, with the substantive ἀγάπη, which is unknown in classical Greek and only sparingly used in hellenistic. It is only in New Testament usage that this word has acquired the well-known meaning and content of a love opposed to ἔρως. In itself it is rather colourless. It has something of the

sense of the English "like." It speaks of the acceptance
or approval of something or someone. Perhaps this lack
of distinctive significance was the very reason why it was
adopted in the New Testament. It lent itself readily to
the receiving of a new impress. But the New Testament
was only following the Septuagint, which had had to find
a supportable rendering for the verb *aheb* (and substantive
ahabah), and its synonyms. *Aheb* can describe, with a
positive emphasis, all kinds of familiar and friendly relationships. Indeed, in the first instance it is also used for that
between a man and his wife, there being a material but
no linguistic distinction in Hebrew between the love which
is theologically significant and that which was later called
"erotic." To avoid the latter, the Septuagint seized
on the colourless terms ἀγαπᾶν and ἀγάπη, using them,
strangely enough, even in the picture of the marriage
between Yahweh and Israel in the Book of Hosea, and
even more strangely in the Song of Songs. We can give as
a reason for the choice of ἀγάπη only the intention to avoid
at all costs the use of ἔρως to describe the love found in
these passages. This intention was shared by hellenistic
Judaism in its interpretation of the Old Testament and
early Christianity in its attestation of Jesus Christ. Whatever we may say concerning ἀγάπη must be determined by
the meaning and content which it was desired to give, and
which were actually given, to this term (the other being
completely eliminated) in the light of the origin, action
and manner of this love which has to be so very differently
described.

We must not form too impoverished a conception of the
love which was linguistically eliminated by the Septuagint
and the New Testament because it was the opposite of the
kind of love that they were seeking to attest. That is to
say, we must not seek it only in sexual love, or in degenerate
and excessive forms of this love. The image of life and
power and thought which is summed up under the catch-
word *eros*, and which dominated to a large extent the
world of Greek antiquity and even the environment of the
New Testament, is a magnitude which does, of course,
include sexual love even in its more curious forms, and
which no doubt has in this a striking symbol, but which
cannot in any sense be understood in its depth and rich-

ness, and its dangerous opposition to Christian love, if it is considered exclusively or even preferentially with reference to its actuality in this sphere. Nor is it a magnitude which was potent and effective only in that particular period. On the contrary, although it did, of course, find particularly forceful expression in the Mystery religions and in thinking influenced by outstanding philosophers like Plato and Aristotle and later Plotinus, it is a general and very real human phenomenon which reaches back to the very beginnings of history and forward into every subsequent age, including our own. We are forced to say, indeed, that the warning given already by the biblical usage was largely in vain, and that the positive proclamation of Christian love has been a largely if not wholly futile swimming against the overwhelming flood of *eros*-love. As a proof of its power, *eros* invaded even Christian thought and life from the end of the 2nd century, and has been able to effect very radical and definite penetrations (sometimes with the conscious help or connivance of Christians, but the more effectively where there has been no awareness of its influence). The *caritas* which the Middle Ages had learned decisively from Augustine was a synthesis of biblical *agape* and antique or hellenistic *eros* in which the antithesis between the two can still be perceived, but not in any sense unequivocally, the tension having been largely destroyed with all its beneficial results. This was inevitable. As long as men love, even though they are Christians they will always live within the framework of *eros*, and be disposed to effect a synthesis between *eros* and *agape*, exercising all their powers both great and small to bring this about. . . .

We will now attempt to give some indication, in a few light strokes, of the form in which *eros* confronted and was perceived by the New Testament and later Septuagint-Judaism with their view of love. Who and what was this *eros*? What was the experience, and action, of the one who loved in this erotic fashion? This is the form which our question must first assume. We are asking concerning a definite experience and practice. In its origin in Orphism and its myth and mysticism *eros* was something far more than the philosophical concept which was first and unforgettably introduced into Western thought by Plato. *Eros* was a doctrine of redemption and salvation claiming to be revealed, and believed and proclaimed as such. Indeed, it was an experienced actuality of redemption and salvation which found expression both in solemn rites and everyday practice. As such, and hence not unlike Christian *agape*, it could and inevitably did stand in direct opposition to the latter, rousing in its advocates the critical concern so strikingly illustrated by the consistent elimination of the term *eros*. As such it could also provoke the question, which was often to be given a positive answer, whether *eros* and *agape* were not intrinsically comparable and combinable realities, and even at bottom one and the same reality—a view which was first explicitly held by Origen. In the actuality of *eros*, and its varied literature, edifying, poetic or dialectical, mythological or rational, it is always a matter of man, his limitation and its meaning and removal, his existence and transcendence, his need and hope. More precisely, it is always a matter of man hovering but in some sense moving upwards between a lower world and a higher, a world of darkness and a world of light. It is a matter of the experience and practice of this twofold reality. As it is seen and portrayed, this reality consists in his inalienable want and the desire which it kindles, or in his inalienable desire and the want to which it gives rise, as the very essence of this central position. This position is necessarily that of want and desire because it is the centre between his below and above, between his proper and improper being, between his fulness and emptiness, between his being in disintegration and in reintegration with himself. *Eros* is the experienced and self-attained turning from his being down below in darkness and return to his being up above in light. *Eros* is the power and act in which he must lose himself on the one hand to find himself again on the other. And so *eros* is a hypostatised form of man himself in this central position and the movement—the turning from and to—which is commensurate with it. As this hypostasis of man himself, the dæmon of man, powerful and manifest in him and known and expressed by him, *eros* is understood as a, and finally *the*, metaphysical link ($\mu\epsilon\tau\alpha\xi\acute{\upsilon}$) between the world of appearance and the world of reality, as the sum of the movement from the one to the other.

It was explained along these lines by Aristotle, who in this respect was more consistent than Plato. As he saw it, it is not merely an anthropological but a cosmological principle. It is the impulse in the power of which—at this point the concept of *eros* verges on that of entelechy—not merely psychic individuals but all cosmic elements, even the lower and higher physical bodies, strive after form in their materiality, actuality in their potentiality and the unmoved One in their movement and plurality, thus seeking their normal state, and being engaged in a universal dissolution and ascent. Plato was more restrained in his depiction of this great turning away and return, confining his gaze to the seizure and exercise of power by *eros* in man. On his view, in the visible *eidola* of transitory things and their relative values, there encounters man, not in visible form but perceptible to the enlightened eye, the *eidos*, the absolute value of that which immutably is, the beautiful, by which he is both attracted and impelled and therefore set in movement. How can he tarry with the *eidola* without being forced to flee them at once in the direction of the *eidos* ? It is only for the sake of the *eidos* that he can love the *eidola*. But again, how can he flee them for the sake of the *eidos* without being forced to tarry with the *eidola* which have a distinct part in the beauty of the *eidos* ? For its sake he may and must love them too. Plotinus brought out very strongly the religious significance of the *eros*-actuality, although here again we see affinities with originally platonic notions. His main contribution was to expand the theory to the point of maintaining that there is a departure of the soul from the higher world prior to its ascent from the lower, or an emanation of the soul from the deity prior to its return from the world, so that the want and desire, the turning from and to, the being in vacillation between world-denial and world-affirmation, can be described as a homecoming, as a return of the soul to its origin and therefore to itself— an innovation which merely serves to reveal the circular movement to which the practice and theory of the *eros*-actuality were exposed from the very outset. It is the actuality of the man who in his relationship to being both visible and invisible, and finally in his relationship to the Godhead, is engaged in realising his own entelechy, i.e., in needing and therefore in seeking, desiring and successfully finding and enjoying himself in his particularity. As he knows and approves and takes himself seriously in this actuality, as he presupposes himself in this form, he orders and understands the process of his life, and therefore loves.

This was the ἐρᾶν and ἔρως with which the authors of the New Testament and the translators of the Old before them refused to equate their own understanding of " love." In the foregoing sketch we have not touched on the concrete difficulties, the intellectual, moral and religious dangers and the corruptive effects which seemed to be involved in practice when the two types of love came face to face. The contrast between *agape* and *eros* arises even when we have to do with the latter in its essential nature and not in its degenerate form, in the vulgarisations to which that which Plato, Aristotle and Plotinus saw and understood as love was submitted on the streets and in the temples and dwelling-places of the antique and hellenistic world. If we are not merely to conceive but to grasp what Christianity and its " love " so resolutely rejected, nothing less than the best of what is held out to us by the plastic works of the time will suffice. If we do not take this into account, but capriciously restrict ourselves to the particular and very obvious antithesis between *agape* and the sinful forms of sexual love or even its most degenerate manifestations, then we shall not understand the consistency (so incisive in its very silence) with which *eros* is completely ignored in the language of the Bible, nor the fact that this could become so important a matter in the Christian sphere, nor finally the necessity of thinking and speaking of Christian love in a restrained and sober manner, i.e., on the basis of its own presuppositions, and therefore not in the *schema* of the actuality and doctrine of *eros*, and therefore not along orphic, platonic, aristotelian or neo-platonic lines. We have to do here with an opponent whom we must estimate at his true stature, and whom we can fully appraise as an opponent only if we do so.

We cannot be content, however, merely to state that there is a difference and antithesis between Christian and every other love. As we bring this introduction to a close we will thus turn to the question at what point and in what sense the two loves diverge. Unless we do this we cannot understand their relationship and antithesis, nor can we understand either *eros* on the one side or *agape* on the other. But to ask concerning this critical point is to ask concerning a common place from which they both come. We cannot ask concerning a place where they can be seen together and understood as components, as partial forms and aspects, of one and the same reality, and therefore in the last resort as one. The question of an original point of identity necessarily involves that of a synthesis compelling to a new identification which *eros* as well as *agape* (being what they are both in actuality and conception) must very definitely resist. Yet we can and must ask concerning the point from which they both come in their true nature, and can therefore be seen in full antithesis. We can and must ask concerning the point from which they cannot possibly co-exist in compromise or mutual tolerance, but only in the history of their controversy. We cannot fathom this matter unless we put this question and make some attempt to answer it. . . .

An obvious answer, and one which is not without real content, is that on both sides—whether we are thinking of *eros* or *agape*—we have to do with man, and with one and the self-same man in the case of the Christian. It is man who loves either in the one way or the other, or in both ways in the Christian conflict between the two. However sharply we may see and define the difference, there is no question of the love of two different beings, or even of different individuals 'when we are dealing with Christians. In this very different and even antithetical determination, direction and form we have to do with the same human being. It is always man who encounters us in the two forms.

This does not mean, in the case of either determination, that the two are peculiar to or inherent and grounded in the nature of man. We can say this neither of *eros* nor *agape*. Neither the one nor the other rests on a possibility of human nature as such. Neither the one nor the other is a perfection of human nature achieved or to be achieved in the actualisation of such a possibility. We can only say and must say—and we now take a second step—that they are both historical determinations of human nature. It is the same human nature which, as man loves in one way or the other, shows itself to be capable of this or that

183

form of love, not with a capacity which is proper to it, but with one which is (shall we say) generally contingent to it, i.e., which comes upon it, in the history and existence of man. It is merely the case that man does actually express himself in the form of *eros* or *agape* or (in the case of the Christian) the two in contradiction ; and that to this extent (in view of the fact that he actually does so) he can express himself in this way. It is merely the case that man does always encounter us in these two forms of love, and to this extent in the corresponding forms of his nature.

He does so in a definite expression of his nature—this is the third step that we have to take. What actually comes upon him as the one who loves in the one way or the other is a distinct and even antithetical determination and direction of the act in which he himself, existing as the man he is, gives expression to his nature in its totality. . . .

Neither in *eros* nor *agape* therefore—this is the fourth step—can there be any question of an alteration of human nature. Whether he loves in the one way or the other he is the same man engaged in the expression of the same human nature. What comes upon him in his history, in the fulfilment of his self-expression, is the fact that in the two cases he is the same man in very different ways. As in neither case God ceases to be the Creator, in neither case does man cease to be the creature that God willed and posited when He made him a man, with the structure of human nature. Whatever form the history of man may take, there is broken neither the continuity of the divine will for man nor that of the nature which man is given by God. And although this may be seen in very different ways in the two forms of his loving, it can be seen in both of them. The only thing is that the human act is very different in the two cases. The only thing is that, as man loves in one way or the other, it comes upon him that the one unchangeable, perennial human nature is put by him to a very different use and given a very different character. The basis of the difference is not to be found in itself (so that it cannot be explained in terms of itself or deduced from itself), but in its historical determination.

Concerning this difference in the use and character of

human nature in *eros*-love on the one hand and *agape*-love on the other, we have first to make—the fifth step—a formal statement. We can and must speak of the difference of the new thing (in relation to human nature) which, as a matter of historical fact, overtakes or comes on man as he loves in the one form or the other. Without being grounded in his nature, this act of love takes place in a distinctive relationship to it, to that which makes him a man. This is not by a long way the whole of what has to be said about this love. Our present enquiry concerns only the common point of departure where comparison is possible, and at once becomes impossible, between the two ways of loving. The common point of departure consists in the fact that they both take place in relationship to the human nature chosen and willed and posited and ordered by God. They are both new in relation to this human nature, but they both take place in connexion with it. They are together in this relationship, and therefore comparison is possible. But they diverge in it, and therefore comparison becomes utterly impossible. The decisive statement must be ventured—decisive for the distinction— that *agape*-love takes place in correspondence and *eros*-love in contradiction to this nature ; the one as its "analogue " and the other as its " catalogue " ; the one as man does that which is right in relation to it, and the other as he does that which is not right in relation to it. *Agape*-love takes place in affinity, *eros*-love in opposition, to human nature. As we see, they both take place in relationship to it (and in this they can be compared). But in the one case the relationship is positive, in the other negative (so that they cannot be compared). In this antithetical use and character, in which the one unchanging human takes on form but which differ as Yes and No, being related only in respect of their object, *eros* and *agape* go their divergent ways.

This formal statement requires material clarification and substantiation in two directions which demand attention in this question. Our starting-point for a sixth step is that it is essential, natural and original to man, that it belongs to his very structure as this particular creature of God, to be with God, who is His Creator and Lord, as with his eternal Counterpart : deriving wholly from this

185

God, participating from the very first and in all circumstances (as His elect) in His preservation and effective help, and being sheltered absolutely by Him and in Him; and moving wholly towards Him, thanking Him (as the one who is called by Him), in responsibility before Him and obedience to Him, calling upon His name. From this vertical standpoint, as it were, the very nature and essence of man is to be freed by and for this God; to be engaged in the act of this twofold freedom (cf. *C.D.*, III, 2, § 44, 3). Man cannot escape or destroy or lose or alter the fact that it is only in this that he is truly and naturally and essentially a man. But in the life-act of every man (both as a whole and in detail) it is decided whether and to what extent, in relationship to that which he really is in his togetherness with God, he is true or untrue, in correspondence or contradiction, to himself (from this standpoint his being from God and to God). It is in this decision that there arises the new thing either of his *agape*-love in which he corresponds to his being from and to God or of his *eros*-love in which he contradicts it. In this respect *agape*-love consists in the fact that he accepts God as his eternal Counterpart, and therefore his own being as that of one who is elected by this God, being absolutely sheltered by His preservation and help, but who is also called by Him to thanksgiving, responsibility, obedience and prayer. It consists in the fact that he is determined and ready to live from and to God to the best of his knowledge and capacity : not raising any claim ; not trying to control God ; not with the ulterior motive of winning God for himself or demanding anything from Him ; but simply because He is God, and as such worthy to be loved. *Agape* consists in the orientation of human nature on God in a movement which does not merely express it but means that it is transcended, since in it man gives himself up to be genuinely freed by and for God, and therefore to be free from self-concern and free for the service of God. *Eros*-love consists in this respect in the new thing (which is absurd in relation to human nature) that man shuts off himself against this freedom. In it he prefers a being from and by and in and for himself to togetherness with God as his eternal Counterpart, and makes God the origin of this self-inflated and self-enclosed being. In it he thus fabricates his God out of the compulsion and impulsion to this being, and therefore his own caprice. In the name of this reflection he chooses himself as the basis from which he comes, and therefore accepts the whole burden and responsibility for his help and preservation, for the securing and sheltering of his being. He also makes himself his goal, and therefore finds no place for thanksgiving, responsibility, obedience and calling upon God, but transposes them into a desire and longing and striving and transcending in which he spreads himself with some degree of coarse or refined appetite and more or less skill and consistency in the sensual and spiritual world, using it and making it serviceable to himself, as his environment, as that which satisfies his needs, as a place to sow and reap, as his sphere of work, or it may be only as his gymnasium and playground. *Eros* is love which is wholly claim, wholly the desire to control, wholly the actual attempt to control, in relation to God. This is inevitable, seeing it is the love in which the one who loves and the object of love are one and the same, so that from first to last it is self-love. In both cases we are dealing with love, even with the love of God, although in very different senses. In both cases it is love in relation to that which is essential to man, to that which is peculiar to him in his nature as it is formed and fashioned by God. The difference is that *agape* (irrespective of its strength or weakness) corresponds to this nature, and *eros* (irrespective of its form or intensity) contradicts it. The one transcends it ; the other falls short of it. It will always be the case in practice that human nature orientated on God, and therefore *agape* as its correspondence, will be recognisable even in the negative of the most radical form of the contradiction and therefore of *eros* ; and on the other hand that the most perfect form of the correspondence, and therefore *agape*, will reflect to some extent the contradiction, and therefore *eros*, in and with human nature. Yet the distinction, and the necessity of deciding, between them is perfectly clear from that which they have conceptually in common, and in the way in which they accompany one another in practice.

The starting-point for a seventh and final step is that it is essential and natural to man not only to be with God but also, on the horizontal level and in analogy with this togetherness with God, to be with his fellow-man : not in isolation ; not in opposition or neutrality to this other ; not united with him in a subsequent relationship; but bound to him basically and from the very first ; directed, that is, to the I-Thou encounter, in which there can be no I without the Thou, no man without the fellow-man, any more than there can be any man without God. He is a man as he sees the other man and is seen by him ; as he hears him and speaks with him ; as he assists him and receives his assistance. He is a man as he is free to do this ; as he can be a comrade and companion and fellow to the other, not under constraint, but voluntarily (cf. *C.D.*, III, 2, § 45, 2). In this respect, too, the nature of man is immutable, quite independently of his history. But in this respect, too, in indissoluble relationship with his decision in the connexion with God, it is decided in the history and life-act of man whether and how far he is true or untrue, in correspondence or contradiction, to his nature, to his humanity in this special sense, and therefore to himself. And in this connexion, too, *agape* means correspondence and *eros* contradiction. In *agape*-love the essential fellow-humanity of man is respected. For the one who loves in this way there can be no opposition or neutrality in relation to the other. In his love there takes place the encounter of I and Thou, the open perception of the other and self-disclosure to him, conversation with him, the offering and receiving of assistance, and all this with joy. In this respect, too, the real man is at work in *agape*, not merely expressing but transcending his nature. In this respect, too, *agape* means self-giving : not the losing of oneself in the other, which would bring us back into the sphere of *eros* ; but identification with his interests in utter independence of the question of his attractiveness, of what he has to offer, of the reciprocity of the relationship, or repayment in the form of a similar self-giving. In *agape*-love a man gives himself to the other with no expectation of a return, in a pure venture, even at the risk of ingratitude, of his refusal to make a response of love, which would be a denial of his humanity. He loves the other because he is this other, his brother. But as the one who loves in this way sees a brother in his fellow, and treats him as such, he also honours him as a man. While *agape* transcends humanity, the man who loves in this way is genuinely human ; he gives a true expression to human nature ; he is a real man. The same cannot be said of *eros*-love. In most cases this does, of course, consist in an address to one's fellow, and perhaps with considerable warmth and intensity. But as in relation to God, so also to his fellow, the man who loves erotically is not really thinking of the other but of himself. His fellow is envisaged only as an expected increase and gain for his own existence, as an acquisition, a booty, a prey, to be used by him in the pursuance of some purpose. In these circumstances how can he really be a comrade, companion and fellow ? How can he see him openly, or disclose himself to him ? How can he enter into honest conversation with him ? How can he assist him and receive his assistance ? It is only in semblance and not in truth that the one who loves erotically is well-disposed to him. As he grasps at him, he has already let him fall and rejected him. And it is inevitable that sooner or later he will do this openly. In the duality apparently sought and found by the one who loves erotically there lurks the isolation which he has never really left and in which he will finally remain. Erotic love is a denial of humanity. To be sure, it is love ; love for man ; an action in relationship, in this relationship, to humanity. Hence humanity and to that extent *agape* may be negatively seen in it, and it may be confessed in this perverted form ; just as *agape*-love as the act of man in his human nature is never so pure as not to betray in some way the proximity of the *eros*-love which is its opposite. Yet the two loves are still different—basically different in their relationship to humanity. And since they have this common point of departure from which they both come, it will always be the case that man can only choose between *eros* and *agape*. . . .

Since *agape* is from God—as we shall see in the next sub-section—and *eros* from self-contradictory man, is it not one of the things which make comparison impossible that the former is absolutely superior to the latter, not only in dignity, but also in power ? *Eros* can only flee and perish and cease, and with it the whole world which is dominated and impelled and built up and characterised by it. But love, *agape*, never fails (1 Cor. 13⁸). With that which issues from it (as it does from God), it is imperishable even in the midst of a world which perishes.

For this reason, our final word can and must be conciliatory as we look back on our development of the problem of Christian love and therefore of its antithesis to *eros*. There can be no question of mediation, or of a weakening of the antithesis. But we can speak a word of reconciliation, not in respect of *eros*, but in respect of erotic man contradicting himself and shunning and opposing God and his neighbour. *Agape* cannot change into *eros*, or *eros* into *agape*. The one love cannot, then, be interpreted as the other. But if this is impossible, it is even more impossible that God should change into, or be interpreted as, another God who is no longer the God of man, even of the man who loves erotically; and that this man should cease to be man, and therefore the creature elected and willed and fashioned by God, and therefore in the hands of God even in his corruption. But if he is in the hands of God, even erotic man must and will be affirmed in and with the love which is from God—Christian love. His erotic love will not be affirmed. But he himself will be affirmed as the man which he does not cease to be even as he loves erotically—God's man. And this affirmation proclaims his reconciliation; the fact that God has loved, and loves, and will love even him. How can we love as Christians if we forget this, if we do not hold out this affirmation, this proclamation, even to the one who loves erotically? How we judge ourselves—for we, too, love erotically—if we withhold this affirmation from the heathen who in contrast know no other love! But if we love as Christians, and therefore with the love which is from God, and therefore in self-giving to God and our fellows, then in respect of the man who loves erotically our love must consist wholly and utterly in this affirmation: in the declaration that he, too, is loved by God and therefore in His hands; that overlooking his erotic love God in His genuine, non-self-seeking love is the One who in His self-giving wills to be God only as his God, God for him, and to be majestic, all-powerful and glorious as such. If Christian love does not make this declaration to the non-Christian, it is not Christian love. It stops where the love of God, from which it derives, does not stop. And in so doing it parts company with the love of God. If a Christian believes, as he can and should, that he himself is not separated from the love of God by the fact that he loves erotically, he cannot refuse this declaration to the fellow-man whom he thinks he sees wholly entangled in the bands of *eros*-love.

The concrete content of this declaration, and therefore of the conciliatory word with which we must close our consideration of the antithesis between *agape* and *eros*, is to the effect that God simply espouses the cause of man, and therefore even the man who loves erotically. But this means that he understands him—far better than he understands himself. He cares for him—far better than he cares, or can care, for himself. This is how it is when he calls him out of the kingdom of *eros* and into the kingdom of His love, which consists in the act of self-giving and not in a campaign of aggression. And this is how it must be between the Christian and the non-Christian, the man who loves erotically. It is not a question of subjecting man to an alien, cold and gloomy law, in the following of which he will be afraid of falling short, and can expect only to be invaded and disarmed and oppressed and destroyed, so that he has every reason to try to evade it. There is no reason for this. For it is a matter of his liberation when God loves him—even him—in spite of his corruption, and calls him to decision in favour of *agape* against *eros*. This call is a message of light and not darkness, of promise and not threat, of joy and not sorrow. What is it, then, that the man who loves erotically wills and desires and seeks and strives after? What is it that he would achieve and maintain? We have seen that in the circle in which he turns to the natural and spiritual world, to God and his fellow-man, it is first and last himself. May he not, then, be himself? Will God refuse him this? Can the God who has created him as he is refuse it? Most certainly not. The truth is that he can never in all eternity find himself, his being as this self in the world before God and among his fellows, but, chasing his own shadow, can and will only lose it in all eternity, so long as he tries to will and desire and seek and strive after and achieve and maintain himself as the erotic man thinks it necessary to do. The love which is from God, the Christian love in which man can respond to the love of God, is his liberation from this supposed necessity, his dispensation from this forward-seeking in need and desire, his release from the obligation of this chase in which he is both the hunter and the hunted and which for this reason can only be utterly futile. Man can cease from this self-willing, and therefore from all the frenzied activity in which he can seek, yet never find, but only lose himself. For if the only meaning of life is that man must seek himself to find himself, he can only lose himself in this seeking, and life is meaningless. Christian love is his deliverance because the one who loves as a Christian gives up trying to save himself, to be his own deliverer. In Christian love a man can finally leave that circle of destruction, which is in the true sense a vicious circle. And not become himself? Quite the contrary! It is only in this way that he can and will become himself. To renounce that seeking, to leave that circle, is indeed a *conditio sine qua non* of Christian love. But positively this love is man's self-giving to God (not for what He can give, nor for the sake of some purpose that can be achieved with His help, but for God Himself), and his self-giving to his fellow (again, not for what he can give, nor for the sake of some purpose, but for the man himself). As this self-giving, the Christian love which is from God is man's response to God's own love. It is in this way that God loves man. He does not seek Himself, let alone anything for Himself, but simply man, man as he is and as such, man himself. And God does not in any sense fall short of Himself when He loves in this way. In this self-giving to man He is God in all His freedom and glory. If the love of man, as his response to the fact that God loves him in this way, itself consists in his self-giving, this certainly means that there can be no more self-love, no more desiring and seeking the freedom and glory of the self. But why, and how far, is this really the case? Simply because he has already found himself in great freedom and glory. What he cannot win by desiring and seeking, he has already attained, not in the power of his renunciation, but in the power of the self-giving in which he may respond to the love of God. He *himself* is the one who is loved by God. He *himself* is the

192

one to whom God has given Himself in His Son, and gives Himself as He gives him His Holy Spirit. He is cut off from *eros*-love, and taken out of that circle, by the fact that, loving as a Christian, he is already at the place which he was vainly trying to reach in the Icarus-flight and self-assertion of *eros*-love. There is no further point in erotic love. *Eros* is made superfluous by the *agape* in which man may find himself and therefore has no more need to seek himself. He himself discovers himself to be secure in his response to the love of God.

It is obvious that at this point a second and theoretically more dangerous aberration would be worse than the first. I cannot try to love as a Christian in order to attain the goal and end which escapes me as one who loves erotically. An *ut finale* necessarily means a relapse into *eros*-love. The only valid *ut* is the radiant *ut consecutivum*. But this is indeed valid, and it makes any such·relapse quite impossible. For in Christian love I am already at the goal. I have found myself, and cannot therefore lose myself by trying to love as a Christian in order to come to myself.

I have only to love continually as a Christian, and therefore without regard or purpose for myself, in self-giving to God and my fellows, and I will come to myself and be myself. This is what we are told in the saying in Mk. 8^{35}, which speaks about the saving and losing and the losing and saving of life; and also in the saying in Mt. 6^{33}, which tells us that if we seek first the kingdom of God and His righteousness all other things are added to us. These sayings are not Law but Gospel. They describe the *agape* which conquers *eros* by making it pointless and superfluous. They describe the man who loves as a Christian as already at the goal which the man who loves erotically— poor dupe—wants to reach but never can or will reach in erotic love. They make no demand. They take nothing away. They do not blame or judge. They merely show him that he is understood and accepted and received by God—not his erotic love, but he himself. He may save himself and find himself and be himself. But this is something which is given, which comes, as he loses his life, as he renounces his whole self-seeking—" for my sake and the gospel's "—so that he is saved and has found himself already. [IV, 2, pp. 733–751]

VII. MAN AND WOMAN

Because man is not merely a creature, but the knowledge derived from the reality of Jesus Christ shows that he is designed by God to be a covenant-partner and exists and can exist as man only in this covenant-relationship, real man is never solitary but is always man in relation, confronted by another for whom he exists, namely, God and the fellow-man. To be a fellow-man is the decisive determination of the nature of man. In the creaturely sphere this is revealed in the indissoluble bi-sexuality of man. Hence Barth gives to this phenomenon extended consideration (in III, 1, III, 2 and III, 4). What he has to say about the anthropological significance of the relationship of man and woman is a good example of the way in which his dogmatic insights produce ethical directions, the knowledge of the act of God for us leading to knowledge of His command to us. The selected passages on man and woman are the basis of Barth's thinking on questions of marriage and sexual life.

[91] The first and typical sphere of fellow-humanity, the first and typical differentiation and relationship between man and man, is that between male and female. . . .

Reflection upon the creaturely being of man as a co-existence of man and fellow-man confirms this reference. There are also other types of differentiation and relationship between man and man. But this relationship alone rests on a structural and functional distinction. So much cannot be said of the relationship between father and son or mother and daughter, nor of the relationship between men of different ages or different gifts and dispositions, nor of that between various peoples and historical epochs. Only that between man and woman rests upon a structural and functional difference. Notice that the distinction is merely structural and functional. It does not call in question the fact that male and female are both human. But structurally and functionally it is too clear and serious to be a mere variation upon a theme common to both— a neutral and abstract humanity which exists and can be considered independently. Man never exists as such, but always as the human male or the human female. Hence in humanity, and therefore in fellow-humanity, the decisive, fundamental and typical question, normative for all other relationships, is that of the relationship in this differentiation. This is just as clear and serious as the distinction. For the differentiation itself, for all its incomparable depth, is one long reference to the relationship. We have to say both that man is necessarily and totally man *or* woman, and that as such and in consequence he is equally necessarily and totally man *and* woman. He cannot wish to liberate himself from the differentiation and exist beyond his sexual determination as mere man ; for in everything that is commonly human he will always be in fact either the human male or the human female. Nor can he wish to liberate himself from the relationship and be man without woman or woman apart from man ; for in all that characterises him as man he will be thrown back upon woman, or as woman upon man, both man and woman being referred to this encounter and co-existence. No other distinction between man and man goes so deep as that in which the human male and the human female are so utterly different from each other. And no other relationship is so obvious, self-explanatory and universally valid as that whose force resides precisely in the presupposed underlying otherness. The female is to the male, and the male to the female the other man and as such the fellow-man. It is with reason, therefore, that we first enquire what the divine command has to say in this sphere of fellow-humanity. [III, 4, p.117f.]

[92] It will serve to clarify and temper our understanding of the question if we begin by stating what it means, generally and fundamentally, that in this sphere too man is confronted by the divine command.

Consider the myths and sagas, the rites and customs, of so many religions in relation to this particular point. Think of the speculation of so much philosophy, psychology and poetry. Think finally of the tumult and violence of emotions which cannot be quite strange to any one who is slightly acquainted with this field, even though he be not capable of expressing them in happy and systematic form. These all point to the fact that here, more than anywhere else, man seems at least to stand on the threshold of a kind of natural mysticism. What else can stir him so much, bringing him as he thinks—whether he be a crude or a highly cultivated person—into such ecstasy, such rapture, such enthusiasm, into what seem to be the depths

195

and essence of all being, into the vision of the Godhead and participation in it, supposedly exalting him into the vicinity at least of another God and Creator—what else can do this like the primal experience of encounter between male and female? Perhaps it is this experience itself in any one of its possible forms and varying degrees, perhaps it is a sublimation, transposition or spiritualisation of it— but always it is the experience of this encounter! Why this experience precisely? If we understand what is at issue here, we shall not ask. It is obviously on account of the truly breath-taking dialectic which arises in this encounter—the dialectic of difference and affinity, of real dualism and equally real unity, of utter self-recollection and utter transport beyond the bounds of self into union with another, of creation and redemption, of this world and the next. If humanity spells fellow-humanity and fellow-humanity is primarily experienced in this dialectic, how tempting it is to understand and experience this fellow-humanity as the bold and blessed intoxication of the deepest abasement and the supreme exaltation of human essence, as its deification! Is man not God to the extent that his being is being in this encounter?

But the command of God has precise reference to the being of man in this encounter. It is rewarding to linger a moment over this fact. Whatever the command requires of a man, it is the command of *God*. It shows that the throne of the true God is already occupied. It brings the real beyond into the picture. It makes us realise that there can be no question of man's experiencing himself as God, that the divine with which man would like to equate himself in the experience of this encounter can only be a miserable idol, a Baal or an Astarte, an Osiris or an Isis. It puts man in his place and confines him within his limits. It marks him as a creature. Even in the depths and heights, the self-recollection and rapture, the immanence and transcendence of this primal experience he is still a creature. And whatever the command wills of him, it is the *command* of God. An alien and superior will confronts him at this climax of his self-affirmation and self-denial, in this immanence and transcendence. It shows him that in all the seriousness and rapture of this dialectic he is still not his own master. In face of the dialectic which transports him it reveals a higher and impregnable place, and it lets it be understood that from this place there is One who rules, commands, permits and also forbids. From this place there is heard in the voice of the Law, in the midst of the storms of passion or the whispers of sublimated ecstasy, a critical and judicial Yes and No by which man is tested and must test himself.

What is the implication of this ? First and supremely, it obviously means that in this sphere he is not without a Master nor abandoned by his Creator ; that he does not here find himself plunged into a demonic world, into an abyss or jungle, but is at home and under the rule of his heavenly Father. Were it otherwise, God would not show him the grace to be present with him as a Ruler at this point too and in this matter. Where God is concerned for him, man and his humanity are not lost. He is still at home. It is still at bottom a question of things that are natural and right. If the command of God is relevant to the relationship of male and female, this means that God is concerned for man in this respect too. Here too, therefore, man is not lost but in his native sphere, and it is essentially a question of things that are natural and right.

Secondly, it is clear that the command of God which is relevant in this sphere, no matter what it prescribes, implies the radical relativisation of this encounter, and of the being of man in this encounter ; not its negation or destruction, but its radical relativisation. As the command enters the picture there is implied on the one hand a demythologisation of this field. If such a process is anywhere necessary, it is so here, where so many gods or demigods or partial gods try to speak and rule. The command of God carries through this process of demythologisation, and it does so radically. It sets aside these gods with a wave of the hand. It unmasks them as elemental spirits. It explains them naturally. What remains is man as the creature standing as such under his determination to be in this encounter, as male or female and as male and female, in this natural dualism. And it remains for man to confirm this natural dualism. On the other hand, the entry of the command of God means the ordering of this sphere. Whatever it asks of man, it certainly requires him to affirm this natural dualism ; not to deny it nor to pervert it, but simply to express and reveal it as it is in his existence. As he does so, this sphere, and man within it, comes under control, and the task of man—for it is his own affair—is to exercise this control. To do so is the act of obedience required of him.

And now, thirdly, the fact that man is faced by the divine command at this point, too, implies that here again he is directed to freedom. He may be in the encounter of man and woman. He need not be afraid or ashamed of it. He need not have a bad conscience about the fact that his life is lived on this plane. He may relate himself to it as to everything else which concerns his human existence. He may even accept the fact that this seems to be a particularly exalted, important and beautiful aspect of his being. He may simply affirm this aspect. He may be a man in this respect too. He does not need any ecstasy or enthusiasm, any mysticism, rapture or deification, to accept this determination. He can and may take the dialectic in all seriousness. But he can and may spare himself the convulsions, pains and complications which would be inevitable if it were a question of a metaphysical and absolute dialectic, if in this dialectic he felt the desire and obligation to be himself God and his own master. In this respect, too, he may be man—only man, but real man. As God gives him His command at this point, as He is concerned for him and submits him to that radical relativisation, He gives him here too this freedom.

[III, 4, pp. 119–121]

[93] But what is the man in his sex and the woman in hers? When it is not a question of psychology, pedagogy, hygiene and the like, but of ethics, of theological ethics, and therefore of the command of God, we cannot and may not prejudge the issue with an abstract definition. Man and woman as the man willed and created by God and now summoned by Him and placed under His command are in themselves as much and as little capable of description as the human individual in his particularity over against another. Male and female being is the prototype of all I and Thou, of all the individuality in which man and man differ from and yet belong to each other. We can, of course, denote the human individual with the demonstrative " this " or " that " or " the same." We can call

198

man and woman " he " and " she." We can describe
individual men and women by their Christian names and
surnames, their date of birth, family, birthplace or titles.
But we have to realise that when we say all this we merely
point to something which cannot be expressed, to the
mystery in which man stands revealed to God and to Him
alone. It is at the point where he is indefinable that he is
sought and found by the divine command, that the decision
is made, that he is obedient or disobedient, good or bad.
It is here that man and woman affirm their sex or deny it.
We cannot really characterise man and woman in the
form of a definition, but only as we recall that in their
very differentiation God has willed and made them in
mutual relation and that His command has also the
dimension or component that in the interests of this
relationship they must be true to their specific differentiation. We have no right, especially if we ask concerning
the command of God, to define or describe this differentiation. Even though we may think we know this or that
about it, it can never be known to us in advance if this is
our question. Otherwise we presume to know in advance
the content of the will of God concerning which ethics can
only ask. The command of God will find man and woman
as what they are in themselves. It will disclose to them
the male or female being to which they have to remain
faithful. It will tell them what they have to acknowledge
and may never deny as man or woman. In all this it
may perhaps coincide at various points with what we may
think we know concerning the differentiation of male and
female. But it may not always do this. It may manifest
the distinction in new and surprising ways. The summons
to both man and woman to be true to themselves may
take completely unforeseen forms right outside the systems
in which we like to think. In no event is it bound to a
scheme which we may presuppose. It is thus a mistake
to attach oneself to any such scheme, however well considered and illuminating it might appear to be. Such
schemes can sometimes render us heuristic, exegetic and
illustrative services. But it is not for us to write the text
itself with the help of any such system. It is not for us
to write the text at all. For the texts which we write, the
definitions and descriptions of male and female being

which we might derive from others or attempt ourselves, do not attain what is meant by the command when it requires of man that here, too, he should accept his being as man, as male or female, as it is seen to God. For it is a well-known fact, admitted by all wise exponents of such views, that these systems can take the form only of suppositions and assertions which rest upon impressions and personal experiences and are necessarily problematic if only because they are the suppositions and assertions of a man or a woman and it is most unlikely that any man has genuinely and deeply understood woman as woman, or any woman man as man. What we have here are simply opinions which may be very interesting and stimulating in themselves, which have their value for the current dealings of man with man, and which, as they are exchanged and compared, may produce all kinds of clarifications and agreements, but which cannot be known without doubt to be valid and necessary. If there is to be a knowledge of man and woman which in the enquiry concerning the command of God we can treat as unquestioned and presupposed, it will most certainly have to be a form of knowledge which rests upon secure foundations. That man and woman—in the relationship conditioned by this irreversible order—are the human creature of God and as such the image of God and likeness of the covenant of grace—this is the secure theological knowledge with which we ourselves work and with which we must be content. What God's command wills for man and woman is that they should be faithful to this their human nature and to the special gift and duty indicated in and by it.

This means that although we recognise their achievements we definitely reject every phenomenology or typology of the sexes. . . .

Example of such a typology: " The man is the one who produces, he is the leader ; the woman is receptive, and she preserves life ; it is the man's duty to shape the new ; it is the woman's duty to write it and adapt it to that which already exists. The man has to go forth and make the earth subject to him, the woman looks within and guards the hidden unity. The man must be objective and universalise, woman must be subjective and individualise ; the man must build, the woman adorns ; the man must conquer, the woman must tend ; the man must comprehend all with his mind, the woman must impregnate all with the life of her soul. It is the duty of man to plan and to master, of the woman to understand and to unite." I quote this passage because over and above the characterisation it brings us into the sphere of an " ought " or "must," of definite tasks supposedly set the sexes in virtue of their inherent characteristics. But here the matter becomes more than doubtful. Why should we not be content with these characterisations ? Why should we not agree that there is a good deal of truth in them ? Why should we not even accept the view that in the antithesis between Apollo and the chthonic-telluric divinities, man represents the former and woman the latter ? Yet how is it that we can hardly resist a certain levity in face of such antitheses, as though seeing in them, however serious their authors, a rather malicious caricature on the one side or the other, or perhaps both ? These things obviously cannot be said or heard in all seriousness. For they cannot be stated with real security. They cannot be stated in such a way that probably every third man and certainly every second woman does not become agitated and protest sharply against the very idea of seeing themselves in these sketches. Nor can they be stated in such a way that they will wholeheartedly accept the idea that this is what they, true man and true woman ought to be, that here they see their true nature portrayed. And how are these rather contingent, schematic, conventional, literary and half-true indicatives to be transformed into imperatives ? Real man and real woman would then have to let themselves be told : Thou shalt be concerned with things (preferably machines) and thou with persons ! Thou shalt cherish the mind, thou the soul ! Thou shalt follow thy reason and thou thy instinct ! Thou shalt be objective and thou subjective ! Thou shalt build and thou merely adorn ; thou shalt conquer and thou cherish etc. ! Thou shalt ! This is commanded thee ! This is thy task ! By exercising the one or the other function, thou shalt be faithful to thyself as man or woman ! This is quite impossible. Obviously we cannot seriously address and bind any man or woman on these lines. They will justifiably refuse to be so addressed in this way. On what authority are we told that these traits are masculine and these feminine ? And how can we be even sure that the last thing which can be said of the sexes on this plane will not be fatally identical with the first, namely, the hostility of the sexes ? Who can say whether the imperatives thus acquired, even if they command notice, will not be simply challenges in that conflict whose unhappy beginnings we observed in the world of the hamster. But if these descriptions fail us the moment we take them seriously and change them into imperatives, it is evident that we have moved on to ground which may be interesting but is extremely insecure. What, then, is the point of these typologies ? They may have value in other directions, but they are certainly not adapted to be a valid law for male and female, and we can only cause the greatest confusion if we try to exalt them into such a law and use them as such. It is for this reason that we for our part refuse to do so.

The specific differentiation particularly of male and female which is at issue in the divine command and its requirement of fidelity lies somewhere above and beyond the sphere in which such typologies are relatively possible and practicable. The command of God comes to man and woman in the relationship and order in which God created them to be together as His image, as the likeness of His covenant of grace, in the male or female existence which they gain in His eyes within the framework of their character as likeness and image. Thus it is the command of God itself which tells them what here and now is their male or female nature, and what they have to guard faithfully as such. As the divine command is itself free from the systematisation by which man and woman seek to order and clarify their thoughts about their differentiation, so, in requiring fidelity, it frees man and woman from the self-imposed compulsion of such systematisation. To what male or female nature must they both be true ? Precisely to that to which they are summoned and engaged by the divine command—to that which it imposes upon them as it confronts them with its here-and-now requirement. As this encounters them, their particular sexual nature will not be hidden from them. And in this way the divine command permits man and woman continually and particularly to discover their specific sexual nature, and to be faithful to it in this form which is true before God, without being enslaved to any preconceived opinions.

The temptation which arises in face of this first and fundamental demand for fidelity has two forms. The first is that the sexes might wish to exchange their special vocations, what is required of the one or the other as such. This must not happen. It involves a movement of flight which may be particularly attractive to those who for any reason cannot find a suitable partner and in the isolation of their existence feel so much the more oppressively the peculiar weakness of their sex. Yet they are none the less called to be whole and genuine men and women, not seeking to evade their sexuality, but in their own way having to express it just as honourably and being enabled to live in it just as cheerfully as others. But the problem may present itself just as acutely within marriage. And here supremely, as in all the concrete relationships between man and woman, it is important to recognise that each man and woman owes it not only to himself but also to the other always to be faithful to his own sexual characteristics. Fellowship is always threatened when there is a failure at this point either on the one side or the other. Of course, it is not a question of keeping any special masculine or feminine standard. We have just seen that the systematisations to which we might be tempted in this connexion do not yield any practicable imperatives. Different ages, peoples and cultures have had very different ideas of what is concretely appropriate, salutary and necessary in man and woman as such. But this does not mean that the distinction between masculine and non-masculine or feminine and unfeminine being, attitude and action is illusory. Just because the command of God is not bound to any standard it makes this distinction all the more sharply and clearly. This distinction insists upon being observed. It must not be blurred on either side. The command of God will always point man to his position and woman to hers. In every situation, in face of every task and in every conversation, their functions and possibilities, when they are obedient to the command, will be distinctive and diverse, and will never be interchangeable. Not every apparent violation is, of course, a real one. Life is richer, and above all the command of God is more manifold, than might appear from preconceived opinions. Not every apparent offence is a real one. But there are real violations and offences. They arise where the one sex or the other forgets, or for any reason refuses to acknowledge, that it has its right and dignity only in relation to the opposite sex and therefore in distinction from it. Such a forgetting or refusal will immediately disclose itself even outwardly as a blunder, error or disturbance. The root of fellow-humanity and of humanity generally is thus affected. A desire which at this point might include jealousy, envy, imitation or usurpation can never in any circumstances be good, whereas a pure desire will constantly and surely lead man and woman back to their place. . . .

Quite apart from the feminist movement, there is hardly a possibility of everyday life which is ethically irrelevant in this respect or falls outside the scope of this distinction, even down to the problems of dress and outward bearing. Nothing is indifferent in this connexion. The decision with regard to this requirement of faithfulness to sex is made at every point by both man and woman. The famous veil which the women of Corinth (1 Cor. 11) refused to wear any longer was obviously a subject of this decision in the then circumstances. This question is connected with that of order to which we shall come later. But it has also these general implications. The women of Corinth, like so many after them, had heard something of the truth which Paul himself had proclaimed in Gal. 3^{28}, that in Christ Jesus all are one—Jew and Greek, bond and free, and male and female. What was more natural than to infer that in their gatherings they should wish to have a similar external appearance to that of the men ? But we must not blame Paul if he did not interpret his saying of Gal. 3^{28} in this way, in the sense of a cancellation of the sexual distinction between man and woman, of an evasion of the command of God relevant at this point, but threatened these women with the greatest displeasure on the part of the watching angels (v. 10), and devoted sixteen whole verses to this question of their wearing veils. It was not a matter of superfluous legalism, nor of any depreciation or humiliation of woman—Gal, 3^{28} makes this

204

inconceivable—but of reminding woman of her peculiar dignity and rights. The recollection of this brought Paul to a final stand where he could not yield an inch. But why should women blame him for this ? In resisting the women of Corinth he was contending for their own true cause. And appearances must be very deceptive if in the much more debated direction of 1 Cor. 14$^{33\text{ff.}}$, where they are told not to speak but to be silent in the assembly, he was really relegating them to an inferior position. " If any man think himself to be a prophet, or spiritual, let him acknowledge that the things that I write unto you are the commandments of the Lord " (v. 37). The command of the Lord does not put anyone, man or woman, in a humiliating, dishonourable or unworthy position. It puts both man and woman in their proper place. Interpretations may vary as to where this place is, for the Lord is a living Lord and His command is ever new. It is certainly foolish to try to make an inflexible rule of the particular interpretation of Paul in this instance. It is undoubtedly the case that women may also not wear veils and actually speak in the assembly. But this is not the most important point to be gathered from 1 Cor. 11 and 14 in the present context. The essential point is that woman must always, and in all circumstances, be woman ; that she must feel and conduct herself as such and not as a man ; that the command of the Lord, which is for all eternity, directs both man and woman to their own proper sacred place and forbids all attempts to violate this order. The command may be given a different interpretation from that of Paul, for it is the living command of the living Lord, but if it is to be respected at all, it cannot even for a moment or in any conceivable sense be disregarded in this its decisive expression and requirement.

But the temptation which we have to see and avoid in this connexion may take a very different form. The desire to violate fidelity to one's own sex does not now think in terms of an exchange with the nature and character-istics of the opposite sex. It aspires beyond its own and the opposite sex to a third and supposedly higher mode of being, possible to both sexes and indifferent to both. What is sought is a purely human being which is male or female only externally, incidentally and on a lower plane, in respect of psychological and biological conditioning, perhaps only *per nefas* on the basis of a historical or metaphysical disturbance and perversion, but in any case only temporarily and provisionally. What is sought is a purely human being which in itself and properly is semi-sexual and therefore, in relation to its apparent bi-sexuality, sexless, abstractly human, and to that extent, a third and distinctive being as compared with male and female. There can be no doubt that what we have here is a more sublime and lofty and spiritualised form of that movement of escape. It is no accident that this type of consciousness has been traditionally impregnated with the magic fragrance of so much mysticism, mythology and gnosis. It is a movement in which man and woman aspire to overcome their sexual and separated mode of existence and to transcend it by a humanity which is neither distinctively male nor female but both at once, or neither.

On the one hand this movement can be presented and defended as the attempt at an idealistic solution of the problem of the single man or woman, or as a reason for the decision to live a sexually lonely life. What need have I of a sexual partner, and what difference does it make that in certain circumstances I have to resign the idea of one, and therefore of love and marriage, if at some depth of existence I can be feminine even as a man or masculine as a woman and thus embody in myself alone the whole of human being ? On the other hand, it can make itself out to be the deepest and truest fulfilment of love and marriage. The first and last word in this matter is not the fact that man and woman meet as such and unite in their dualism, but rather the overcoming of this dualism, the realisation of the destiny and aspiration of both to transcend their particularity and distinction, and together to be or to aspire to the one and undivided human being, in which not humanity, not the fellowship of the sexes, but sexual indifference and therefore the totality of humanity, or at any rate orientation towards this indifference and totality, is the meaning of *eros* and marriage.

It is obvious that this rejected religio-metaphysical interpretation of the whole sphere of man and woman can take very profound and concrete forms. Nor is it easy to criticise this theory and the corresponding practice. It

206

seems somewhere very near the indisputable truth that in the being of man and woman, distinctive and related, we have to do with the genuine humanity of both. And it seems to commend itself only too well from an ethical standpoint as a serious illumination and purification of this whole sphere, emanating from a higher angle of vision. But the fact remains that if the divine command is valid and relevant in this sphere we must object no less earnestly to this view and the resultant conduct than to everything which necessarily entails effeminacy in the male or mannishness in the female. We can certainly accept the humanisation of this sphere, but not in such a way as would neutralise the sexes, for this would finally mean dehumanisation. Outside their common relationship to God there is no point in the encounter and fellowship of man and woman at which even as man and woman they can also transcend their sexuality. And precisely in the relationship to God, they cannot do this in such a way that they cease to be male and female or that their sexuality becomes non-essential, in such a way that they become or even can aspire to be a third higher type of being. In his relationship to God man does not become a god. He becomes genuinely and definitely a man. He is put in his proper place, which is that of a man or woman. The fact that man and woman transcend themselves in their relationship to God does not therefore mean that their encounter and fellowship would cease to be real encounter and fellowship. But they transcend themselves, becoming more than man and woman in their particularity and distinction, in the fact that God Himself in His unity is their unity, that their encounter and fellowship are guaranteed by His unity, and that this may be recognised and confessed by them. God is the One for them, and this very fact saves them from having to become one amongst themselves and prevents them from trying to do so. That God created man as male and female, and therefore as His image and the likeness of the covenant of grace, of the relationship between Himself and His people, between Christ and His community, is something which can never lead to a neutral It, nor found a purely external, incidental and transient sexuality, but rather an inward, essential and lasting order of being as He and She, valid for all time and also for eternity. The fact that they are male and female does not destroy the fact that they are man, nor merge into it. They are man as they are male and female, not as they are neither or both at some basic depth of the human, and not as they can expect to be neither or both in some *eschaton* of the human. And if the command of God concerns and reaches them at all, then it finds them as male and female, and in this way as man. And the first thing which it requires of them is simply that, confessing and acknowledging their unity in the unity of God, they should not leave behind or beneath them these concrete forms of their humanity, and especially that they should not aspire to sexless or bi-sexual humanity on the ground that it would be so fine and noble and glorious, so emancipating and purifying for human existence in this sphere, if male and female could somewhere transcend their sex, surrendering their sexual particularity and distinction in favour of a higher and better form of humanity which embraces both male and female and overcomes the division between them. We should never want to know better than God the Creator whose will in this respect as in others is simple and clear. We should be content to investigate and embody this simple and clear will of His—it is sufficiently deep and rich and living as such—and not try to emulate it with our own arbitrary profundities.

Here, too, we must see and respect the limit drawn by the command of God. It is incontestable that for male and female both in themselves and in their relationship to each other (through love and marriage or outside this special connexion), it is a question of the actualisation of humanity, and this must take place in the realisation of the fact that they belong indissolubly together and are necessary the one to the other for their mutual completion. But we have to remember that on this line of thought there is a point where good inevitably becomes evil and sense nonsense if this actualisation is sought outside obedience to God's command. There is a point at which the incontestable truth that male and female as such are together man becomes a lie when it is not significantly counterbalanced by the recognition that man as such is male or female and not a third term. There is a point at which the good work of mutual completion ceases to be good if it becomes the representation of a myth which has its foundation neither in the will of the Creator nor in the reality of His creature and therefore has no foundation at all, except to warn us against the sin of *hubris*, of wanting to be the whole either individually or together. There is a point at which even orientation towards the one God in which man and woman individually and together are true man can degenerate into the orientation towards an idea or principle or idol or demon if we do not take due warning of the possibility of exchanging the unity of God for a neutral unity of our own arbitrary invention. There is a point on this line where right can become wrong, the sublime ridiculous, freedom captivity. Here again we cannot lay down as a general rule what the point is when the faithfulness required of man is still preserved or already denied, and therefore what is the limit defined by the command of God. But there is a criterion which can help us to identify the limit in any given case. All is well so long and so far as man and woman, as they seek to be man individually and together whether in or outside the union of love and marriage, are not merely fully aware of their sexuality, but honestly glad of it, thanking God that they are allowed to be members of their particular sex and therefore soberly and with a good conscience going the way marked out for them by this distinction. But things are far from well if man or woman or both seek to be man in such a way that in virtue of a fancied higher being their sex becomes indifferent or contemptible or vexatious or even hateful, a burden which they bear unwillingly and from which they would gladly emancipate themselves as they ask after God and seek to be human. This is the starting-point of the flight from God which inevitably becomes a flight into inhumanity. This, then, is the limit to be drawn in this matter. And this is the question which has to be put to establish it, and to decide whether one has transgressed it or not. . . .

We proceed to a second principle, which again extends to the whole sphere. Looking now in the opposite direction, we maintain that in obedience to the divine command there is no such thing as a self-contained and self-sufficient male life or female life. In obedience to the divine command, the life of man is ordered, related and directed to

209

that of the woman, and that of the woman to that of the man. What we have to say in this connexion is summed up in a verse which we have already quoted from 1 Cor. 11^{11}: " Nevertheless neither is the man without the woman, neither the woman without the man, in the Lord." This is true of man and woman in marriage, but not only of them. We remember that to say man *or* woman is also, rightly understood, to say man *and* woman. The dissociation and diversity which we have so far emphasised, the demand for fidelity to one's own sex which has hitherto been our concern in its twofold aspect, certainly cannot be taken to mean that there is such a thing as an abstract masculinity and corresponding femininity which it is our task and aim to exalt, cherish and preserve as such. The position to which we were directed as the true and distinctive position for each sex is for each man and woman, whether within marriage or without, a position which is open to its opposite. One cannot occupy it, nor fulfil the requirement of fidelity to one's sex, without being aware of woman if one is a man, or of man if a woman. And openness to the opposite is not an incidental and dispensable attribute of this position; it constitutes its very essence. All the other conditions of masculine and feminine being may be disputable, but it is inviolable, and can be turned at once into an imperative and taken with the utmost seriousness, that man is directed to woman and woman to man, each being for the other a horizon and focus, and that man proceeds from woman and woman from man, each being for the other a centre and source. This mutual orientation constitutes the being of each. It is always in relationship to their opposite that man and woman are what they are in themselves. We must be clear that relationship does not mean transition and dissolution. It does not mean a denial of one's own sex or an open or secret exchange with its opposite. On the contrary, it means a firm adherence to this polarity and therefore to one's own sex, but only in so far as such adherence is not self-centred but expansive, not closed but open, not concentric but eccentric. Relationship to woman in this sense makes the man a man, and her relationship to man in this sense makes the woman a woman. To become sexually awake, ripe and active, to be true to one's own sex, means for both man and woman to be awake to this polar relationship, ripe for it and active in it, to remain true to it. To this extent our second principle corresponds with the first, and the first can be properly grasped only in the light of the second. It is the equivalence of the being of both sexes with this relationship which legitimately replaces the many typologies which have been attempted, and makes them completely superfluous.

It cannot be objected that this relationship differs on the two sides. This is, of course, true, for man's relationship to and from woman is different from the corresponding relationship of woman. He is ordered, related and directed to her very differently from what she is to him. We shall return to this point in a third principle in which it will be a question of the order within the relationship. The relationship, and therefore the being of man and of woman, does not subsist apart from this order. But it is not this order which creates the relationship and makes the man man and the woman woman. It is where there is this relationship, where the man is man and the woman woman, that the order is operative and revealed. We shall have to concern ourselves with it as a *conditio sine qua non*, but only when we have recognised the relationship itself and therefore the being and distinctive difference of the sexes as determined by it, i.e., as they are ordered, related and directed the one to the other. And in this recognition the reciprocity of the sexes, and therefore that which they have in common, must take absolute precedence of the difference in their modes of interrelation. In other words, the similarity in their interrelationship must be more important in the first instance than the illuminating and fundamental dissimilarity in which it is realised. Or, to put it in yet another way, we must first consider their mutual co-ordination, for it is only on this basis that we can properly understand the order which obtains within it.

We have here a nodal point in our whole investigation and representation of " freedom in community " generally, and particularly typical of the freedom in the community of man and woman. The truth which we have to enunciate is that in Christ Jesus there is neither male nor female (Gal. 3[28]), which means that like Jew and Gentile or slave and free they are one in Him, and stand upon an equal footing. But if they are one in Him, standing upon an equal footing, this means that they are what they are for themselves as they are ordered, related and directed to each other. The Jew is a Jew in the Lord only, but precisely, to the extent that he confronts and is confronted by the Greek. The free man is free in the Lord only, but precisely, to the extent that the slave is associated with him and he with the slave. Similarly the male is a male in the Lord only, but precisely, to the extent that he is with the female, and the female likewise. That they are one in the Lord holds them together. It allows and commands them to be together. And it is the basis of their distinction, which is rooted in the fact that they have their essence in the fact that they are directed to be in fellowship. Because their freedom is that which they have from and before and for God, therefore it can take shape only in their fellowship with each other, and their humanity can consist concretely only in the fact that they live in fellow-humanity, male with female, and female with male. Every right of man and woman stands or falls with the observance and maintenance of this rule, and every wrong consists in its contravention.

This rule is from this standpoint the command of God. If we are to be obedient to the divine command we cannot regard ourselves as dispensed from its observance. It is clear that in it we have to do with the fundamental law of love and marriage in so far as it must be in particular the law of the being and attitude of a particular man in relation to a particular woman and *vice versa*. But the woman is the partner of the single man too, not woman in general, not an idea of woman, certainly not the Virgin Mary, but the concrete and definite form of woman encountering him in a particular way. She does actually encounter him too, being unmistakeably present for him at varying distances and in many different ways, even though she does not come into question as a companion in love or marriage. She is woman for him too, whether as mother, sister, acquaintance, friend or fellow-worker, just as she is also present in all these and other forms—and always as woman —for the man who is bound by love and marriage. Similarly, the man is undoubted partner of the single woman, not (it is to be hoped not !) as an epitome or ideal form of manhood, as the heavenly bridegroom and such like, but as the real man who encounters her in concrete and definite form, not as a companion in love and marriage, but no less truly as a man in kinship, acquaintance, friendship and vocation than he is in relation to the woman to whom he is specially and individually bound. That the man is and should be with the woman, and the woman with the man, applies to the whole sphere of relationships now under consideration, and in this regard the primary and fundamental formulation of the relevant command should be as follows—that whether in love and marriage or outside this bond, every woman and every man should realise that he is committed to live consciously and willingly in this interrelationship, not regarding his being abstractly as his own but as being in fellowship, and shaping it accordingly.

As against this, everything which points in the direction of male or female seclusion, or of religious or secular orders or communities, or of male or female segregation—if it is undertaken in principle and not consciously and temporarily as an emergency measure—is obviously disobedience. All due respect to the comradeship of a company of soldiers ! But neither men nor women can seriously wish to be alone, as in clubs and ladies' circles. Who commands or permits them to run away from each other ? That such an attitude is all wrong is shown symptomatically in the fact that every artificially induced and maintained isolation of the sexes tends as such— usually very quickly and certainly morosely and blindly— to become philistinish in the case of men and precious in that of women, and in both cases more or less inhuman. It is well to pay heed even to the first steps in this direction.

These first steps may well be symptoms of the malady called homosexuality. This is the physical, psychological and social sickness, the phenomenon of perversion, decadence and decay, which can emerge when man refuses to admit the validity of the divine command in the sense in which we are now considering it. In Rom. 1 Paul connected it with idolatry, with changing the truth of God into a lie, with the adoration of the creature instead of the Creator (v. 25). " For this cause God gave them up unto vile affections : for even their women did change the

213

natural use into that which is against nature : and likewise also the men, leaving the natural use of the woman,
burned in their lust one toward another ; men with men
working that which is unseemly, and receiving in themselves the recompence of their error which was meet "
(vv. 26–27). From the refusal to recognise God there
follows the failure to appreciate man, and thus humanity
without the fellow-man (*C.D.* III, 2, p. 229 ff.). And
since humanity as fellow-humanity is to be understood in
its root as the togetherness of man and woman, as the
root of this inhumanity there follows the ideal of a masculinity free from woman and a femininity free from man.
And because nature or the Creator of nature will not be
trifled with, because the despised fellow-man is still there,
because the natural orientation on him is still in force,
there follows the corrupt, emotional and finally physical
desire in which—in a sexual union which is not and cannot
be genuine—man thinks that he must seek and can find
in man, and woman in woman, a substitute for the despised
partner. But there is no sense in reminding man of the
command of God only when he is face to face with this
ultimate consequence, or pointing to the fact of human disobedience only when this malady breaks out openly in
these unnatural courses. Naturally the command of God
is opposed to these courses. This is almost too obvious to
need stating. It is to be hoped that, in awareness of God's
command as also of His forgiving grace, the doctor, the
pastor trained in psycho-therapy, and the legislator and
judge—for the protection of threatened youth—will put
forth their best efforts. But the decisive word of Christian
ethics must consist in a warning against entering upon the
whole way of life which can only end in the tragedy of
concrete homosexuality. We know that in its early stages
it may have an appearance of particular beauty and
spirituality, and even be redolent of sanctity. Often it
has not been the worst people who have discovered and
to some extent practised it as a sort of wonderful esoteric
of personal life. Nor does this malady always manifest
itself openly, or, when it does so, in obvious or indictable
forms. Fear of ultimate consequences can give as little
protection in this case, and condemnation may be as
feeble a deterrent, as the thought of painful consequences

in the case of fornication. What is needed is that the recognition of the divine command should cut sharply across the attractive beginnings. The real perversion takes place, the original decadence and disintegration begins, where man will not see his partner of the opposite sex and therefore the primal form of fellow-man, refusing to hear his question and to make a responsible answer, but trying to be human in himself as sovereign man or woman, rejoicing in himself in self-satisfaction and self-sufficiency. The command of God is opposed to the wonderful esoteric of this *beata solitudo*. For in this supposed discovery of the genuinely human man and woman give themselves up to the worship of a false god. It is here, therefore, that for himself and then in relation to others each must be brought to fear, recollection and understanding. This is the place for protest, warning and conversion. The command of God shows him irrefutably—in clear contradiction to his own theories—that as a man he can only be genuinely human with woman, or as a woman with man. In proportion as he accepts this insight, homosexuality can have no place in his life, whether in its more refined or cruder forms.

The commanded orientation of the sexes on one another, which constitutes the essence of each, can be summed up under three heads. They are to consider one another, to hear the question which each puts to the other and to make responsible answer to one another.

To consider one another means to know, or more precisely to want to know, about one another : not, then, as if they already knew about one another ; not on the basis of a preconceived general or even personal judgment of men about women or of women about men ; but with unprejudiced eyes and generous hearts, always ready to learn something new, to turn the corner and see something better. Among the immediate data of existence there is certainly no greater riddle for man than the fact of the existence of woman and the question as to her nature. And on the other hand the same applies to women. We need not think that a man can exist without encountering this riddle and being occupied with it, nor need we think that he has already solved it. To live humanly means never to escape the astonishment of one's own sex

215

at the other, and the desire of one's sex to understand the other.

But each sex has also to realise that it is questioned by the other. The puzzle which the opposite sex implies for it is not theoretical but practical, not optional but obligatory, not factual but human. It is the great human puzzle which as man and woman they put to one another in their mutual confrontation. As man and woman are human in their co-existence and mutual confrontation, neither the one nor the other can be content with his own sexuality or heedlessly work out his sexually conditioned capacities, needs, interests, tendencies, joys and sorrows. Man is unsettled by woman and woman by man. There is always this unsettlement by the opposite sex where there is the encounter of man and woman. Each is asked by the opposite sex : Why, *quo iure*, are you *de facto* so utterly different from myself ? Can and will you guarantee that your mode of life which disconcerts me is also human ? Can you show me this in such a way that I can understand it ? There is such a thing as a silent but severe criticism which tacitly but persistently and in all conceivable forms passes between man and woman in their mutual relationships. The woman stands always in a certain tension to the man, and the man to the woman. No one can escape this unsettlement, this criticism and tension. To live humanly means to hear and face this question at the expense on both sides of self-glorification or simply of self-satisfaction.

And the question challenges both man and woman to act in responsibility to each other. As they consider one another and necessarily realise that they question each other, they become mutually, not the law of each other's being (for each must be true to his particularity), but the measure or criterion of their inner right to live in their sexual distinctiveness. Man can be and speak and act as a true man only as he realises that in so doing he must answer the question of woman, i.e., give her an account of his humanity. Much that is typically masculine would have to be left unsaid and undone, or said and done quite differently, if man remembered that in it, if it is to be truly masculine, he must prove his humanity in the eyes of woman, to whom he constitutes so great a question mark. For example, might not the very dubious masculine enterprise of war become intrinsically impossible if the remembrance of the confrontation with woman were suddenly to be given the normative significance which is undoubtedly its due ? When man excuses himself from this recollection, he strengthens rather than dispels woman's natural doubt of his humanity. And the more he strengthens her doubt, and the bond of fellowship between them is therefore weakened, so much the more doubtful does his humanity become even objectively, and so much the more is humanity as such called in question for both sides. On the other hand, exactly the same can be said of feminine being and speaking and acting. Woman, too, is challenged by the natural criticism of man to prove herself human in his eyes. If she may and must live out her life as woman, she too must consider that she has to render an account to man as he must render an account to her, that she is measured by his norms as he by hers. For this reason all the movements of man and woman in which there is an open or secret attempt to escape this reciprocal responsibility are suspect at least from the very outset. On both sides, everything is at stake here. They are not to elude their mutual responsibility, but to fulfil it. And, of course, they must fulfil it even when no representative of the opposite sex is present. As a norm and criterion the opposite sex is always and everywhere invisibly present. The divine decision that it is not good for man to be alone has been taken irrevocably ; and it applies to woman as well as to man. For both, therefore, there is only an incidental, external, provisional and transient isolation and autonomy. They elude themselves if they try to escape their orientation on one another, i.e., the fact that they are ordered, related and directed to one another. Their being is always and in all circumstances a being with the other. In obedience to God's command they will know that they are always and in all circumstances bound to remember and to do justice to the character of their existence as an existence in relationship.

We shall now take a third step, again with reference to the whole sphere of the relationship of man and woman. It brings us to the most delicate of the general questions which call for consideration at this point. The disjunction

and the conjunction of man and woman, of their sexual
independence and sexual interrelationship, is controlled by
a definite order. As the attitude and function of the man
and those of the woman must not be confused and interchanged but faithfully maintained, and as on the other
hand they must not be divorced and played off against
each other but grasped and realised in their mutual related-
ness, so they are not to be equated, nor their relationship
reversed. They stand in a sequence. It is in this that
man has his allotted place and woman hers. It is in this
that they are orientated on each other. It is in this that
they are individually and together the human creature as
created by God. Man and woman are not an A and a
second A whose being and relationship can be described
like the two halves of an hour glass, which are obviously
two, but absolutely equal and therefore interchangeable.
Man and woman are an A and a B, and cannot, therefore,
be equated. In inner dignity and right, and therefore in
human dignity and right, A has not the slightest advantage over B, nor does it suffer the slightest disadvantage.
What is more, when we say A we must with equal emphasis
say B also, and when we say B we must with equal emphasis
have said A. We have considered this equality of man
and woman as carefully as possible in our first two propositions, and not one iota of it must be forgotten or
abrogated as we now turn in the third to the order in
which their being no less than their being in fellowship is
real, and therefore to the requirement of the divine command in so far as it includes the observance of this order.
Man and woman are fully equal before God and therefore
as men and therefore in respect of the meaning and determination, the imperilling, but also the promise, of their
human existence. They are also equal in regard to the
necessity of their mutual relationship and orientation.
They stand or fall together. They become and are free or
unfree together. They are claimed and sanctified by the
command of God together, at the same time, with equal
seriousness, by the same free grace, to the same obedience
and the reception of the same benefits. Yet the fact
remains—and in this respect there is no simple equality—
that they are claimed and sanctified as man and woman,
each for himself, each in relation to the other in his own

particular place, and therefore in such a way that A is not B but A, and B is not another A but B. It is here that we see the order outside which man cannot be man nor woman be woman, either in themselves or in their mutual orientation and relationship.

Every word is dangerous and liable to be misunderstood when we try to characterise this order. But it exists. And everything else is null and void if its existence is ignored, if we refuse to recognise it as an element in the divine command, if it is left to chance. If order does not prevail in the being and fellowship of man and woman— we refer to man and woman as such and in general, to the rule which is valid both in and outside love and marriage— the only alternative is disorder. All the misuse and misunderstanding to which the conception of order is liable must not prevent us from considering and asserting the aspect of reality to which it points. A precedes B, and B follows A. Order means succession. It means preceding and following. It means super- and sub-ordination. But when we say this we utter the very dangerous words which are unavoidable if we are to describe what is at issue in the being and fellowship of man and woman. Let us proceed at once to the very necessary explanation. When it is a question of the true order which God the Creator has established, succession, and therefore precedence and following, super- and sub-ordination, does not mean any inner inequality between those who stand in this succession and are subject to this order. It does indeed reveal their inequality. But it does not do so without immediately confirming their equality. In so far as it demands subjection and obedience, it affects equally all whom it concerns. It does not confer any privilege or do any injustice. It lays a duty on all, but it also gives to all their right. It does not deny honour to any, but gives to each his own honour.

Thus man does not enjoy any privilege or advantage over woman, nor is he entitled to any kind of self-glorification, simply because in respect of order he is man, and therefore A, and thus precedes and is superior in relation to woman. This order simply points him to the position which, if he is obedient, he can occupy only in humility, or materially only as he is ordered, related and directed to woman in preceding her, taking the lead as the inspirer, leader and initiator in their common being and action. He cannot occupy it, then, for himself, let alone against her, or in self-exaltation, let alone in exaltation over her and therefore to her degradation, but as he humbles himself in obedience to the command which concerns them both, as he first frees himself from sexual self-sufficiency and takes seriously his orientation on woman, as he first enters into fellowship with her, as he first bows before the common law of humanity as fellow-humanity. Only as he accepts her as fellow-man, only together with her, can he be the first in his relationship to her—the first in a sequence which would have no meaning if she did not follow and occupy her own place in it. If it is understood in any other way, and not as a primacy of service, the pre-eminence of man is not the divine order but a particular form of human disorder. The exploitation of this order by man, in consequence of which he exalts himself over woman, making himself her lord and master and humiliating and offending her so that she inevitably finds herself oppressed and injured, has nothing whatever to do with divine order. It is understandable that woman should protest and rebel against this exploitation, although she ought to realise at once that here as elsewhere protesting and rebelling are one thing and the way from disorder to order quite another. It cannot be a question of woman attaining her rights as opposed to man and his, but of man's understanding the order and sequence and therefore the obligation in which he is the first, of his primarily submitting and rendering obedience to the common law instead of standing upon his own rights, of his not neglecting in his own favour—or his own disfavour—the required initiative of service in the common cause of humanity, but of assuming and discharging it. By simply protesting and rebelling, woman, even though she were a thousand times in the right, does not affirm and respect the order under which she also stands and by which alone she can vindicate her rights. Indeed, it may well be that her protesting and rebelling spring from the same source of contempt for order with which man offends her so deeply. The real service which she ought to render in this matter—indirectly in her own favour—is certainly not yet performed by the mere fact of her opposing man when he turns order into disorder.

For woman does not come short of man in any way nor renounce her right, dignity and honour, nor make any surrender, when theoretically and practically she recognises that in order she is woman and therefore B, and therefore behind and subordinate to man. This order gives her her proper place, and in pride that it is hers, she may and should assume it as freely as man assumes his. She, too, has to realise that she is ordered, related and directed to man and has thus to follow the initiative which he must take. Nor is this a trifling matter. Properly speaking, the business of woman, her task and function, is to actualise the fellowship, in which matter man can only precede her, stimulating, leading and inspiring. How could she do this alone, without the precedence of man? How could she do it for herself and against him? How could she reject or envy his precedence, his task and function, as the one who stimulates, leads and inspires? To wish to replace him in this, or to do it with him, would be to wish not to be a woman. She does not admit any false superiority on his part when she not merely grants him this primacy of service, for it can be nothing more, but is glad that man has and exercises this function in the common service of the common cause of humanity, he himself being also subject to order in his own place. Why should not woman be the second in sequence, but only in sequence? What other choice has she, seeing she can be nothing at all apart from this sequence and her place within it? And why should she desire anything else, seeing this function and her share in the common service has its own special honour and greatness, an honour and greatness which man in his place and within the limits of his function cannot have? Is it then settled—if such things can be settled—that the honour and greatness peculiar to her position, the honour and greatness possible to her in her subordinate role, cannot possibly exceed his? At least there can be no doubt that the subordination about which woman is entitled to complain is certainly not that which is envisaged in the divine order in which she has second place as woman. On the other hand the establishment of an equality with man might well lead to a state of affairs in which her position is genuinely and irreparably deplorable because both it and that of man are as it were left hanging in the void. If she occupies and retains her proper place, she will not merely complain even when man for his part does not keep to his place and thus encroaches upon her rights. The goodness and justice of the divine order are not transformed into evil and injustice even for those who have to suffer from its misunderstanding and abuse by others. Even then it is better that she on her side should not infringe but observe it. If there is a way of bringing man to repentance, it is the way of the woman who refuses to let herself be corrupted and made disobedient by his disobedience, but who in spite of his disobedience maintains her place in the order all the more firmly. . . .

The divine command, which is our concern, will thus always require from man that he should observe and maintain this order, wherever and in whatever circumstances man and woman meet and live together. Since God is the same God at all times, in all places and situations and in regard to all men, but is also a living God, Ruler and therefore Commander, it is not to be expected that the conduct which He requires, the obedience consistent with His command, will always and everywhere and for all individuals have the same form and expression. The divinely willed order remains the same. Its application to what God requires yesterday and to-day, here and there, from this man and that, varies, and so does also the content of the conduct which is commanded or forbidden, obedient or disobedient. Here again ethics must not become casual. Nor may we wish to fetter the divine command and thus the divine order concerning the relationship of man and woman by any system, whether old or new, traditional or progressive. It may not be adapted to any arrangements, customs, manners or even advances in human conduct and action, in which this order might be supposed to be preserved as opposed to other arrangements and customs in which it might be supposed to be infringed. But ethics can and must call our attention to the crossroads at which man and woman, every man and every woman both in marriage and outside it, are always placed by the very fact that God's command uncompromisingly requires of them the observance of divine order in their relationships. Here, too, ethics can and must suggest the points of view from which we should ask concerning good and evil in the light of this order. It can and must indicate the very question which man and woman must answer in this respect, and in the answering of which it will be seen whether they stand in obedience or in disobedience. This is the task to which we must now briefly address ourselves. It will inevitably entail a certain systematisation, almost a kind of woodcut.

The man who confronts woman in accordance with this order and therefore in obedience is always the strong man, which means the man who is conscious of his special responsibility for the maintenance of this order, and is engaged in practising it. It should be noted that it is not a question of his manly dignity and honour, even less of his masculine wishes and interests, but rather of his masculine responsibility for this order. The obedient man will in his proper place as a man set himself in its service. He will not leave it to chance whether the order subsists and prevails. Nor will he wait for woman to do her part in serving it. On the contrary, he will forestall her in this. And because for him, too, it is only a question of service, he will do so without arrogance or pretentiousness, but naturally and without embarrassment. In so doing, he will not feel superior to woman. He will really be superior only in so far as he will primarily accept as his own a concern for the right communion of the sexes as secured by this order, and therefore for the order itself. He is strong to the extent that he accepts as his own affair service to the order and in this order. He is strong as he is vigilant for the interests of both sexes. This is what is intended and tenable in the otherwise rather doubtful idea of chivalry. To the man who is strong in this sense there corresponds, when woman is obedient, the woman who is mature, i.e., whose only thought is to take up the position which falls to her in accordance with this order, desiring nothing better than that this order should be in force, and realising that her own independence, honour and dignity, her own special wishes and interests, are best secured within it. Thus in regard to the precedence which she sees man assume in this matter, she will feel no sense of inferiority

223

nor impulse of jealousy. She will not consider herself to be attacked by this, but promoted and protected. She will see guarded by it just what she herself desires to see guarded. She has no need to assert herself by throwing out a challenge to man. She will perceive the opportunity which man places within her grasp. She will not merely accept his concern for the order and for herself, but make it her joy and pride as woman to be worthy of this concern, i.e., to be a free human being alongside man and in fellowship with him. If things go well, the strong man will summon woman to this maturity, and the mature woman will summon man to be a strong man. But the obedience of man and woman do not depend on the successful evocation of a response by this summons, on the actualisation of this reciprocity. There is on both sides also a solitary unanswered and apparently ineffective obedience which perhaps as such has all the more weight and inner grandeur. Wherever the true path may lead or not lead, there can be no doubt that it is to be sought in this direction both by man and by woman.

We may now oppose to this the contrasting picture, and we shall begin, as is fitting, with man. The tyrant is always disobedient in relation to this order. He need not be cruel or bad-tempered. There are quiet, gentle, amiable, easy-going tyrants who suit women only too well, and it is an open question in which form the male tyrant is worse and more dangerous. The distinctive characteristic of the tyrannical as opposed to the strong man is that he does not serve the order but makes the order serve himself. It interests him only in so far as he falsely supposes that it confers distinction upon him and gives him an advantage over women. He changes it into an instrument for the seizing and exerting of power in favour of his supposed masculine dignity and honour, wishes and interests. It is not for him a duty, but a need and a pleasure, to take precedence of woman. It is for him an end in itself to take advantage of her. Just because there cannot intrinsically be such a thing as the man who in himself and as such is a superior being, he must be all the more intensively concerned to play the role of lord and master, or at any rate of the all-wise and almighty, in relation to woman. And because the order persists even though it is misunderstood and abused, he finds ready to hand the means to do so. So he bluffs, and he has the advantage of possessing at least the instrument with which to do it. He preens himself, as the peacock its feathers. In his own refined or crude, convincing or ridiculous manner, he plays as best he can the part of the male. And only too often, unfortunately, complacent woman plays up to him, allowing such behaviour to impress and please her, and in fact actually inviting it. She forgets that she, too, has her responsibility. She is only too pleased to be relieved of it. She adapts herself to the attitude and role of the flexible and compliant person who waits on the other's moods. She plays on her side the counterpart which the tyrant expects to see and which is necessary to the success of his own performance. She discovers in advance what is expected of her and fulfils it to the letter. She finds it convenient to make things as convenient as possible for him. She also finds it attractive—and the clever tyrant will certainly support this view—to be his pliable kitten, his flattering mirror. In pleasing him, she thus pleases herself. And she, too, will play her part all the more craftily because it is only a part, because the submissive woman in this sense has no real existence, having no place in the order of the relationship of man and woman. She, too, abuses the order. She, too, lives on an appearance of it. She, too, is strong by the truth which she makes into a lie. In this case man and woman are thus corresponding forms of disobedience. The tyrannical man and the compliant woman mutually encourage each other. But this does not always happen. The submissive woman does not always encounter the tyrant, nor will the tyrant always encounter the submissive woman. The resultant conflict is at least more promising than the peace which ensues when these counterparts meet and find each other. But whether in isolation or co-operation, this is the contrasting picture of a disobedience which can take place on either side or both in violation of the order, but ought not to do so.

Let us now follow this development rather further, and first on the side of the woman. Since the tyranny of the man and compliance of the woman both imply what is disobedient and wrong, it is *ipso facto* decided that they cannot maintain the positions taken up. This impossibility is especially clear in the case of woman, for even when she co-operates she is in fact the one who is injured and suffers. The disorder will be avenged on her first, although it puts man, too, in an impossible position. But she will be the first to seek to extricate herself. By a return to order and therefore by becoming mature? Perhaps! But perhaps also by a deeper involvement in disorder. For somewhere in the submissive woman there lies concealed—not merely crouching in readiness, but already active—the rebellious woman. In her own way even the submissive woman illegitimately exercises power over man. By her very compliance—she knows well enough what she is about—she grasps at control over man. She avenges herself for his tyranny by performing so exactly the part which he desires her to play. In her voluntary weakness and readiness to yield, she acquires authority over him and is secretly the stronger. But this secret state of affairs can and must break out and come into the open. The order which is only apparently respected, but in reality abused and perverted, can clearly be challenged and infringed openly. Where it is not really obeyed, it may one day occur to woman to question not only the claimed prerogatives and postured lordship but also the real primacy of man, openly abandoning her position and snatching power from his hands. This dramatic turn obviously demands a change of scenery. Claim is now met by counter-claim, power by power, tyrant by tyrant. What objection can man bring when he himself and primarily is a transgressor of the order? The conflict thus starts in real earnest. It is now to be seen which will prove the stronger party. But whatever the result, on neither side is there right in the true and Christian sense. Let us suppose that woman's open or concealed revolt is successful. In fact it must often be more successful than would appear. The prospects of man in this encounter are none too good. In this case, man will obviously emerge as the weak man. That he was not really superior as he ought to have been according to the demands of the order, he has betrayed already by the fact that he felt compelled to proclaim his lordship so loudly and could thus become a tyrant. It is now clear that he could only assume the

226

role of lord, as also the submissive woman was only playing a part. The magnificent garb of the tyrant now becomes torn and thin. He may continue to play his role *pro forma*. But woman sees through him. She no longer believes, nor does he, that in their relationship he is the first and she the second. As he misused his position as the first and she refuses any longer to be the second, as neither is controlled nor assigned to his place by an order, there is no ambivalence, but the woman has now become the first in the bad sense, and the man has secretly or openly surrendered his position. What man will not desperately and indignantly strive against having to admit the truth of this? To be sure, it cannot be the real truth. But where the tyranny of man and the submissiveness of woman can take place, there one day her revolt and his weakness and dependence will in some way be a fact. As the offended and humiliated party, woman does not have right on her side, but she has the appearance of right. And in this appearance of right, conjoined with the demonic power of her very weakness, she can in fact become the stronger and man the weaker. How can he now dare to assert his primacy over her? Seeing he has failed to grasp this primacy, refusing the service in which alone he might have done so, it is his weakness that he must now try to assert it. The primacy of man is either there or not. The man who must defend or struggle for it shows by this very fact that he has lost it or never possessed it, that he is a poor weakling who can be twisted around one's finger— probably very gently, usually without anything sensational, but as effectively as only rebellious woman can do—and from whom there is no longer to be expected the leadership which he should exercise in virtue of the order and which he owes to woman, so that she, too, is now really poor. The weak man will become continually weaker through the rebellion of his wife, and the rebellious wife continually more rebellious through the weakness of her husband. In short, the order will be continually loosened and disrupted. And if the worst befalls, and man succeeds in reviving the tyranny with which it all began, the *circulus vitiosus* will be completed, and the game will start all over again.

But let us now return to our discussion of obedience to

the divine command and therefore observance of the order. We referred to the mature woman. This woman will never let herself be pushed into the role of the compliant wife, whether she has to do with the strong or the tyrannical man. She will endorse the strength of the strong man which is the strength of his sense of responsibility and service, and successfully or otherwise she will negate the tyranny of the tyrant. She will do both because she is an independent element in the order which binds both man and woman. The mature woman is as such the woman who knows and takes her proper place, not in relation to man but in relation to the order. She realises that as between man and woman there can be no question of claim and counter-claim or the brutal struggle for power, but of rivalry only in regard to the right following of the path common to both but specifically allotted to each. Therefore, while she compares herself to the man, she will not compare her place and right to his. If she is challenged by him, it is not whether his attitude and function might not equally well be hers, but whether she is truly fulfilling the position and function assigned her. If she is orientated on him, it is not with the intention of imitating him, but with that of doing her part in fellowship with him. In this self-knowledge there is no resignation on the part of woman. By it she asserts rather her independence, showing her mastery, her true equality with man. There can be in it no shadow of sadness and resignation and therefore no spark of rebellion even in relation to the tyrannical and weak man. In face of an erring man the mature woman will not only be sure of herself in her quiet self-restriction, but she will also know her duty and witness towards him. Successfully or otherwise—and we now turn over another leaf—she is in her whole existence an appeal to the kindness of man. In human relationships kindness is not the same thing as condescension. It means the free impulse in which a man interests himself in his neighbour because he understands him and is aware of his obligation towards him. The self-restricting woman appeals to the kindness of man. She puts him under an obligation to be kind. The opposite is also true, but in this respect the advantage is perhaps with woman. She may win the respect of man. If he is capable of this at all, it is in face of the mature and therefore self-restricting woman. He understands such a woman, not condescendingly, or superciliously, or complacently in respect of her pliability, but with a sincere and non-patronising respect for the independence, mastery and equality which she thus evinces. Such a woman puts man under an obligation. He can and must take such a one seriously. If anything can disturb his male tyranny and therefore his male weakness, if anything can challenge him to goodness and therefore to the acceptance of woman, it is encounter with the self-restricting woman. Why? Because her maturity is displayed in her self-restriction. She need not wait for the kind man to know and limit herself, as he need not wait for the modest woman to be kind. For kindness belongs originally to his particular responsibility as a man. But we come to the point where woman may in fact be the educator of man, so long, be it noted, as she does not evade her proper subordination. And now the circle may be closed. For the kind man, who is instructed in kindness by the self-knowledge and self-restriction of the woman, is identical with the strong man with whom we commenced this discussion. What is manly strength if not the power with which man in his relationships with woman may in obedience to the order of things seize responsibility and take the initiative? As a strong man he confirms the order, the order in which woman in her place is not simply subordinate to him, but stands at his side.

It is somewhere on the border-line between this *circulus veritatis* and the *circulus vitiosus* that the decision is made on those questions of good and evil which face man and woman in their relationship to the order under which they stand and which in their being, attitude and action they must answer both individually and in their manifold inter-relations.   [III, 4, pp. 150–181]

APPENDIX

1. The Light of Life

[94] In sum, our statement distinguishes the Word spoken in the existence of Jesus Christ from all others as the Word of God. When we think of these others, we do well to include even the human words spoken in the existence and witness of the men of the Bible and the Church. In distinction from all these, Jesus Christ is the one Word of God. There are other words which are good in their own way and measure. There are other prophets in this sense. We shall return to this point. But there is only one Prophet who speaks the Word of God as He is Himself this Word, and this One is called and is Jesus. This is the substance of our statement, no more but also no less.

We shall now try to fix its more precise meaning by describing what it actually says. That Jesus is the one Word of God means first that He is the total and complete declaration of God concerning Himself and the men whom He addresses in His Word. God does satisfaction both to Himself and us in what He says in and with the existence of Jesus Christ. What He is for us and wills of us, but also what we are for Him and are ordained to be and will and do in this relationship, is exhaustively, unreservedly and totally revealed to us in Jesus Christ as the one Word of God. As this one Word He does not need to be completed by others. If we are to speak of completion, we must say that, as and because He is the living Lord Jesus Christ, He is engaged as the one Word of God in a continual completion of Himself, not in the sense that the Word spoken by Him is incomplete or inadequate, but in the sense that our hearing of it is profoundly incomplete. For He Himself is in Himself rich and strong enough to display and offer Himself to our poverty with perennial fulness. It is not His fault if we see and know so little of God and ourselves. There is thus no need to try to catch other words of God. Indeed, we must not do so, for any such word can only be the word of another god which is *per se* false in relation to the one God, and therefore it can only lead us astray from the truth of the one God and the consequent truth of man as His elect and beloved creature. Who and what the true God is, and through Him true man ; what the freedom of God is, and the freedom given by Him to man, is said to us in and with the existence of Jesus Christ as true Son of God and Son of Man in such a way that any addition can only mean a diminution and perversion of our knowledge of the truth.

That He is the one Word of God means further that He is not exposed on any third side to any serious competition, any challenge to His truth, any threat to His authority. Such a third side could only be a word of God different from that spoken in Him and superior or at least equivalent in value and force ; the word, perhaps, of a *Deus absconditus* not identical with the *Deus revelatus*, or identical only in irreconcilable contradiction. Now we have no cause to reckon with such an alien word, such a self-contradiction, on the part of God. But we have every cause to keep to the fact that He is faithful, and that in Jesus Christ we have His total and unique and therefore authentic revelation, the Word in which He does full justice both to Himself and us. To be sure, this Word meets opposition in the world, and also and supremely, as we must not forget, in the Church. To be sure, its light is resisted by darkness in the many forms of many sinister powers, all of which are connected with the sin of man, all empowered and unleashed by his falsehood, all to be taken seriously as opponents of the one Word of God. Jesus Christ can certainly be unrecognised, despised and rejected in the world and among His own people. He can be partially or even totally unheard as the one Word of God. That did happen, and happens still. But since God does not contradict but is always faithful to Himself, there is one thing that can never take place, namely, that such a sinister power and its lying words, revelations and prophecies should seriously threaten the validity and force of the one Word of God, invading and even destroying it. The living Lord Jesus Christ, risen again from the dead, has no serious rival as the one Prophet of God who does not merely attest but is the Word of God. There is none whose inferiority and final displacement is not already decided by His existence, presence and action. Who or what can rise up against God, or against Him as the one Word of God? This means in practice that no risk is involved if among the bids made by many supposed and pretended lords and prophets we trust and obey Him as *the* Lord and Prophet. He and He alone is worthy of complete trust and total obedience. None will ever repent of responding to His self-giving, and to the Word spoken in it, with a corresponding self-giving which is resolute and exclusive. " Whosoever believeth on him shall not be ashamed " (Rom. 10[11]). For, although He has enemies, He has none who can put Him to shame, or who will not be put to shame by Him.

That He is the one Word of God means further that His truth and prophecy cannot be combined with any other, nor can He be enclosed with other words in a system superior to both Him and them. As the one Word of God, He can bring Himself into the closest conjunction with such words. He can make use of certain men, making them His witnesses and confessing their witness in such a way that to hear them is to hear Him (Lk. 10[16]). He has actually entered into a union of this kind with the biblical prophets and apostles, and it is the prayer and promise in and by which His community exists that He will not refuse but be willing to enter into a similar union with it. Nor can any prevent Him entering into such a union with men outside the sphere of the Bible and the Church, and with the words of these men. Whether in the Church or the world, however, this type of union can be legitimate and fruitful only through His act, as His work, as a form of His free revelation of grace. Conversely, all syntheses which Christians or non-Christians may arbitrarily devise and create between Jesus Christ as the one Word of God and any other words, however illuminating, necessary or successful they may be ; all well-meant but capricious conjunction of Jesus Christ with something else, whether it be Mary, the Church, the fate worked out in general and individual history, a presupposed human self-understanding, etc., all these imply a control over Him to which none of us has any right, which can be only the work of religious arrogance, in which we try to invest Him with His dignity as the Lord and Prophet, in the exercise of which He ceases to be who He is, not objectively, but for those who are guilty of this rash assault, and in and with which faith in Him, love for Him and hope in Him are abandoned, however loudly or with whatever degree of subjective sincerity they may be professed. There is no legitimate place for projects in the planning and devising of which Jesus Christ can be given a particular niche in co-ordination with those of other events, powers, forms and truths. Such projects are irrelevant and unfruitful enterprises because as the one Word of God He wholly escapes every conceivable synthesis envisaged in them. They are irrelevant and unfruitful because the men who attempt them will always be content with the revelations of the other elements.

We have here the irresistible and relentless outworking of the " Thou shalt have none other gods but me " of Ex. 20^2. The sin of Israel against the God of the covenant made and continually renewed with the patriarchs did not consist so much in direct apostasy from Yahweh as in the combination and admixture of His service, invocation and acknowledgment in practical obedience, with the adoration of the numina of Canaan and other surrounding peoples. It consisted in the fact that Israel made constant experiments to do the one and not leave the other undone, not losing Yahweh yet not missing the Baalim, and therefore halting between two opinions (1 K. 18^{21}). It consisted in the fact that in its refusal to elect in accordance with its own election, it already elected, not electing Yahweh but deciding against Him and for the Baalim, and thus becoming a people alien like all others to the command of God. The remarkable but very relevant and accurate reference to the " jealousy " of Yahweh, which according to Ex. 20^5 is directed against the attempt to worship Him in fashioned images as well as in His invisible majesty, shows us clearly that He radically and automatically refuses to allow His Godhead to be equated with other divinities, or His Word to be heard with other words. Israel can look to Him alone, or not at all. It can hear Him alone, or not at all. The whole prophecy of the history of Israel as attested by the Old Testament, and therefore explicitly and implicitly all its prophets, speak along these lines.

This combining of the Word of Jesus Christ with the authority and contents of other supposed revelations and truths of God has been and is the weak point, revealed already in the *gnosis* attacked in the New Testament, at almost every point in the history of the Christian Church. The prophecy of Jesus Christ has never been flatly denied, but fresh attempts have continually been made to list it with other principles, ideas and forces (and their prophecy) which are also regarded and lauded as divine, restricting its authority to what it can signify in co-ordination with them, and therefore to what remains when their authority is also granted. Nor is this trend characteristic only of early and mediaeval Catholicism. It is seen in Protestantism too, from the very outset in certain circles, even in the Reformers themselves, and then with increasing vigour and weight, until the fatal little word " and " threatened to become the predominant word of theology even in this sphere where we might have hoped for better things in view of what seemed to be the strong enough doctrine of justification. It needed the rise of the strange but temporarily powerful sect of the German Christians of 1933 to call us back to reflection, and at least the beginning of a return, when the more zealous among them, in addition to their other abominations, awarded cultic honour to the portrait of the Führer. The overthrow of this whole attitude, and its provisional reversal, was accomplished in the first thesis of Barmen which is the theme of the present exposition. But there are other Christian nations in which it is customary to find a prominent place in the church for national flags as well as the pulpit and the Lord's table, just as there are evangelical churches which substitute for the Lord's table a meaningfully furnished apparatus for the accomplishment of baptism by immersion. These externals, of course, are trivial in themselves. But as such they may well be symptoms of the attempt which is possible in so many forms to incorporate that which is alien in other prophecies into what is proper to that of Jesus Christ. If these prophecies are prepared for this—and sooner or later they will make an open bid for sole dominion—the prophecy of Jesus Christ asks to be excused and avoids any such incorporation. If it is subjected to such combinations, the living Lord Jesus and His Word depart, and all that usually remains is the suspiciously loud but empty utterance of the familiar

234

name of this Prophet. " No man can serve two masters " (Mt. 6²⁴). No man can serve both the one Word of God called Jesus Christ and other divine words.

That He is the one Word of God means finally that His prophecy cannot be transcended by any other. It cannot be transcended in the content of its declarations, for it tells us all that it is necessary and good for us to know concerning God, man and the world, embracing, establishing and crowning all that is really worth knowing. It cannot be transcended in the depth with which it speaks the truth, for it is itself the source and norm of all truth. It cannot be transcended in the urgency with which it presents itself to man and demands to be acknowledged, recognised and confessed by him, for everyone who gives it a hearing sees that this is the one thing necessary compared with which all other hearing, however important, must be given a secondary and subordinate place. Above all, it cannot be transcended in the goodness, seriousness, comfort and wisdom of what it imparts, for all other things imparted to us, though these qualities may be ascribed to them, are inferior to it, and in respect of goodness can only be abased and exalted, disqualified and qualified, by it. In one respect alone can there be transcendence. This is not in relation to the content, depth, urgency or goodness of the one Word of God spoken in Jesus Christ. It is not its transcendence by any other word. It is the self-transcendence of Jesus Christ as the one Word of God in respect of the universality and direct and definitive clarity of the knowledge which Christianity and the world do not yet have in the time between His resurrection and ascension, but to which they look and move at His return, i.e., His total presence, action and revelation which will conclude and fulfil time and history, all times and all histories. In this *eschaton* of creation and reconciliation there will not be another Word of God. Jesus Christ will be the one Word and we shall then see the final and unequivocal form of His own glory which even now shines forth from His resurrection into time and history, all times and all histories. The theme of Christian hope, to the extent that it is not yet fulfilled nor cannot be so long as time endures, is the revelation of the fact that neither formally nor materially, theoretically nor

235

practically, can the one Word of God be transcended, as this is now confirmed in and through his self-transcendence, in virtue of which all ears hear and all eyes see all the things which already it is actually given to us to see and hear in Him. The inclusion of the eschatological element, then, does not imply any restriction, but the final expansion and deepening, of our statement that Jesus Christ is the one Word of God.   [IV, 3, pp. 99–103]

2. The Threefold Coming Again of Jesus Christ

[95] Let us try to be clear what it means if it is true that in the Easter event there has taken place the self-declaration of Jesus Christ, of His being and action in the relationship between God and man, and therefore the revelation of the reconciliation of the world with God, the immediate and perfect prophecy, by a new and specific divine act, of the divine-human High-priest and King. Let us have no reservations on the ground that what has taken place is perhaps too great for the measure of our being and understanding, nor prudent fears of the questions raised. These will come later. But they can properly come only when we first realise on what basis and with what reference they can be put and answered. Our first and unconditional objective must be to see and know what the Easter message no less unconditionally says.

In a first and very general formulation of its declaration, we venture the statement that the Easter event, as the revelation of the being and action of Jesus Christ in His preceding life and death, is His new coming as the One who had come before. As is made quite clear by the accounts in the Gospels, the One who now comes afresh and appears to His disciples is none other than the One who had come before. He is " Jesus Christ yesterday " (Heb. 13[8]), the One who yesterday acted and suffered and was finally crucified in His existence as temporally limited by His birth and death, with all the power and range and significance of this event for the whole world, but still enclosed yesterday within the limits of His existence, concealed and unknown in the world reconciled to God in

236

Him, not yet exercising the latent power and range and significance of His presence and therefore putting into effect what was done in Him for all men and for the whole created order. This One who came before now comes afresh in the Easter event. He is " Jesus Christ to-day," in all His being and action of yesterday, and its whole power for the world, new in the fact that to-day, His death and the empty tomb behind Him, He moves out from the latency of His being and action of yesterday and from the inoperativeness of His power, appearing to His disciples and in them potentially to all men and the whole cosmos, declaring Himself, making known His presence and what has been accomplished in Him for all men and for the whole created order, putting it into effect. With its manifestation and self-declaration, the fact of there and yesterday now becomes the factor of here and to-day. And in virtue of this event, newly come in His self-revelation as the One who came, Jesus Christ will not cease to be this factor and to work as such. Hence " Jesus Christ for ever " (Heb. 13⁸). As this factor, as the Prophet, Witness and Preacher entered into the world, as the light of His mediatorship, of the atonement made in Him, shining from this place, He is the living Jesus Christ, who has death behind Him, the light which shines in the world and can never be extinguished. And the world for its part is what it is enabled to be in the presence of this factor, in encounter with Him, in the shining of His light, in the determination given it by Him.

The citation in 1 Tim. 3¹⁶ from what is probably a liturgical text old even at the time of the composition of the Epistle should be allowed to speak for itself in this connexion : " He was manifest in the flesh, justified in the Spirit, seen of angels, preached unto the Gentiles, believed on in the world, received up into glory." The passage is introduced into the Epistle as a comprehensive definition of what is " by agreed confession " (ὁμολογουμένως) the one great " mystery of (Christian) godliness " (μέγα τὸ τῆς εὐσεβείας μυστήριον). Its six clauses can hardly be understood as a list of successive saving events such as we have in the oldest versions of the Christian creed. They are rather six references from different standpoints to a single event which can only be that of the resurrection or self-declaration of the living Jesus Christ as the divine act. All the references apply to this. If the passage is really a hymn, it must surely be an Easter hymn, or part of such a hymn.

It is not merely possible but imperative that what took place in the Easter event, the fresh coming of Jesus Christ as the One who came before, should be summed up under the New Testament concept of the *parousia* of Jesus Christ. However the New Testament writers may apply the term in other respects, or refer to it without application, the concrete perception with which they do so is that of the resurrection of Jesus Christ, just as conversely their notion of the resurrection is strictly identical with the full range of content of the concept of *parousia*.

The word παρουσία (cf. for what follows the article by A. Oepke in Kittel) derives from Hellenistic sources and originally means quite simply " effective presence." A *parousia* might be a military invasion, or the visitation of a city or district by a high dignitary who, as in the case of the emperor, might sometimes be treated so seriously that the local calendar would be dated afresh from the occasion. The term was also applied sometimes to the helpful intervention of such divine figures as Dionysius or Aesculapius Soter. What is signified by the term, if not the term itself, is familiar and important in the thinking of the Old Testament. From His place, whether Sinai, Sion or heaven, Yahweh comes in the storm, or enthroned over the ark of the covenant, or in His Word or Spirit, or in dreams or visions, or simply and especially in the events of the history of Israel. To the men of His people He comes finally as universal King in the unfolding of His power and glory. The coming of " one like the Son of man with the clouds of heaven " (Dan. 7^{13}) ; the coming of the righteous and victorious Messiah-King abolishing war and establishing peace (cf. Zech. $9^{9f.}$) ; above all the recurrent Old Testament picture of the coming God of the covenant Himself manifesting Himself in movement from there to here—all these constitute materially the preparatory form of what in the New Testament is called παρουσία in the pregnant technical sense, namely, the effective presence of Jesus Christ.

What is formally meant by the word is best seen from

the fact that in the later New Testament (especially the Pastorals, yet also as early as 2 Thess. 2⁸) it is found in close proximity to, and sometimes replaced by, the term ἐπιφάνεια. In its Hellenistic origin at least ἐπιφάνεια denotes the making visible of concealed divinity. In 2 Thess. 2⁸ both terms appear in a way which is not just plerophoric (so W. Bauer) but materially instructive. With the breath of His mouth the Lord Jesus will slay a hidden but one day manifested ἄνομος, destroying him τῇ ἐπιφανείᾳ τῆς παρουσίας αὐτοῦ. What else can this genitive conjunction mean but that the epiphany of Jesus Christ is the manifestation of His *parousia* or effective presence, or conversely that His *parousia* takes place in His epiphany and therefore His manifestation ?

As far as I can see, there are no passages (not even 2 Tim. 1¹⁰) where either term refers abstractly to the first coming of Jesus Christ as such, i.e., to His history and existence within the limits of His birth and death, of Bethlehem and Golgotha. In relation to these there would be no point in speaking either of ἐπιφάνεια (manifestation) or of παρουσία (effective presence). In them He is not even " manifest in the flesh " (1 Tim. 3¹⁶), and none of the other references in this passage can really apply to His pre-Easter existence as such. To be sure, the Word then became flesh, and His whole work was done in all its dimensions. But the incarnate Word was not yet revealed and seen in His glory (Jn. 1¹⁴). This took place in the event of Easter. In this event we certainly have the coming of the One who came before in that sphere. But it is now His coming in effective presence, because in visible manifestation in the world. It is now His coming in glory as the active and dominant factor within it. It is thus His new coming as the One who came before. It is now His " coming again," and in spite of Oepke I do not see how we can avoid this expression as we have provisionally and generally explained it.

We must now continue that, as concerns the scope and content of this event, the New Testament knows of only one coming again of Jesus Christ, of only one new coming of the One who came before, of only one manifestation of His effective presence in the world corresponding to His own unity as the One who came before. This does not

239

exclude the fact that His new coming and therefore His manifestation in effective presence in the world takes place in different forms at the different times chosen and appointed by Himself and in the different relationships which He Himself has ordained. Everything depends, of course, upon our seeing and understanding the one continuous event in all its forms. But in the time of the community and its mission after the Easter revelation it also takes place in the form of the impartation of the Holy Spirit, and it is with this that we are particularly concerned in this sub-section. It will also take place in a different and definitive form (of which we shall have to speak in eschatology), as the return of Jesus Christ as the goal of the history of the Church, the world and each individual, as His coming as the Author of the general resurrection of the dead and the Fulfiller of universal judgment. In all these forms it is one event. Nothing different takes place in any of them. It is not more in one case or less in another. It is the one thing taking place in different ways, in a difference of form corresponding to the willing and fulfilment of the action of its one Subject, the living Jesus Christ. Always and in all three forms it is a matter of the fresh coming of the One who came before. Always and in different ways it is a matter of the coming again of Jesus Christ.

The Easter event is only the first form of this happening. From the standpoint of its substance, scope and content, it is identical with its occurrence in the forms which follow. It is no less significant than these, nor is it to be depreciated in relation to them. On the contrary, the one and total coming in its other forms has its primal and basic pattern in the Easter event, so that we might well be tempted to describe the whole event simply as one long fulfilment of the resurrection of Jesus Christ. There are, of course, similar temptations in relation to the second and third forms of the event. We shall not attempt to reduce it in this way, since in so doing we should wander too far not only from the speech and terminology but also the material outlook of the New Testament. Thus, there can be no question that in all its forms the one totality of coming again does really have the character, colours and accents of the Easter event. There can also be no question that this is only the first if also the original form of this one totality.

If we allow the New Testament to say what it has to say, we shall be led in this matter to a thinking which is differentiated even in its incontestable unity, formally corresponding to that which is required for an understanding of the three modes of being of God in relation to His one essence in triunity : *una substantia in tribus personis, tres personae in una substantia.*

When the matter is usually spoken of in the New Testament under the terms *parousia* or epiphany, the reference is usually or chiefly to the third and final form, to the eschatological form in the narrower traditional sense, of the return of Jesus Christ, i.e., to His manifestation and effective presence beyond history, the community, the world and the individual human life, and as their absolute future. But reference to this climax of His coming dominates New Testament thought and utterance even where it is materially concerned with the subject without using these particular terms. We can hardly deny or explain this away in such typical passages as the *parousia* passages in the Synoptists, or the Thessalonian Epistles of Paul, or 1 Cor. 15, or the Apocalypse with its final ἔρχου κύριε Ἰησοῦ (22²⁰). Even the Gospel of John, which seems particularly to invite us to do this with its placing of both the gift of eternal life and the judgment in the present, resists it inasmuch as it is rather strangely the only book in the whole of the New Testament to speak of the last day (ἐσχάτη ἡμέρα) when Jesus will awaken the dead (6³⁹, ⁴⁰, ⁴⁴, ⁵⁴) and His Word spoken to men will judge them (12⁴⁸) ; and it is advisable not to solve the implied difficulty of interpretation by critical amputation. According to the New Testament, the return of Jesus Christ in the Easter event is not yet as such His return in the Holy Ghost and certainly not His return at the end of the days. Similarly, His return in the Easter event and at the end of the days cannot be dissolved into His return in the Holy Ghost, nor the Easter event and the outpouring of the Holy Spirit into His last coming. In all these we have to do with the one new coming of Him who came before. But if we are to be true to the New Testament, none of these three forms of His new coming, including the Easter event, may be regarded as its only form. The most that we can say is that a particular glory attaches to the Easter event because here it begins, the Easter event being the primal and basic form in which it comes to be seen and grasped in its totality.

Yet, as we must plainly distinguish the resurrection, the outpouring of the Spirit and the final return of Jesus Christ, so we must understand and see them together as forms of one and the same event. A no less sharp warning must be issued against an abstract separation of the three forms of the new coming of Jesus Christ for which there is no basis in the New Testament. How else could we distinguish them except within the unity of the whole and therefore on the assumption of one event in these three forms ?

Oepke is surely right when he says of the so-called last discourses in John that in them the " coming of the Resurrected, the coming in the Spirit and the coming at the end of the days merge into one another," and when he also says of the Synoptic Jesus that it is impossible to decide to what extent He made a clear distinction between His resurrection and His *parousia* in its final form. Yet may it not be that we can very definitely decide that He, or the Synoptic and also the Johannine tradition concerning Him, did not in fact make any absolute distinction between them at all in respect of either matter or form ? What do we learn from the well-known passages (considered in detail in *C.D.*, III, 2, pp. 499 ff.) in which Jesus unmistakeably prophesies the manifestation of the kingdom of God $\dot{\epsilon}\nu$ $\delta\nu\nu\dot{\alpha}\mu\epsilon\iota$ (Mk. $^{1f.}$), the coming of the Son of Man (Mt. 10^{23}, 26^{64}), or at least the sign which directly precedes (Mk. 13^{30} and *par.*) within the lifetime of those around Him ? If we may eliminate in advance what is in its way the greatest triviality of any age, what are we to make of the assumption which underlay a particular school of Neo-Liberal theology, and which is unfortunately encountered only too often outside the narrow circle of this school, namely, that Jesus was deluded ? If we find in the coming of the Resurrected, His coming in the Holy Spirit and His coming at the end of the age three forms of His one new coming for all their significant differences, there need be no artificiality in explaining that these passages refer to the first and immediate form in which His coming did really begin in that generation as the Easter event and in which the two remaining forms are plainly delineated and intimated. We are then forced to accept the statement of W. Michaelis which Oepke contests: " The resurrection . . . is the *parousia*," or again the statement of R. Bultmann (with particular reference to John's Gospel) : " The *parousia* has already taken place," although we must be careful to make the proviso that these statements are not to be taken exclusively but need to be amplified by the recollection that this is not the whole story. The outpouring of the Holy Spirit is also the *parousia*. In this it has not only taken place but is still taking place to-day. And as it has taken place in the resurrection and is taking place to-day in the outpouring of the Holy Spirit, it is also true that it will take place at the end of the days in the conclusion of the self-revelation of Jesus Christ.

It is thus impossible to relate a concept of the eschatological which is meaningful in the New Testament sense merely to the final stage of the *parousia*. Eschatological denotes the last time. The last time is the time of the world and human history and all men to which a term is already set in the death of Jesus and which can only run towards this appointed end. In the Easter event as the commencement of the new coming of Jesus Christ in revelation of what took place in His life and death, it is also revealed that the time which is still left to the world and human history and all men can only be the last time, i.e., time running towards its appointed end. In this sense the Easter event is the original because the first eschatological event. The impartation of the Holy Spirit is the coming of Jesus Christ in the last time which still remains. As we shall see, it is the promise, given with and through the Holy Spirit, by which the community, and with it the world in which it exists and has its mission, may live in this time which moves towards its end. Hence the new coming of Jesus Christ has an eschatological character in this second form too. If the *parousia* is an eschatological event in its third and final stage as well, this means specifically that in it we have to do with the manifestation and effective presence of Jesus Christ in their definitive form, with His revelation at the goal of the last time. It will consist again in a coming of Jesus Christ, and at this coming this last time, too, will reach the end which is already set for it in His death and revealed in His resurrection. The happening of the *parousia* is thus eschatological throughout its course. And it is this, as already indicated from the very first by the Easter event, because already and particularly in this event the term set to time in the death of Jesus Christ is revealed and the character and stamp of the last time is given to all the time which remains.

When we treat of the unity of the three forms or stages of the one event of the return of Jesus Christ, it is perhaps worth considering and exegetically helpful, again in analogy to the doctrine of the Trinity, to think of their mutual relationship as a kind of perichoresis (cf. *C.D.*, I, 1, p. 425). It is not merely that these three forms are interconnected in the totality of the action presented in them all, or in each of them in its unity and totality, but that they are mutually related as the forms of this one action by the fact that each of them also contains the other two by way of anticipation or recapitulation, so that, without losing their individuality or destroying that of the others, they participate and are active and revealed in them. As the Resurrected from the dead Jesus Christ is virtually engaged already in the outpouring of the Holy Spirit, and in the outpouring of the Holy Spirit He is engaged in the resurrection of all the dead and the execution of the last judgment. The outpouring of the Holy Spirit obviously takes place in the power of His resurrection from the dead, yet it is already His knocking as the One who comes finally and definitively, and it is active and perceptible as such. Similarly His final coming to resurrection and judgment is only the completion of what He has begun in His own resurrection and continued in the outpouring of the Holy Spirit.

To be sure, this is a view which is never systematised in the New Testament or presented in the form of instruction. But this does not mean that we are false to the Bible, or obscure its statements concerning the *parousia*, by adopting this view. Are we not more likely to throw light on them if we advance it with the necessary prudence yet also boldness ? Are there not many passages in the New

Testament which with their apparent contradictions cannot be satisfactorily explained except on the assumption of such a view ? This is not a key to open every lock. But it is one which we do well not to despise.

[IV, 3, pp. 290–296]

3. Union with Christ

[96] Not by way of addition, but to give the most precise expression possible to what we have already stated in various ways, we must now take a further step. This is not merely because certain passages of the New Testament clearly direct us beyond the point already reached, but because the matter itself imperiously calls for further reflection. What is the nature of this fellowship of Christians with Jesus Christ if we have correctly understood it as the relationship of discipleship and possession, and finally as the powerful work of the Holy Spirit ? Are we not justified in asking whether the word " fellowship " is not too weak to embrace everything that is involved between Jesus Christ and the man called by Him, whether the word is not transcended and thus rendered unusable by the content which it acquires at this point ? Yet this is not the case. From all these different angles the relationship is always one of fellowship because, for all the intimacy and intensity of the connexion between them, there can be no question of an identification of the follower with his preceding leader, the possession with its owner, or the life of the one awakened by the Holy Spirit with the One who gives him this Spirit. There can thus be no question of an identification of the Christian with Christ. We have still to show, however, to what extent the fellowship of the Christian with Christ is one which is uniquely close and direct in the perfection of the mutual address of the two partners, so that it cannot be interchanged with any other.

We may begin by stating that it belongs to the perfection of this fellowship, and must not be overlooked or denied, that in it Christ does not merge into the Christian nor the Christian into Christ. There is no disappearance nor destruction of the one in favour of the other. Christ remains the One who speaks, commands and gives as the

Lord. And the Christian remains the one who hears and answers and receives as the slave of the Lord. In their fellowship both become and are genuinely what they are, not confounding or exchanging their functions and roles nor losing their totally dissimilar persons.

A delimitation is required at this point. In particular relation to its perfection, the fellowship here described, which is the goal of vocation, has often been linked with the concept of mysticism both in exposition of the relevant New Testament texts and elsewhere. As is well known, even Calvin referred once to a *unio mystica* (*Instit.*, III, 11, 10). But we should never do this unless we state precisely what we have in view when we speak of " mysticism "—and it would have to be a mysticism *sui generis* in this context. There can certainly be no question of what is usually denoted by the term in this relationship. That is to say, there can be no question of an experience of union induced by a psychical and intellectual concentration, deepening and elevating of the human self-consciousness. For while it is true that in his fellowship with Christ, now to be appreciated in all its perfection, the Christian acts as well as receives, neither his receiving nor his acting in this fellowship is the product or work of his own skill, but both can be understood only as the creation of the call of Christ which comes to him. Again, there can be no question of a disappearance of the true confrontation of God and man, of the One who addresses and the one who is addressed and answers. There can be no question either on the one side or the other of any depersonalising or reduction to silence. There can be no question of any neutralising of the distinction between Creator and creature or of the antithesis between the Holy One and sinners, nor of any establishment of the kind of equilibrium which may exist between things but can never obtain between persons, and especially between the divine Jesus Christ and the human person. Even as a child of God, and therefore in the analogy of his existence to that of the eternal Son in the flesh, the Christian is not what the latter is, and alone can be. His fellowship with the latter thus has and maintains the character of an encounter in which the grace of Jesus Christ in all its fulness, but His grace and therefore a grace which is always free, is addressed to him. Nor does this grace fail to include a judgment passed on man. It does not cease to demand that he keep his distance. In face of it even his supreme and most joyous gratitude must always have, and continually acquire, the character of adoration. It is also important to notice that precisely in this fellowship of encounter there is not merely safeguarded the sovereignty of God, of Jesus Christ and of the Holy Spirit, but also the freedom of the human partner is preserved from dissolution. Indeed, it is genuinely established and validated. Unless we consider, safeguard and expressly state these things, we do better not to speak of " Christ-mysticism " when there is obviously no compelling reason to do so.

Having made this point, we may now proceed to state that the fellowship of Christians with Christ, which is the goal of vocation, is a perfect fellowship inasmuch as what takes place in it is no less than their union with Christ. The terms "attachment" and "co-ordination" are inadequate if they are not expressly understood in the sense of "union," i.e., the Christian's *unio cum Christo*. As we have shown, union does not mean the dissolution or disappearance of the one in the other, nor does it mean identification. It does not mean a conjunction of the two in which one or the other, and perhaps both, lose their specific character, role and function in relation to the other, the reciprocal relation being thus reversible. The union of the Christian with Christ which makes a man a Christian is their conjunction in which each has his own independence, uniqueness and activity. In this way it is, of course, their true, total and indissoluble union : true and not ideal ; total and not merely psychical and intellectual ; indissoluble and not just transitory. For it takes place and consists in a self-giving which for all the disparity is total on both sides. In this self-giving Christ and the Christian become and are a single totality, a fluid and differentiated but genuine and solid unity, in which He is with His people, the Lamb on the throne with the one who recognises in Him his Lord and King, the Head with the members of His body, the Prophet, Teacher and Master with His disciples, the eternal Son of God with the child of man who by Him and in Him, but only thus, only as His adopted brother, may be called and be the child of God. Like His own unity of true deity and humanity, this unity is *hic et nunc* concealed. It may be known in faith but not in sight, not by direct vision. The revelation of its glory has still to come. But even *hic et nunc* there can be and is no question of creating it or giving it force, but only of making definitively and universally visible its possibility, nature and reality as something incomparably great and totally new. This, and this alone, is what the whole of creation, with all men and Christians too, is waiting and groaning for. The purpose for which Christians are already called here and now in their life-histories within universal history is that in the self-giving of Jesus Christ to them, and theirs to Him, they should enter into their union with Him, their *unio cum Christo*.

For the sake of practical perspicuity in our definition of the Christian we first spoke of his humanity in common with all men, then of his divine sonship, then, in description of his fellowship with Jesus Christ, of the relationship of discipleship, his existence as the possession of this Owner, and the powerful work of the Holy Spirit within him. It is only now that we have reached the heart of the matter in his union with Christ. In view of what we said about the problem of the *ordo salutis* in the preceding sub-section, there is obviously no question here of a description of the genetic sequence of the states of the Christian, nor is it to be assumed that in the *unio cum Christo* we reach the culminating point of such a sequence. Our present concern is not with the event of vocation at all, but with its meaning and goal. And our supreme and final definition of this as the union of the Christian with Christ describes the most essential element in it which underlies and comprehends all the others, so that from the purely material view we really ought to have put it first. This is what Calvin actually ventured to do (*Instit.*, III, 1) when he opened his whole doctrine *De modo percipiendae gratiae* with a depiction of this *unio*. If we have not followed him in this, and for the sake of clarity have thus departed in some sense from the matter, it is to be noted expressly that only now have we reached the central point which supports all that precedes and is tacitly presupposed in it.

If we are to understand the nature of this union, then,

248

in relation to the emphasised independence, uniqueness and activity of Jesus Christ on the one side and the Christian on the other, we do well to begin, not below with the Christian, but above with Jesus Christ as the Subject who initiates and acts decisively in this union. We do well to begin with the union of Christ with the Christian and His self-giving to the Christian, and not *vice versa*. It is here that the union and self-giving of the Christian have their roots.

That Jesus Christ in calling man to be a Christian unites Himself with him means first from His own standpoint that He is unique as the One who in His life and death was humiliated and exalted in the place and for the sake of all, as the One in whom the reconciliation of the world to God and the justification and sanctification of all were accomplished. In all this He has no assistant nor fellow-worker to accompany Him, let alone any *corredemptor* or *corredemptrix*. He is absolutely isolated from all others. Without them, He intervenes for them. But as this One, when it is a matter of the revelation of this work as inaugurated in His resurrection from the dead and continued in the work of His Holy Spirit, when it is a matter of His work in its prophetic dimension, He cannot and will not remain alone, nor can He be solitary in the reconciled world on His way to His future, conclusive and universal revelation. He cannot and will not be the Master without disciples, the Leader without followers, the Head without members, the King without fellows in His people, Himself without His own, Christ without Christians. The fact that the One who is disclosed in His resurrection from the dead and the outpouring of the Holy Spirit is really the omnipotent God who stooped down in unmerited love to man, the Lord who became a servant, has in the time which moves to its end in His final revelation a counterpart in the fact that as the Proclaimer of the act of God accomplished in Him, in His prophetic office and work, He does not go alone but wills to be what He is and do what He does in company with others whom He calls for the purpose, namely, with the despicable folk called Christians. He attests to the world the reconciliation to God effected in Him, the covenant of God with man fulfilled in Him, as He associates with Christians, making common cause and conjoining Himself with them. He does not merely do this ideally or partially, but really and totally. He does not merely comfort, encourage, admonish or protect them remotely or from afar. But as He calls them to Himself in the divine power of His Spirit, He refreshes them by offering and giving Himself to them and making them His own. That He wills and does this is—in analogy to the mystery and miracle of Christmas—the true *ratio* of Christian existence as this is celebrated, adored and proclaimed within the community of Christians in the common administration of the Lord's Supper, instituted to represent the perfect fellowship between Him and them which He has established—an implication which we cannot do more than indicate in the present context.

We now turn to what must be thought and said concerning this union of His with Christians from their standpoint. There is, of course, no one, apostle, saint or the Virgin, who can contribute in the very slightest to what is accomplished for all by the one Jesus Christ in His life and death. In relation to His high-priestly and kingly work even a Paul can only know what has been done for us by God in Him (1 Cor. 2¹²). But those to whom He reveals and makes known this life and death of His as the act of God for their salvation and His own glory do not confront this act of revelation, this work of atonement in its prophetic dimension, as hearers and spectators who are left to themselves and ordained for pure passivity. What kind of vocation, illumination and awakening would it be, what kind of knowledge, if they were merely left gaping at the One who discloses Himself to them ? No, as surely as He does not will to tread alone His way as the Proclaimer of the kingdom, so surely they for their part must be with Him, companions of the living One who are made alive by Him, witnesses in His discipleship to that which He wills to reveal to the world as having been effected in Him, namely, to the reconciliation accomplished and the covenant fulfilled in Him. This is what He makes them as He calls them to Himself, as He does this really and totally, as He does not leave them to themselves, as He does not remain outside them, as He gives Himself to them, as in the divine power of His Spirit He unites Himself with them. That they may become and be those with whom He unites

Himself by His Word ; that they may be those who are born again from above by His presence and action in their own lives ; that they may be continually nourished by Him—this is, from their standpoint, the *ratio* of Christian existence. Here again we are naturally reminded of the mystery and miracle of Christmas, and must make provisional reference to the Lord's Supper.

" I in you " (Jn. 14[20], 15[4]). " I in them " (Jn. 17[23, 26]). " I in him " (Jn. 6[56], 15[5]). According to Jn. 15[1f.] He is the vine which produces, bears and nourishes the branches, or according to the even stronger expression in Jn. 6[33] He is the " bread of God which cometh down from heaven, and giveth life unto the world." He gives them His flesh and blood, imparting and communicating Himself to them, giving Himself to nourish them, in order that as He lives they also may and will live to all eternity (Jn. 6[53]). The same teaching is found in Paul. " Know ye not your own selves, how that Jesus Christ is in you ? " (2 Cor. 13[5] ; cf. Rom. 8[10], Col. 1[27]). He is the One who has apprehended the apostle (Phil. 3[12]), putting His power in him (2 Cor. 12[9]), setting His truth in him (2 Cor. 11[10]), speaking in him (2 Cor. 13[3]), and always magnifying and glorifying Himself in his person (Phil. 1[20]). And in relation to other Christians He is the One who dwells " in your hearts by faith " (Eph. 3[17]), or who seeks to be formed in them (Gal. 4[19]). Whether they are Greeks, Jews, Barbarians, Scythians, slaves or freemen, Christ is in them all (Col. 3[11]). Χριστὸς ἐν ὑμῖν is the great mystery of God among the nations (Col. 1[27]). In the strongest possible expression (Gal. 2[20]), Christ lives in the apostle in such a way that he has to say of himself that he no longer lives, i.e., in himself and apart from the fact that Christ lives in him, but that he now lives in faith in Him who gave Himself for him, this being his own most proper life to which, as one who still lives in the flesh, he can do justice only as he believes in Him. In Col. 3[4], however, " Christ our life " is also said in relation to Christians generally, and again in relation to all those who by the Spirit have been given to know what is given them by God there is made the immeasurable claim : " We have the mind of Christ " (ἡμεῖς δὲ νοῦν Χριστοῦ ἔχομεν, 1 Cor. 2[12, 16]), i.e., in virtue of His life in us we have His reason.

251

It has always involved an unwise and, on a proper consideration, an attenuating exposition of these verses to speak of an extension of the incarnation in relation to the Christian's *unio cum Christo* and then in relation to the Lord's Supper. We are concerned rather with the extended action in His prophetic work of the one Son of God who became flesh once and for all and does not therefore need any further incarnation. We are concerned with the fact that He as the one Word of God takes up His abode in the called, that His life becomes their life as He gives Himself to them. This is the mystery and miracle of His union with them. Similarly, we do well to refrain from describing the Christian in relation to his fellows (Luther, *De libertate*, 1520, W.A., 66, 26), or, as Roman Catholics do, the priest in the mass in relation to other believers, as an *alter Christus*. In this perfect fellowship the one Christ as the only original Son of God, beside whom there can be no other, is always the One who gives, commands and precedes, and the other, the *homo christianus*, whom He makes His brother and therefore a child of God, is always the one who receives, obeys and follows. The former is the Word of God in person; the latter, like John the Baptist in the Fourth Gospel, is His witness. In this distinction, of course, neither remains alone. Both become a totality. For it is not too great or small a thing for Christ to give Himself to the Christian, to cause His own life to be that of the Christian, to make Himself his with all that this necessarily implies. This is the high reality of His vocation to the extent that this takes place and is to be understood as His union with the Christian.

In the reality and power of the union of Christ with the Christian, however, their fellowship has also the meaning and character of a union of the Christian with Christ. Their fellowship would not be complete if their relationship were actualised only from above downwards and not also from below upwards, if it were not reciprocal. A justifiable concern for the unconditional predominance of the freedom, grace and decision of Jesus Christ which establish the relationship should not mislead us into suppressing or minimising the fact that His action has its correspondence in an action of the Christian. According to the guidance of the New Testament the declaration concerning the communication of Christ with the Christian necessarily includes a complementary declaration concerning the communication of the Christian with Christ.

That Christ links Himself with the Christian settles the fact that the latter, too, does not go alone. To do justice to Christ as his Counterpart he is not directed to believe in Him and to obey and confess Him on his own initiative or resources. He is certainly summoned to believe, obey and confess. And both as a whole and in detail this will always be the venture of a free decision and leap. It will always be a venture in which no man can wait for or rely on others, as though they could represent him or make the leap for him. Even in the community and therefore with other Christians, he can believe, obey and confess only in his own person and on his own responsibility. But does this mean on his own initiative and resources? No, for the act of the Christian is not to be described as a leap into the dark or a kind of adventure. We have only to consider what kind of a free decision or leap is involved to see that, if there is any action which is well-grounded and therefore assured in respect of its goal, it is the faith, obedience and confession of the Christian. The Christian undertakes these things as through the Spirit he is called to do so by the risen One in whom he believes and whom he obeys and confesses. And in the knowledge given him with his calling, he is not merely required but empowered to do it. In Jesus Christ he knows and apprehends himself as a member of the world reconciled to God in Him, as a man who is justified and sanctified in Him in spite of his sin, as a legitimate partner of the covenant fulfilled in Him. Believing in Jesus Christ and obeying and confessing him, he simply does the natural thing proper to him as the man he is in Christ and therefore in truth. He simply realises his true—the only truly human—possibility. He simply exercises the freedom given him as the man he is in Christ and therefore in truth. The decision or leap of his faith, obedience and confession consists in the fact that he takes himself seriously as the man he is and recognises himself to be in Jesus Christ instead of immediately forgetting his true self (who and what he is in Christ), like the man who looks at himself in a mirror and then goes on his way (Jas. $1^{23f.}$). It consists in the fact that he begins to act on this basis, i.e., on the basis of Jesus Christ and as the man he is in Him. He believes, obeys and confesses as, now that Christ has united Himself with him, he unites himself with Christ, giving himself to the One who first gave Himself to him, and thus choosing Him as the starting-point and therefore the goal of His thinking, speech, volition and action, quite simply and non-paradoxically because this is what He is, because there is no other starting-point or goal apart from Him, because in truth he is not outside Him but within Him.

Here again, however, we must consider the opposite side and therefore add that as the Christian unites himself with Christ it is also settled that he cannot part from Christ. In his relationship with Him He alone is the One who gives, commands and leads, and the criterion of the genuineness of all the faith, obedience and confession of Christians will always necessarily consist in their allowing Him alone to be what He alone is, neither openly nor secretly trying to subject Him to their own dominion, in the exercise of which their faith would at once become unbelief, their obedience, disobedience and their confession denial. This does not mean, however, that they can refrain from immediately and directly recognising their own cause in His cause, i.e., in the occurrence of His prophetic work in the world. For as they recognise Him, they can and should recognise themselves in Him, what they themselves are in truth. Except by the self-deception of Jas. $1^{23f.}$, how could they break their solidarity with Him? As those they are and know themselves to be in Him, as members of the world reconciled to God in Him, as justified and sanctified sinners, they cannot possibly leave Him in the lurch instead of following Him. In the freedom given them as those they are, they have only one option, namely, to believe in Him, to obey Him and to confess Him, and in so doing, in making this movement, to unite themselves with Him as He in His turning to them, in calling them and making Himself known to them, unites Himself with them. Called, illumined and awakened by His prophetic Word, for this Word they can only be in truth the men they are. What other can they do, then, as those to whom Christ has given Himself, than to give themselves to Him, to exist as His, and therefore continually to seek

254

and find their life in Him, in whom it is their truest life ?

The New Testament gives us every reason to draw very distinctly this line from below upwards. For rather strangely, but quite unmistakeably, it is not merely no less but much more noticeable in the New Testament than the opposite line which is original and must thus be regarded as decisive in our description of the whole relationship. It certainly receives more frequent mention. While the authors of the New Testament presuppose the being of Christ in the Christian, with no fear of injuring the supremacy of the divine initiative they do in fact look more in the opposite direction, namely, to the being of the Christian in Christ. The whole emphasis of the speech concerning the vine in Jn. 15[1f.] is obviously laid on the fact that, as the branches can bear fruit only as they abide in the vine, so the disciples, if they are to be what they are fruitfully, must abide in the One who speaks to them. This is brought home in many different ways, and it is impressively repeated in the First Epistle of John (3[6, 9], 4[16]). For χωρὶς ἐμοῦ, " without me ye can do nothing " (Jn. 15[5]). That they are called to abide in Him presupposes that the free and responsible participation of Christians in their status is envisaged in the description of the fellowship between Christ and them. It presupposes that they are already in Him, and obviously because first and supremely He is in them and has made their being a being in Him. " I in you " (Jn. 14[20]), comes first, but secondly and on this basis it must also be said : " Ye in me." That Christians are in Christ, that their Christian existence is everywhere realised in the fact that it unites with His in which it has its origin, substance and norm, is the insight which in the New Testament dominates especially the thinking and language of Paul, though it also finds expression in the First Epistles of Peter and John. The statement usually has an indicative character. But we have to remember that even indicatively it speaks of the history in which the union of the Christian with Christ takes place, so that we need not be surprised that it may become the imperative so characteristic of the Johannine passages. Christians are now quite briefly described as οἱ ἐν Χριστῷ Ἰησοῦ, or usually even more simply as ἐν Χριστῷ or ἐν κυρίῳ (Rom. 8¹, 2 Cor. 5¹⁷, Eph. 2¹³, 1 Pet. 5¹⁴). And they are described in this way because they are in Him (ἐστέ, 1 Cor. 1³⁰, 9¹, ²; ἐσμέν, 1 Jn. 2⁵). And they are in Him because Christ has adopted them into unity with His being (Rom. 15⁷), which means that in virtue of their baptism they have put Him on like a covering garment (Gal. 3²⁷), and must continually do so (Rom. 13¹⁴). This historical being in Christ is decisively determined, of course, by the fact that first and supremely God was " in Christ " reconciling the world to Himself (2 Cor. 5¹⁹). It is thus determined by their election made and revealed in Christ (Eph. 1⁴, ⁹, 3¹¹), by their redemption accomplished and manifested in Him (Col. 1¹⁴), by the grace of God addressed to them and recognisable in Him (1 Cor. 1¹⁴), by His love (Rom. 8³⁹), by His peace (Phil. 4⁷), by the eternal life of which they are assured in Him (Rom. 6²³). As they are in Christ, they acquire and have a direct share in what God first and supremely is in Him, what was done by God for the world and therefore for them in Him, and what is assigned and given to them by God in Him. But their being as thus determined by God is a concretely active being. In the one reality ἐν Χριστῷ God and man do not confront each other abstractly as such. On the contrary, there is a direct and concrete confrontation of the divine and corresponding human action, the former kindling the latter and the latter kindled by it. Conscious of being an ἄνθρωπος ἐν Χριστῷ (2 Cor. 12²), Paul is very definitely activated as an apostle. He can be absolutely certain of his convictions " in him," as in respect of the distinction of meats in Rom. 14¹⁴. He can have " in him " the joy with which he confidently makes his request of Philemon (v. 8). He can be sure " in him " of speaking the truth both from God and before Him (Rom. 9¹, 2 Cor. 2¹⁷). " In him," too, he can be quietly confident in respect of His communities (2 Thess. 3⁴, Gal. 5¹⁰) and thank God that He always causes him to triumph in Christ and to spread abroad the savour of His knowledge (2 Cor. 2¹⁴). Nor does Paul ascribe here to himself anything that he does not also basically ascribe both indicatively and imperatively to all Christians and to the whole community. " In him " he makes his boast in respect of them (1 Cor. 15³¹). Has not he Paul as an apostle begotten them again

256

in Christ Jesus through the Gospel (1 Cor. 4¹⁵) ? Called
" in Christ," are not all Christians " in him " saints (Col. 1²)
and believers (Col. 1⁴, Eph. 1¹⁵), hoping " in him " (1 Cor.
15¹⁹) and " in him " called to obedience in their own
particular situation (Eph. 6¹ᶠ·) ? " We all, with open face
beholding as in a glass the glory of the Lord, are changed
into the same image from glory to glory, even as by the
Lord who is the Spirit," without whom it would be impossible (2 Cor. 3¹⁸ᶠ·). Hence Paul can see in one or
another his fellow-labourer (Rom. 16³) or fellow-servant
(Col. 4⁷) " in Christ," and in Epaphras his fellow-prisoner
" in him " (Philem. 23). They are all light " in the Lord "
(Eph. 5⁸). They can and should all glory " in the Lord "
(1 Cor. 1³¹, 2 Cor. 10¹⁷, Phil. 1²⁶). They can and should
all rejoice " in the Lord " (Phil. 3¹, 4⁴, ¹⁰). The apostle
greets them " in him " in his letters (1 Cor. 16¹⁹, Phil. 4²¹).
And " in him " he also admonishes them, here too presupposing that they are " in him," that as Christians they
are within and not without, so that they have only to be
told to continue to walk " in him " (Col. 2⁶, 1 Pet. 3¹⁶) and
to be reminded of the mind which is self-evident " in Christ
Jesus " (Phil. 2⁵) and of that which is " fit in the Lord "
(Col. 3¹⁸). To what can those who are in Him be meaningfully admonished, invited and summoned but—in a rather
different expression—to stand as who and what they are
(1 Thess. 3⁸, Phil. 4¹) ? In relation to the historical character of this being of theirs, however, it is indeed meaningful
to admonish, invite and summon them to do this. How
could they be what they are in Christ if they did not continually become it ?

This is not by any means a full list of the New Testament
references to the εἶναι ἐν Χριστῷ. To give such a list it
would be necessary not only to mention and co-ordinate
many others, but also to introduce a series which we have
left aside, namely, the passages which, without any basic
alteration of meaning, substitute διὰ Χριστοῦ or ἐν ὀνόματι
Χριστοῦ for ἐν Χριστῷ. But we have certainly adduced
sufficient to show what powerful witness there is in the
New Testament to the union of the Christian with Christ
which is our present concern.

It is perhaps relevant to our purpose to add a brief
linguistic enquiry into what has been said both materially

and in the biblical discussions concerning the two aspects of this union, i.e., that of Christ with the Christian and that of the Christian with Christ. What is meant by the word " in " when we say that Christ is in the Christian and the Christian in Him ? Is this a mode of expression which demands demythologisation because of its evident localising ? We may confidently reply that the word certainly has in all seriousness a local signification. If, in the fellowship between Christ and the Christian and the Christian and Christ, it must be maintained—for this is the limit beyond which there can be nothing more to demythologise—that we have an encounter in time between two personal partners who do not lose but keep their identity and particularity in this encounter, then the " in " must indeed indicate on both sides that the spatial distance between Christ and the Christian disappears, that Christ is spatially present where Christians are, and that Christians are spatially present where Christ is, and not merely along-side but in exactly the same spot. Hence we say that Christ is in Christians and they in Him. Yet while this is true, it has surely become obvious both in our material presentation and in our survey of the biblical evidence that in this context the word " in " transcends even though it also includes its local signification.

The first statement, namely, that Christ is in the Christian, has the further meaning that Christ speaks, acts and rules—and this is the grace of His calling of this man—as the Lord of his thinking, speech and action. He takes possession of his free human heart. He rules and controls in the obedience of his free reason (2 Cor. 10[5]). As a divine person it is very possible for Him to do this in the unrestricted sovereignty proper to Himself and yet in such a way that there can be no question whatever of any competition between His person and that of the Christian, whether in the attempt of the latter to control His person, or conversely in its suppression or extinction by His person. It is very possible for Him to do it in such a way that the human person of the Christian is validated and honoured in full and genuine freedom, in the freedom of the obedient children of God. That Christ is in the Christian means, then, that as the Mediator between God and man He does not exist merely for Himself and to that extent concentrically, but that in His prophetic work, in the calling of His disciples and Christians, with no self-surrender but in supreme expression of Himself, He also exists eccentrically, i.e., in and with the realisation of the existence of these men, as the ruling principle of the history lived by them in their own freedom.

The second statement, namely, that the Christian is in Christ, has not only the local but also the higher meaning that his own thinking, speech and action has its ruling and determinative principle—and herein it is the work of his gratitude corresponding to grace—in the speech, action and rule of Christ. His free human heart and reason and acts are orientated on Him, i.e., on agreement with His being and action. In the power of the Word of God which calls him, and therefore in the power of the Holy Spirit, this orientation is his only possibility, already in process of realisation. Again, there is no rivalry between the human person and the divine. There is thus no danger that the former will be overwhelmed by the latter. There is no danger that it will necessarily be destroyed by it and perish. Rather, the human person, experiencing the power of the divine, and unreservedly subject to it, will necessarily recognise and honour it again and again in its sovereignty, finding itself established as a human person and set in truly human and the freest possible movement in orientation on it. That the Christian is in Christ means *mutatis mutandis* for him, too, that as one who is called by the one Mediator between God and man in the exercise of His prophetic office he cannot exist for himself and to that extent concentrically, but that, without detriment to his humanity, awakened rather to genuine humanity, he also exists eccentrically, in and with the realisation of his own existence, being received and adopted as an integral element in the life and history of Christ.

This, then, is the Christian's *unio cum Christo*. We recall that in this high view and doctrine we are not presenting a climax of Christian experience and development in face of which the anxious question might well be raised whether we have reached the point, or will ever do so, where in respect of our own Christianity we can sincerely say : " Christ in me, and I in Christ." On the contrary, we are presenting the last and most exact formulation of what makes us Christians whatever our development or experience. We have seen that Paul particularly in the New Testament does not think of restricting his insight in this regard to himself and a few other Christians of higher rank, but that as he speaks of himself he also speaks of the generality of Christians, not excluding the very doubtful Christians of Galatia and Corinth and not excluding the doubtful nature of their Christianity. If, as we have attempted in concentric circles, we think through what it means that the goal of vocation, and therefore of Christianity as divine sonship, is always attachment to Christ, co-ordination and fellowship with Him, discipleship, appropriation to Him with the corresponding expropriation, life of and by the Holy Spirit, then we are infallibly led at last to the point which we have now reached and described, namely, that a man becomes and is a Christian as he unites himself with Christ and Christ with·him. And we remember that from the purely material standpoint this is the starting-point for everything else which is to be thought and said concerning what makes the Christian a Christian.

[IV, 3, pp. 538–549]

INDEX OF PASSAGES

A

262

hARpER ⚡ ⚡ ⊂ORCbBOOKS

† The New American Nation Series, edited by Henry Steele Commager and Richard B. Morris.
‡ American Perspectives series, edited by Bernard Wishy and William E. Leuchtenburg.
α History of Europe series, edited by J. H. Plumb.
§ The Library of Religion and Culture, edited by Benjamin Nelson.
|| Researches in the Social, Cultural, and Behavioral Sciences, edited by Benjamin Nelson.
Σ Harper Modern Science Series, edited by James R. Newman.
° Not for sale in Canada.
+ Documentary History of the United States series, edited by Richard B. Morris.
# Documentary History of Western Civilization series, edited by Eugene C. Black and Leonard W. Levy.
Λ The Economic History of the United States series, edited by Henry David et al.
¶ European Perspectives series, edited by Eugene C. Black.
** Contemporary Essays series, edited by Leonard W Levy.
* The Stratum Series, edited by John Hale.